The Works of Graham Greene, Volume 3

Additions & Essays

The Works of Graham Greene, Volume 3

Additions & Essays

Jon Wise and Mike Hill

BLOOMSBURY ACADEMIC
LONDON • NEW YORK • OXFORD • NEW DELHI • SYDNEY

BLOOMSBURY ACADEMIC
Bloomsbury Publishing Plc
50 Bedford Square, London, WC1B 3DP, UK
1385 Broadway, New York, NY 10018, USA
29 Earlsfort Terrace, Dublin 2, Ireland

BLOOMSBURY, BLOOMSBURY ACADEMIC and the Diana logo are trademarks of Bloomsbury Publishing Plc

First published in Great Britain 2022
This paperback edition published 2023

Cover design: Rebecca Heselton

A catalogue record for this book is available from the British Library.

A catalog record for this book is available from the Library of Congress.

ISBN: HB: 978-1-3502-8573-6
PB: 978-1-3502-8577-4
ePDF: 978-1-3502-8574-3
eBook: 978-1-3502-8575-0

Typeset by Newgen KnowledgeWorks Pvt. Ltd., Chennai, India

To find out more about our authors and books visit www.bloomsbury.com and sign up for our newsletters.

To Lucy

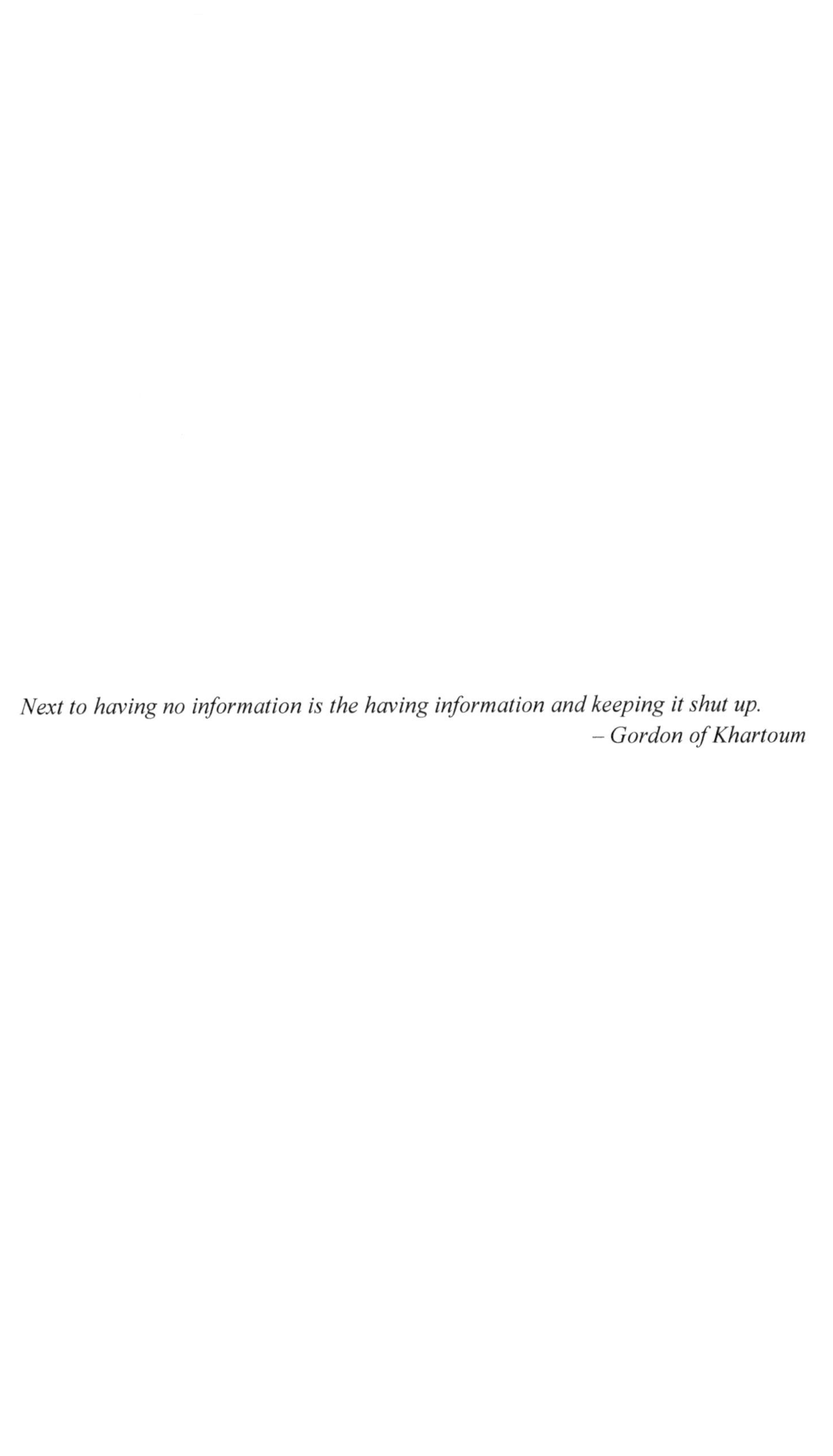

Next to having no information is the having information and keeping it shut up.

– Gordon of Khartoum

Contents

Acknowledgements

The authors of this final volume of bibliography first met at one of the Graham Greene International Festivals, and our acknowledgements should start with the Graham Greene Birthplace Trust, which organizes these annual events. The Trust's work is detailed in the Introduction to this book, but we wish to put on record our thanks to it for its support, including financial, over the years. In particular, in the year of her death, we wish to pay tribute to Caroline Bourget, a Patron of the Trust, whose interest and enthusiasm in her father's work encouraged us and others to keep going in our researches. Caroline will be much missed by all who met her in Berkhamsted at the festivals. More generally, the Trust's activities have generated a community of those with an interest in Graham Greene, and we have benefitted from being a part of that community over the years.

We owe a big debt of gratitude to Francis Greene, Graham's son and literary executor, for supporting our work, for allowing us access to the Marie Biche Papers at Balliol College, Oxford, and for giving permission to quote from Greene's writing in this book. Much of the richness of what we record and comment on here stems from that permission. We also thank the staff of the National Library of Sweden for the information and help they were able to provide regarding the Ragnar Svanström archive, and Professor Adrian Kendry for his assistance with translation.

As we detail in our Introduction, we also owe a debt of gratitude to the pioneering bibliographical work of Alan Redway and Neil Brennan. We hope our three volumes have done something to bring that work to fruition. In more recent times, we should add our thanks to a young American scholar named Michael J. Abolafia: his detective work at the BBC Written Archives Centre in Reading identified twelve previously unrecorded Greene book reviews in the *Listener* magazine, and they are listed in these pages. We also thank Philip Hormbrey for his meticulous work in locating and dating some of Greene's very earliest writings.

We have had support from many Greene specialists in the academic world. Judith Adamson in Canada, Carlos Villar Flor in Spain, Richard Greene in Canada, Motonori Sato in Japan, Neil Sinyard in the UK and Joyce Stavick in the United States have all read parts or all of this book, and we have benefitted from their support and comments. More particularly, Professor Richard Greene has been most helpful in gaining the trust and support of the Greene Literary Estate and unfailingly helpful and inspiring. Professor Adamson has given us the benefit of her knowledge about Graham Greene's *The Tenth Man* and his involvement in the world of film in the 1930s. We thank them all.

Our thanks are also extended to all the archivists who helped us at each of the libraries or special collections departments which we visited either in person or electronically. Many of these we have thanked by name in Volume 2. To these we should now add, in no particular order, Anna Sander and Naomi Tiley at Balliol College, Oxford, Jeremy Parrett at All Saints Library at Manchester Metropolitan University and the administrative staff of Berkhamsted School.

Finally, we should again thank our partners, Lindsay and Jean, for their continued support and patience as we have pursued our researches.

Introduction

The aim of this guide

In the Introduction to the first volume of our bibliographic guide we wrote that our aim was 'to give as complete an account as possible of Greene's published work'. In other words, simply to make a record in one place of what he had written during a career lasting some seventy years. In the second volume, which covered relevant archival material held in nearly sixty repositories across four countries, we warned, 'We do not claim that this is a complete record of everything that Greene wrote.'

Inevitably, since we wrote those words, enough information has indeed come to light to justify a third volume. This book complements Volumes 1 and 2 in layout and in style. It corrects or builds on existing entries while describing and listing entirely new entries, of which there are a great number. We have added a new component: a series of essays, which grew out of our research, on subjects not explored hitherto.

Perhaps the most interesting discovery we have made is the sheer extent of Graham Greene's early published work. While it is correct to state that Greene's early efforts at finding a career in writing were frustrated by setbacks, it is not true that the years between leaving Balliol College, Oxford, in 1925 and achieving his first success as a novelist with *The Man Within* (1929) were mostly barren with the exception of one small volume of poetry, *Babbling April* (1925). Our research has revealed two things: firstly that Greene's skills and potential were clearly recognized while still at Balliol and secondly that, during the 1920s, his published output was far greater than hitherto appreciated.

Greene's writing ability had been evident while at school. Five contributions to the school magazine *The Berkhamstedian* have been identified: four short stories and a poem. Indeed his first work was later accepted by the London evening paper *The Star* and published in January 1921 – quite an achievement for a sixteen-year-old. None of *The Berkhamstedian* publications has been reprinted, at the specific request of the writer's Literary Estate. The frankly juvenile stories embrace a variety of often fantastical themes and characters: Pied-Piperesque strangers and pagan gods, medieval knights and talking clocks, death, chivalry, romance, visions and voices. Clearly, Greene was still delving into his rich, childhood imagination, perhaps subconsciously denying entry to a world still shaken by the apocalyptic experiences of the First World War.

Even before Greene left Balliol he was contributing to a variety of publications, both in the Oxford area and beyond. Remarkably, aside from the five that appeared in his school magazine between December 1920 and July 1922, it is now possible to identify no fewer than 153 individual pieces of published writing which can definitely be attributed to him, up to the point when his breakthrough novel *The Man Within* was published in June 1929. In addition to poems and book reviews, these included play reviews, travel writing, short stories, essays, articles and film reviews. That grounding, particularly in the art of criticism, was to prove most valuable in the 1930s when Greene initially struggled to sustain a full-time career as a novelist.

How the guide is arranged and what it includes

The guide is arranged in three sections. Section 1 mirrors the layout used in Volume 1 of our bibliographic guide and is subdivided. Section 1a provides additional material to Greene's published work across a number of categories together with notes correcting any errors we made previously. Section 1b lists new entries. These are considerable in number, including, for example, over 150 hitherto unlisted contributions to periodicals, journals and magazines.

Section 2 also copies the layout in Volume 2 of the guide. Part 1 of Section 2b, 'Contents and analysis' provides an in-depth examination of some major new findings relating to Greene's work which will be of particular value to researchers in the field as well as the general reader. Balliol College has been the beneficiary of a very large collection of private correspondence consisting of Greene's letters to his French literary agents Denyse Clairouin, prior to the Second World War, and Marie Biche, née Schebeko, afterwards. The Cherry Record Collection of Josephine Reid's Papers and Books is also of note. Reid was Greene's devoted and notably discreet secretary from 1959 to 1975, after which she continued to work for him into her retirement. Her papers include Greene's correspondence and much else besides. Lastly Balliol, through the diligence of its archivists, has constructed an 'Old Member Dossier' for Greene which records the college's own association with the writer. In addition to correspondence, it charts his time at the university and later in his career when he built an increasingly warm relationship with his old college.

Elsewhere, there is a description of the archive of artist Paul Hogarth held by Manchester Metropolitan University. Hogarth, as well as being best known for his cover illustrations of Greene's books for Penguin paperbacks in the 1960s, was a personal friend. The collection includes correspondence between the two men from the late 1960s until Greene's death.

Finally, Ragnar Svanström is best remembered in his native Sweden and beyond as co-author of *A Short History of Sweden*, first published in English in 1934. He was literary adviser to Norstedts and Sons, Greene's Swedish publisher. He was another personal friend. The archive, held by the National Library of Sweden, principally contains correspondence between the two men dating from 1952 to 1977. It forms an important insight into Greene's work as he progressed through a key period in his career and as such complements the Clairouin/Biche archive referred to earlier.

Section 2b, Part 2, 'Listings' is mainly intended for reference purposes. In addition to brief notes, in some cases it provides relevant archival search codes where these are available. Again, they are evidence of the extremely wide range of people known to Graham Greene. All these records are held within the public domain, and the individual archives listed can be contacted using the relevant internet addresses provided.

Section 3 comprises nine essays on topics derived from our research undertaken during the compilation of this trilogy of guides. Our visits to archives both in the UK and abroad in preparation for Volume 2 produced a very rich vein of material pertaining to Greene, the bulk of which has never been read or indeed is known about, let alone explored in critical works. Therefore, the essays flowed naturally from these 'discoveries' and were selected because they highlight less-explored aspects of Greene's oeuvre. But the principal reason why they are included in this volume is to provide a 'springboard' for further scholarly examination in keeping with the contemporary trend in Greene studies which has seen quite diverse themes aired as opposed to the familiar ones concerning faith, betrayal and loyalty.

It is now more than a half-century since the author was at the most productive stage of his long writing career. Unsurprisingly therefore, given the passage of time, his works are often being written about from a historical perspective focusing on such subjects as the Cold War and postcolonialism. The nine essays, in very different ways and on very different subjects, frequently reflect the historical context in which they were written; the supporting evidence in each case has been largely drawn from the primary research material we accrued from the archives.

Vivat Bristowa concerns a sizeable, yet unfinished novel, probably to be called 'Lucius', which Greene worked on in the late 1950s at the pinnacle of his writing powers, before abandoning it. Although it is rooted in familiar childhood schooldays territory, the unfolding plot promises much; the reason why the author never finished the novel can be linked to his fragile mental state at the time. *The Virtue of Disloyalty* was the title the author gave to a controversial and deliberately provocative speech delivered in Hamburg in 1969. It explores Greene's personal views on the role of the writer in society and was aired at a time when loyalty to one's country or to a particular cause was being called into question. Both the aforementioned topics originated as talks given at past Graham Greene International Festivals at Berkhamsted.

The novel and film of *The Comedians* were so controversial that they caused an international diplomatic row during the 1960s. Foreign Office documents and other sources examine the repercussions of this incident. Greene thought that his short story 'The Basement Room' was unfilmable. *The Fallen Idol* essay analyses in detail how the story was adapted for the big screen in the immediate post-war era and became one of the most famous and lauded Greene-related films of all time. Greene's 1936 'shocker' *A Gun for Sale* is a typical noir of the period, and the essay looks at this 'Entertainment' particularly in terms of its historical context. Another 1930s work, the slightly earlier *It's a Battlefield*, has often been overlooked. It is notable both for its left-leaning political undercurrents and for the author's new-found use of realism, which was to become the hallmark of his writing style illustrated here in his highly accurate depiction of pre-war South London.

The play *A House of Reputation* was abandoned by Greene in the late 1950s only to be 'rediscovered' in the 1980s and completed. The writer did not live long enough to see it staged, but interestingly, and uniquely for this writer, the two leading roles are both female. Does this work contradict the long-held view that Greene could write only about male characters? *The Tenth Man* was another 'lost work', although the term is used advisedly. The essay seeks to untangle a web of conflicting evidence concerning the provenance of this novella. It also poses interesting questions about the writer's fallible memory and the fine line he walked between fact and fantasy. Finally, after he wrote *A Burnt-Out Case*, Greene believed that his career as a novelist was over. '"No longer a by-product" but a "main occupation"' explores the short-lived period during in the late 1950s and early 1960s when the author believed his future lay in short story writing, a format he had previously dismissed as being of secondary importance.

As in Volumes 1 and 2, this guide gives the first publication date of a particular piece of writing. It neither includes an exhaustive list of all subsequent printings nor lists translations into other languages unless of particular note. Inevitably, as the scope of these guides has expanded, earlier entries have been superseded or radically updated. Thus, Volume 1, Part G is now entirely redundant, and the bibliographic list of works about Greene has been extensively revised and updated.

The writer's predilection for practical jokes resulted in his use of pseudonyms, particularly in magazine articles and sometimes competition entries. Some of his pseudonyms, such as the name 'Hilary Trench', assumed a more sinister 'janiform' identity. A number of these have been identified in both Volumes 1 and 2, but we do not claim a comprehensive coverage of this form of deception and acknowledge that further research is required in this field.

There is an automatic assumption made that the name 'Graham Greene' is used in all the writings attributed to him. However, in instances where the work is unsigned or variations such as 'G.G.', 'H. Graham' or 'H.G.G.' are known to have been used, these are acknowledged in the entry.

Unsurprisingly, the unsigned writings have caused problems with verification. Greene's official bibliographer Alan Redway spent a good deal of time, with the writer's assistance, attempting to identify his early reviews, particularly those for the *Glasgow Herald* during 1926–27. The problem was exacerbated because the paper did not keep proper records. Given the passage of time, Greene was often unable to verify authorship or had a different recollection of events. For example, in 1973, he claimed that his negative review of 'Dragon of the Alchemist' had caused his connection with the paper to cease owing to a threatened libel action. But Redway found no trace whatsoever of the offending review.

Some information was provided in Volume 1 about the sales numbers and print runs of individual works. That information was culled from a variety of sources, including Greene's somewhat faulty memory. In this volume the sales numbers of his books, in their 'original' editions, are taken from a list provided by Charles Pick, who worked for William Heinemann from 1962 to 1985. However, the information on the three children's books does not come from the same source. It is acknowledged that more work needs to be undertaken on this subject; of course, the very fact that Pick's letter was written in 1973 precludes the writer's later work.

There are some deliberate omissions. According to Alan Redway, in 1939, the *Spectator* started to include, under 'Shorter Notices', some unsigned reviews. Due to wartime exigencies, no records were kept pertaining to authorship. As well as being brief, apparently they were also quite bland in tone. Greene was asked both in 1953 and again in 1983 if he could identify any of these as his own work, a task he undertook. Therefore, only reviews which Greene was sure he had written are included here.

As an 'eminent author' Greene was also asked to contribute to an *Observer* newspaper 'Books of the Year' feature. These were little more than brief recommendations. Only Greene's comments in 1955 concerning Vladimir Nabokov's *Lolita* have been included because of its historical relevance concerning the author and John Gordon.

A good deal of Greene's very early published work appeared in either the *Weekly Westminster* or the *Westminster Gazette*. These very similarly named magazines were in publication in the first half of the 1920s. They merged in January 1926 to become the *Weekly Westminster Gazette* before it too was subsumed by the *Daily News* in 1928. It appears that Wobbe's bibliography is not accurate in this respect, so Redway's delineation has been used in these cases.

The lives of a writer

A section with this title was included in the Introduction to our first volume, giving consideration to some of the most important books available on Graham Greene's life. It is an indication of the continuing interest in Greene that an update on that section is now necessary.

Pre-eminent among these works is Richard Greene's single-volume biography, published as *Russian Roulette: The Life and Times of Graham Greene* in the UK in 2020 and as *The Unquiet Englishman: A Life of Graham Greene* in North America in 2021. As the brilliant editor of the 2007 collection of Greene's letters, Richard Greene is the foremost scholar on the writer in the world. A decade of research has produced a work of impeccable scholarship and wit, nicely balancing the different aspects and periods of Greene's life and giving particular emphasis to his involvements in many countries around the globe.

Professor Greene's book is the new starting point for anyone wanting to know more about Graham Greene's life.

There has been one major new memoir by someone who knew Greene well – Bernard Diederich's *Seeds of Fiction: Graham Greene's Adventures in Haiti and Central America 1954–1983* was published just too late in 2012 to be included in our first volume. Diederich, who died in 2020, was a journalist, historian and author who became Greene's close friend and a very important figure in interesting him in Haiti, which resulted in the writing of *The Comedians*. His book gives a vital insight into Greene's involvements in Haiti and Central America in the latter period of his life.

Other aspects or periods of Greene's life have been covered in recent specialist studies. Pierre Smolik's 2013 book *Graham Greene: The Swiss Chapter* traces Greene's connections with Switzerland, a country in which his daughter came to live and in which he died. Christopher Hull's *Our Man Down in Havana: The Story Behind Graham Greene's Cold War Spy Novel*, published in 2019, is a definitive study of Greene in Cuba, and the novel and film that followed. Complementing Hull's book is Sarah Rainsford's *Our Woman in Havana: Reporting Castro's Cuba* (2018), which recounts the BBC correspondent's three-year assignment to the Caribbean island and her attempts to find evidence of the pre-revolutionary capital city familiar to Greene. Finally, belonging to a completely different genre is *The Prague Coup* (2018) by Jean-Luc Fromental and Miles Hyman, a graphic novel loosely based on Greene's time in Vienna in 1948 and the coup d'état taking place in neighbouring Czechoslovakia.

Mention should also be made of publications to come. Graham Greene's friendship and travels with Father Leopoldo Durán is the subject of Carlos Villar Flor's *The Real Monsignor Quixote: Graham Greene's Travels around Spain and Portugal* (working title; Oxford: Oxford University Press, 2022). Kevin Ruane's account of Greene's travels and adventures in Vietnam in the 1950s, given the provisional title 'Graham Greene in Love and War', is promised for the future as a blend of history, literature and biography.

Greene's bibliographers

It is impossible to know quite what prompted Alan Redway, a banker by profession, to contact Graham Greene in June 1949, offering to 'compile a competent bibliography for the benefit of collectors and dealers' and tentatively to ask, 'Would such a project meet with your approval?' The writer's international reputation was reaching its height: the controversial and much analysed novel *The Heart of the Matter* was in the process of selling over three hundred thousand copies in its initial three years of publication while *The Third Man* was about to be screened in the UK for the first time.

Book collecting and bibliographic research was in Redway's blood. His father, Frank, was a London dealer in rare and fine books and manuscripts and a nephew of George Redway, a publisher. Cautiously, Greene advised him to seek professional advice as to whether 'the time was ripe, if it ever will be ripe', for such an undertaking. But clearly the author grew to like and trust him, commenting in 1977 that he was an 'honest and nice chap'.

Alan Redway was not the only bibliographer interested in Greene in the 1950s. An essay by William Birmingham entitled 'Graham Greene Criticism: A Bibliographical Study' (1952) claimed that there was already sufficient critical material extant to warrant a historiography at least. In the United States, Neil Brennan secured a grant from the Graduate School at Auburn University. His quite comprehensive bibliography is included in the work edited by Robert O. Evans, titled *Graham Greene: Some Critical Considerations* (1963). Brennan generously acknowledged the work of Phylis Hargreaves, 'Graham Greene: A Selected Bibliography' (1957), and others working at the time on similar projects. It was Greene himself who alerted Redway to Brennan in 1953. This led to the two men deciding to work together. In 1968 Brennan and Redway were joined by a third collaborator, Cecil Woolf. However, Woolf was to prove unreliable as a partner, and by the late 1970s Brennan appears to have taken over his responsibilities for compiling data on magazine articles written by Greene.

The publication of two further bibliographies, both in 1979, must have constituted something of a blow to the Redway/Brennan partnership. Robert H. Miller's *Graham Greene: A Descriptive Catalog* provided, in the author's words, detailed information regarding the 'physical nature' of most of Greene's major works. Miller modestly described his book as a mere contribution towards a definitive bibliography and graciously acknowledged the achievement of Redway and his partner in their long-term task.

There is no such acknowledgement to be found in the introduction to Roland Wobbe's *Graham Greene: A Bibliography and Guide to Research*, also published in 1979. Wobbe's primary motive for compiling his book was the absence of a single-volume, bibliographic reference work on Greene. It was this that inspired him to take on the task after gaining a doctorate at the University of Exeter. Importantly, he noted that a catalogue of the author's extensive contributions to periodicals, particularly his film and book reviews, had never been prepared. He argued that this would enlighten the reader regarding what was then a little-known aspect of the writer's work. The section of Wobbe's guide devoted to this topic was meticulously compiled, and one can only admire his research skills in a pre-internet era. After the bibliography appeared, publications such as *Night and Day* (1985), *Reflections* (1990) and *The Graham Greene Film Reader: Mornings in the Dark* (1993) have been comprehensive in scope and serve to vindicate Wobbe's stated aim for his guide.

Demonstrating typical loyalty, Greene seemed to want nothing to do with this unofficial bibliographer who approached him once for help but got nowhere. He later cautioned Ragnar Svanström against providing Wobbe with information concerning Swedish publications of his works. At this distance, there seems to have been a degree of naivety on Wobbe's part not to have made contact with Greene at an early stage in his research, explaining his intentions, even seeking approval.

Sadly, Alan Redway died in 1983. A letter of condolence from Graham Greene was sent to his widow, Helen. Subsequently, he encouraged her to donate her husband's valuable research papers to what was then the Joseph Mark Lauinger Memorial Library, Georgetown University (now the Booth Family Center for Special Collections), with which Greene had established close links. Shortly before Redway passed away, a memorandum of agreement with Oxford University Press (OUP) was signed by the two bibliographers. OUP had recently taken over the Soho Bibliography series although the company retained the original name.

Neil Brennan then assumed sole responsibility for the project while lecturing in English at Villanova, a private establishment in Pennsylvania. In the early 1980s, his daughter Helen assisted him by making research notes at the extensive Greene collection housed in the Harry Ransom Humanities Center, the University of Texas at Austin. Thus Brennan was unaffected by Norman Sherry's later 'embargo' on researchers using the major Greene archives in the United States while he was completing his monumental, three-volume biography. Brennan retired from lecturing in 1987 but continued to prepare the bibliography for publication.

By the turn of the millennium it was fully expected that OUP would be publishing this text shortly. There was promising news that it was practically complete, but when Neil Brennan also died in 2006, OUP admitted that there was more to do than merely 'tying up a few loose ends'. After regular postponements, the publisher conceded in 2011 that the Redway/Brennan bibliography was very unlikely to appear within the next few years. One can only deeply regret that the results of over sixty years of scholarship and endeavour have never been shared with the wider public. Thus Roland Wobbe's book, which has never been republished or updated, remains the sole, fully fledged, conventional bibliography on Greene in existence, and this rare edition is still regularly employed as a reference guide by some second-hand booksellers.

There can be little doubt that Graham Greene would have been saddened and disappointed that Alan Redway in particular did not live to see his work in print. Greene's personal interest in all matters related to book collecting and publishing has been well documented. As his niece Louise Dennys once remarked, Greene loved the very spirit of publishing. This personal engagement is evident in his published works, not only in the well-known *Victorian Detective Fiction: A Catalogue of the Collection* (1966), a collaboration between Dorothy Glover and Greene, but also in *Dear David, Dear Graham* (1989), a 'bibliographic correspondence' he engaged in with David Low, a rare books dealer, and in the prefaces he wrote for *A Bibliography of Arthur Conan Doyle* (1983) and David Low's autobiography *With All Faults* (1973). His brother Hugh was also a bibliophile, and by the 1970s they were regularly planning expeditions together around second-hand bookshops in the UK.

We respectfully acknowledge, therefore, the valuable work of these bibliographers who have gone before us. Their research, to a greater or lesser extent, has usefully informed the compilation of this three-volume guide which, of course, has enjoyed the unique benefit of being more comprehensive simply because it has been constructed retrospectively to Greene's writing career.

The French and German collected editions

Greene wrote a series of introductions for the French and German collected editions of his fiction in the early 1960s, as mentioned in passing in Volume 2. These were subsequently published in France by Robert Laffont in 1964 under the general title *Les Oeuvres Choises de Graham Greene*, appearing in three volumes each comprising four books. The German series was published between 1962 and 1965 by Paul Zsolnay Verlag of Vienna. In this case, six books were issued with varying numbers of texts included in each one.

A typed note by Greene's secretary survives, noting that Greene wrote a total of fifteen introductions for the German editions in late 1962 and early 1963. Until we were working on this guide it was believed that only the introduction to *England Made Me* (1966) had been subsequently published in English. We now know that this was not the case as the author's introduction to *The Power and the Glory* has been 'discovered' in an edition which forms part of the Modern Novel series published by Heinemann Educational in 1963 – clearly aimed at the older secondary school pupil market (see page 31).

Most of the original typescripts of these introductions in their original English-language versions have survived and appear in various archives of the writer's work. They are very similar in approach being both retrospective and critically objective. Those familiar with Greene's Heinemann/Bodley Head UK Collected editions, published in the 1970s, would instantly recognize the very close textual similarities; in some cases complete paragraphs have been reused.

The same is true of the second volume of Greene's autobiography, *Ways of Escape* (1980). For example, his evocative description of how he sat at a small bureau in his parents' home while on sick leave from *The Times* and wrote his first published novel *The Man Within* is practically identical. Apart from it being a constant trait in the writer's professional life – that he never appeared to waste a word when it could be put to good use – it is also consistent with Greene's early ideas for his autobiography. From the start he wanted to eschew the tried-and-tested autobiographical formula in favour of a roughly chronological string of narratives about each novel he had written, in which he could provide interesting contextual detail concerning events leading to their publication but at the same time avoid too many revelations about his private life.

In the event, of course, he did produce a conventional first part, *A Sort of Life*

(1971), followed nine years later by *Ways of Escape*, which, as mentioned earlier, relies heavily on the introductions he had composed for the continental editions some seventeen years previously. The idea for this format had been originally suggested to Greene by Paul Zsolnay in connection with the German Collected Edition.

The German series differs from the more selective French 'Les Grands Roman' approach inasmuch as it sets out to be a true collected presentation of the writer's fictional work. Thus, the sixth volume comprises the more minor works *The Third Man* and *Loser Takes All*, plus twenty short stories and three of his plays (1960).

Interestingly, the typescript of a general foreword to the French series, dated May 1964, has survived. It is written in a distinctly 'un-Greenean' style, presumably to suit the French reader, replete with flowery sentimentality and extended metaphors. Greene was extremely displeased when he received the French translation of this short piece and wrote demanding that his publisher use instead a fresh translation he had since commissioned. To add insult to injury, he added, 'I would also ask you to have the courtesy to print my name as it is spelt.'

The work of The Graham Greene Birthplace Trust

The Graham Greene Birthplace Trust was founded on 20 September 1997 by a group of enthusiastic aficionados from Berkhamsted, Greene's birthplace. It has been central in helping to maintain an active interest in their famous 'son'. It is a charitable, non-profit-making organization whose purpose is to promote interest and research into the life and works of this important twentieth-century writer.

Each year since 1998, with just two exceptions, the Trust has organized a four-day festival in Berkhamsted dedicated solely to the writer's work and life. The annual programme includes talks, some of an academic nature, films, guided walks around the town and local countryside well known to and referenced by Greene in his writings, social gatherings, bookstalls and exhibitions. A focus is an annual birthday toast as the event occurs as close as possible to Greene's birthday on 2 October. The festival is officially titled 'The Graham Greene International Festival' and truly lives up to its name. It is a gathering of people from across the world with an interest in and enthusiasm for this writer as well as a showcase for new books and their authors. It is testament to his universal appeal that a high percentage of the new research in the field is not being undertaken in the UK.

Members of the Greene family have been staunch supporters of the work of the Trust and have served as Patrons, none more so than Caroline Bourget, Greene's daughter, who died at home in late February 2021 at the age of eighty-seven. Caroline was a regular and enthusiastic attendee at the annual festivals as well as a generous financial supporter of the work of the Trust.

The quarterly magazine, *A Sort of Newsletter* (*ASON*), which Friends receive free as the main benefit of their subscriptions, has been an integral part of the Trust's work since its inception. Each twenty-page, illustrated edition contains a rich mix of articles, reviews, correspondence and news. *ASON* is not intended as an academic journal; there is something for everyone with an interest in the writer.

Complementing the magazine, the Trust maintains an active website: www.grahamgreenebt.org. In addition to providing a year-round, up-to-date 'news service', the website also provides a comprehensive guide to the forthcoming festival, the centrepiece of the Trust's rationale. An audio recording of each festival talk is made and becomes available on the website in the months following the event. It is aimed at those unable to attend in person. The website also encourages researchers to submit papers giving information about 'work in progress'.

A recent addition to the Trust's 'portfolio' is its link with the University of North Georgia. Professor Joyce Stavick, who recently retired from the Faculty of English, was instrumental in establishing an academic, peer-reviewed journal dedicated to the works and life of Graham Greene. The inaugural edition of *Graham Greene Studies* was published in 2017 by the University of North Georgia Press in association with the Graham Greene Birthplace Trust. *Graham Greene Studies* Volume 2 was published online in September 2021.

We have mentioned before the personal debt we owe the Trust for their support in this bibliographic project. This extended particularly to a generous research award which enabled us to travel to the United States on three occasions to view Greene archives in Austin, Texas; Boston, Massachusetts; and Washington, DC.

In 1881, during the long years of Pax Britannica, Major General Charles Gordon (later feted as Gordon of Khartoum) was instrumental in persuading the British Admiralty to set up an intelligence branch on account of the fact that valuable information was often accrued by HM ships and overseas consuls but never systematically recorded. Gordon was ahead of his time with regard to intelligence matters, importantly recognizing that it is one thing to acquire information, another to make use of it. This realization became the principal motivation for us to compile this final volume.

Section 1

The Works of Graham Greene: A Reader's Bibliography and Guide

Section 1a ADDITIONAL MATERIAL

INTRODUCTION

p. 4, nine lines from bottom: after 'subsequent reprints', add 'or of translations into other languages'.
p. 11, line 11: *The Captain and the Enemy* is partly set in 'Panama' not 'Paraguay'.

PART A

BOOKS BY GRAHAM GREENE

A1 *BABBLING APRIL*

Poem 10 title is 'I shall be Happy'.
Poem 11 title is 'If you were Dead'.
First Sonnet (Poem 12) begins 'It is not that he gains your craftiest smile,'.
Poem 15 title is 'The Banbury Road, 12 p.m.'
Second Sonnet (Poem 22) has the title 'Sonnet', and begins 'All these belong to youth; all these I hate;'. See **C44** in Volume 1 and in this volume. This poem, with the different first line of 'These things are youth's, old owl; these things I hate.', appeared elsewhere with the title 'A Tramp Finds Himself Inspected By an Owl' – see **B4** and **C11** in this volume.

A2 *THE MAN WITHIN*

The Collected Edition was published in 1976 not 1975.
First UK printing, numbers sold 12,594.
Anthony Sant had the alternative titles of *Prologue to Pilgrimage* and *Goodnight, Sweet Ladies*. The school novel referred to was not 'an early attempt', but *Lucius*, an unfinished novel written in 1958 (see Volume 2, pp. 86–7, and the essay '*Vivat Bristowa*' later in this volume). *A Sense of Security* was material which eventually became the novel *The Human Factor* and was being written as Greene wrote *A Sort of Life*.

A3 *THE NAME OF ACTION*

First UK printing, numbers sold 4,763.

A4 *RUMOUR AT NIGHTFALL*

First UK printing, numbers sold 2,868.
After years of wishing to 'disown' the novel and refusing to permit its republication, Greene made an unexpected proposal in the late 1980s: to offer the publication rights to the Graham Greene Foundation in order to raise funds. The background to the foundation in his name and its brief history are recounted in Carlos Villar Flor's book *Viajes con mi cura: Las andanzas de Graham Greene por España y Portugal*. (See Introduction to this volume, p. 6.)

A5 *STAMBOUL TRAIN*
First UK printing, numbers sold 20,829.

A6 *IT'S A BATTLEFIELD*
First UK printing, numbers sold 7,426.

A8 *ENGLAND MADE ME*
First UK printing, numbers sold 4,431. Greene wrote to his American publisher in 1952 claiming that he never liked *England Made Me* as a title and preferred *The Shipwrecked.* However, at the time of first publication, he could not persuade Heinemann to change it.

A9 *THE BASEMENT ROOM AND OTHER STORIES*
The story 'Proof Positive' was first published in the *Manchester Guardian*, 24 December 1931; 'I Spy' in the *Manchester Guardian*, 9 September 1932; 'The Basement Room' as a five-day serial in the *News Chronicle* in May or June 1935.

A10 *JOURNEY WITHOUT MAPS*
First UK printing, numbers sold 1,430. The Pan Books reprint was published in 1948, not 1946.

A11 *A GUN FOR SALE*
First UK printing, numbers sold 4,874.

A12 *BRIGHTON ROCK*
First UK printing, numbers sold 6,804. The novel was serialized in the *Evening Standard* in September 1938.

A14 *THE CONFIDENTIAL AGENT*
First UK printing, numbers sold 4,948.

A15 *THE POWER AND THE GLORY*
First UK printing, numbers sold 12,398.

A17 *THE MINISTRY OF FEAR*
First UK printing, numbers sold 17,886.

A18 *THE LITTLE TRAIN*
First UK printing, numbers printed 19,742.

A19 *NINETEEN STORIES*
First UK printing, numbers sold 12,311. The short story 'A Drive in the Country' was originally published in the magazine *The Passing Show* on 21 March 1936 under the title 'Crazy Elopement'. 'Crazy Elopement' was included in *Missing from Their Homes*: short stories based on the BBC broadcasts for missing persons (London, Hutchinson), July 1936.

A20 *THE HEART OF THE MATTER*
Insert 'London' before 'Heinemann'.
First UK printing, numbers sold 89,783. Viking Press published 750 specially bound copies for distribution to friends of the company.

A21 *AFTER TWO YEARS*
The poems included in this volume are: 'The Little Peace', 'Behind the Tight Pupils', 'After Two Years', 'For February Twelve', 'On Coming into Naples at Sunset from Capri With the Smell of Freetown over the Water', 'The Grave in the Forest', 'A Letter from London' and 'And The Grass'.
All but two of the poems, 'After Two Years' and 'A Letter from London', were later republished in *A Quick Look Behind: Footnotes to An Autobiography* (Volume 1, **A64**). All but one was given a new title, perhaps to protect the identity

of Catherine Walston. 'The Little Peace' was renamed 'Assisi'; 'For February Twelve' was titled 'A Birthday Thought'; 'Behind Tight Pupils' became 'After Birth'; 'The Grave in the Forest' was retitled 'Digging a Grave'; and 'And the Grass' became 'The Grass'. The last poem was also published in the *Tablet* in October 1987 (see Volume 1, **C720**).

A22 *THE THIRD MAN* and *THE FALLEN IDOL*
The Collected Edition was published in 1976, not 1975.
First UK printing, numbers sold 49,372.
The first publication of the preface to *The Third Man* was published as '"The Third Man" as a story and a film' in the *New York Times*, 19 March 1949.

A23 *THE LITTLE FIRE ENGINE*
First UK printing, numbers printed 5,000.

A24 *THE LOST CHILDHOOD AND OTHER ESSAYS*
First UK printing, numbers printed 7,400.

A25 *THE END OF THE AFFAIR*
First UK printing, numbers sold 67,189.
The novel had the original alternative titles of *The Edge of the Desert* and *The Point of Departure*.

A26 *FOR CHRISTMAS*
The poems included in this volume are: 'Winter Country', 'Those who are Hungry', 'After Four Years', 'A Birthday Letter', 'A Letter from the Workhouse', 'Paris is Empty' and 'In the Restaurant Car'.
Just three of the poems in this private collection were re-published. 'Those who are Hungry' became 'A Name'; 'A Birthday Letter' was retitled 'The Old Words' and contains some textual alterations. Both appear in *A Quick Look Behind*. 'A Letter from the Workhouse' was published in *Commonweal* in December 1973 (see Volume 1, **C694**).

A28 *THE LIVING ROOM*
First UK printing, numbers sold 15,160.

A30 *THE LITTLE STEAMROLLER*
First UK printing, numbers printed 10,000.

A31 *TWENTY-ONE STORIES*
The collection was first published in the Heinemann Uniform Edition. First UK printing, numbers sold 20,532. There was no subsequent edition of this collection.

A32 *LOSER TAKES ALL*
The Collected Edition was published in 1976, not 1975.
First UK printing, numbers sold 44,890.
A *Picture Post* serialization, 21 August–18 September 1954, was called 'A pre-scenario for a film'.

A33 *THE QUIET AMERICAN*
First UK printing, numbers sold 113,399.
The Quiet American is one of few holograph manuscripts of Greene's major works believed to be still in private hands. A first working draft, comprising 135 pages with heavy authorial revisions plus three pages of autograph notes, was sold in 1995 for $68,500. The manuscript is dated 8 March and 31 May 1952.
Greene notes on the holograph title page that he began the novel (which he originally classed as an 'Entertainment')

on 8 March 1952. This was a 'false start' and the work was recorded as 'begun again' on 31 May 1952. It was finished in June 1955.

A34 ***THE POTTING SHED***

First UK printing, numbers sold 8,904.

A35 ***OUR MAN IN HAVANA***

First UK printing, numbers sold 82,129.
The opera by Malcolm Williamson based on the novel was first performed in 1963, not 1962. (See **A69**.)

A36 ***A VISIT TO MORIN***

This was not the first publication in book form. It was included in *Seize Nouvelles* (translated into French by Marcelle Sibon) published by Robert Laffont, Paris, 1958.

A37 ***THE COMPLAISANT LOVER***

First UK printing, numbers sold 8,170.
The play opened at the Royal Court Theatre in Liverpool before its first performance at the Globe Theatre in London on 18 June 1959.
The play was directed not produced by John Gielgud.

A38 ***A BURNT-OUT CASE***

First UK printing, numbers sold 73,602.

A39 ***IN SEARCH OF A CHARACTER***

Extracts were published in the *Observer*, 22 October 1961.

A40 ***THREE PLAYS***

Greene's preface was published in the *Sunday Telegraph*, 17 September 1961, under the title 'Novelist in the Theatre'. See **C121** in this volume. (See also Volume 1, **C598** and **A40**.)

A42 ***A SENSE OF REALITY***

The original title was to be 'Under the Garden and Other Stories' and would have comprised thirteen (and perhaps more) stories divided into three sections. Greene was influenced to make this radical change by his friend and colleague A. S. Frere. (See the essay '"No longer a by-product" but a "main occupation"' later in this volume.)

A44 ***CARVING A STATUE***

The play had a two-week run in Brighton from 31 August 1964 before opening in the West End.

A45 ***THE COMEDIANS***

The Collected Edition was published in 1976, not 1975.
Extracts were published in *The Sunday Times*, 24, 31 January, 7 February 1965.

A48 ***COLLECTED ESSAYS***

It had been suggested that *Collected Essays* should be titled *The Lost Childhood*, thus repeating the name of the original collection (see Volume 1, **A24**). However, Greene argued logically to his publisher Max Reinhardt, 'We are in danger of losing sales to libraries etc. who already possess that title.'

A50 ***A SORT OF LIFE***

Extracts were published in *The Sunday Times*, 22 and 29 August 1971.
The US edition of the autobiography was the first of the author's books to be published by Simon and Schuster and not

by Viking Press, who had been Greene's publisher for the past thirty-two years. The move followed a dispute with Viking over how his last novel, *Travels with My Aunt*, had been marketed.

A52 *THE PLEASURE-DOME: THE COLLECTED FILM CRITICISM 1935–40*
Greene's Introduction was published in the *Daily Telegraph Magazine*, 27 October 1972, together with reviews of nine films.

A53 *THE VIRTUE OF DISLOYALTY*
An early version of Greene's 1969 speech is contained in an essay entitled 'La Mision del escritor en la sociedad actual' which was published in the Argentine journal *Sur* in 1963, translated by Miguel Alfredo Olivera. (See also the essay 'Graham Greene's *The Virtue of Disloyalty*: Origins, context and significance' in Section 3 of this volume.)

A54 *THE HONORARY CONSUL*
The Leeds University typescript copy has composition dates 'Sep. 1969–Sep. 1972', not 1970–3.

A55 *THE PORTABLE GRAHAM GREENE*
The 1994 updated edition was published by the Penguin Group in Britain as well as by Viking Penguin.

A56 *LORD ROCHESTER'S MONKEY*
Extracts were published in *The Times* Saturday Review, 31 August 1974.

A57 *THE RETURN OF A. J. RAFFLES*
The 250 hardback copies of the limited edition had orange covers and matching dust jackets. Nos 1–80 were for friends and signed by the author. The remainder of the first edition had stiff grey wrappers.

A58 *THE HUMAN FACTOR*
An extract of the novel was published in *Playboy* in February 1978.
The novel was started ten years before its publication and was originally given the title *The Cold Fault*. (See also **A2** in this volume.)

A59 *DOCTOR FISCHER OF GENEVA or THE BOMB PARTY*
The novel was not issued as part of the Collected Edition.
Chapter 9 of the novella was published in *The Times* on 29 March 1980.

A60 *WAYS OF ESCAPE*
The Toronto limited edition was published by Lester & Orpen Dennys.
The section in *Ways of Escape* on *The Human Factor* predates Greene's Collected Edition Introduction to that novel by two years.

A62 *J'ACCUSE: THE DARK SIDE OF NICE*
An extract of the essay was published in *The Sunday Times* on 9 May 1982.
Greene referred to *J'Accuse* as a 'pamphlet' on a number of occasions prior to publication. Later, he appeared to change his mind. He wrote to Max Reinhardt in 1988 regarding the classification of titles of his work, 'I think *J'Accuse* ought to come under the heading "Essays" and not "Autobiography".'

A63 *MONSIGNOR QUIXOTE*
The extract 'How Father Quixote became a Monsignor' was published in April 1980.

A65 *YES AND NO* and *FOR WHOM THE BELL CHIMES*
Hugh Greene suggested that a dramatization of 'Alas, Poor Maling' could be used as a 'curtain raiser' for *For Whom the Bell Chimes* as the latter play was very short. This suggestion was never taken up although Graham Greene had written the screenplay for the story as part of the *Shades of Greene* TV series. (See Volume 1, **F31**.)

A66 *GETTING TO KNOW THE GENERAL: THE STORY OF AN INVOLVEMENT*
An early title of this work was *Getting to Know the General: A Friendship in Panama.*

A67 *THE MONSTER OF CAPRI*
The book includes another story called 'The Monster's Treasure'. It is in an identical format, consisting of reproductions of postcards.
An additional twenty unnumbered copies were printed for distribution to friends and family.

A69 *THE COLLECTED PLAYS OF GRAHAM GREENE*
The opera version of *Our Man in Havana* by Malcolm Williamson was first performed in 1963, not 1962.
Greene's three-act play *A House of Reputation* is the subject of an essay later in this volume.

More recent stage adaptations of Greene's novels have included a musical version of *Travels with My Aunt* in Chichester in 2016, with a book by Ron Cowan and Daniel Lipman, music by George Stiles and lyrics by Anthony Drewe; a touring version of *Brighton Rock* in 2018, written by Bryony Lavery and with music by Hannah Peel; and in 2022 a musical version of *Our Man in Havana*, adapted by Richard Hough with music by Ben Morales Frost.

A75 *REFLECTIONS*
The 2014 reprint of the collection, selected and introduced by Judith Adamson, includes additional material. There is one, hitherto unpublished, essay, 'Thoughts on Nicaragua' (1986). Five other pieces, 'The Country with Five Frontiers' (1977), 'The Great Spectacular' (1978), 'Freedom of Thought' (1981), 'Musings at Eighty' (1984) and 'A Constant Question Mark' (1987), appear either in book form or unabridged for the first time.
The first US edition was published by Viking, not Simon and Schuster.

A75 and **A76 *THE LAST WORD AND OTHER STORIES***
Given their respective dates of publication, these two works should be listed in reverse order.
'The Man who Stole the Eiffel Tower' was first published in book form in *Seize Nouvelles* (translated into French by Marcelle Sibon), published by Robert Laffont, Paris, 1958.

A77 *A WORLD OF MY OWN: A DREAM DIARY*

This work was published by Reinhardt in association with Viking and simultaneously with Alfred A. Knopf in Canada.

A79 *COMPLETE SHORT STORIES*

To the list of stories not included in *Complete Short Stories* should be added 'Castles in the Air' (**C1** in this volume), 'Upended: A Macabre Meditation' (**C120** in this volume) and 'An Impossibly Bad Hotel' (**C157** in this volume).

Greene wrote four short stories for *The Berkhamstedian* (**C1**, **C2** and **C3** in Volume 1 and **C1** in this volume) which were never reprinted and to which there is no public access at the express wish of the Greene Estate.

PART B

CONTRIBUTIONS BY GRAHAM GREENE TO BOOKS

B1 *OXFORD POETRY, 1923*, and **B2 *PUBLIC SCHOOL VERSE: AN ANTHOLOGY, III, 1921–1922***

The order of these two entries should be reversed, since **B1** was published in November 1923 and **B2** around May 1923.

B4 *THE BEST POEMS OF 1925*

In this anthology, Greene's poem is signed 'H. Graham Greene'. 'A Tramp Finds Himself Inspected by an Owl' was published in the *Weekly Westminster*, 6 September 1924, which predates its appearance in this book: see **C11** in this volume. It was published as the second Sonnet (Poem 22), with a different first line, in *Babbling April*. (See **A1** in this volume.)

B9 *THE OLD SCHOOL: ESSAYS BY DIVERS HANDS*

The essay and preface have never been reprinted separately from the book, but the whole book was issued as an Oxford University Press paperback in 1984.

B23 *THE PENGUIN NEW WRITING 30*

Contrary to what is written under this entry in Volume 1, Greene does *not* state in *A Sort of Life* that he wrote the story around 1926 or 1927.

B34 *VENUS IN THE KITCHEN: or LOVE'S COOKERY BOOK*

On Greene's review of *Footnote on Capri*, see **C110** in this volume.

B41 *UN HOMME DANS LA RIZIÈRE*

Colonel Leroy was military governor of 'Bên Tre' province, not 'Bentre'.

B43 *L'OBELISCO*

There are several errors made in Volume 1 concerning this entry. The title of Greene's essay, used both in the 1953 pamphlet and the 1960 (not 1955) book, is 'Nino Caffè'. The book containing the essay also takes the title *Nino Caffè*. The publisher, L'Obelisco, uses Greene's name as the author on the title page although the essay forms only part of the contents. Arguably, in view of the above, the 1960 publication is wrongly included in Part B of the guide. Indeed, booksellers classify the 1960 L'Obelisco publication as the true first edition by Graham Greene.

B54 *EDGAR WALLACE: THE BIOGRAPHY OF A PHENOMENON*

Margaret Lane's biography was first published in 1938, not 1939. Greene's Introduction was first published in *The Sunday Times*, 15 November 1964. (See C124 in this volume.)

B58 *AUTHORS TAKE SIDES ON VIETNAM*

The first question was 'Are you for, or against, the intervention of the United States in Vietnam?' The number of responses included in the book was 259, with a further small total excluded.

B60 *MY SILENT WAR*

Greene visited Philby in Moscow in 1986 and 1987.

B62 *PAPA DOC: HAITI AND ITS DICTATOR*

The book was reissued as a paperback in 2006 by Marcus Weiner Publishers, Princeton, NJ, with the title *Papa Doc and the Tontons Macoutes*. Greene's piece appears there as a Preface.

B65 *WITH ALL FAULTS*

The Introduction was published in the *Observer Magazine* on 1 July 1973 under the title 'My Adventures as a Bookhunter'.

B67 *AN IMPOSSIBLE WOMAN: THE MEMORIES OF DOTTORESSA MOOR OF CAPRI*

Greene's Preface was published in the *Daily Telegraph Magazine* on 12 September 1975. (See C137 in this volume.) The original title of the book was to be *The Wild One*.

B73 *THE BACHELOR OF ARTS*

Greene's new introduction to Narayan's novel was published in the *Spectator*, 28 October 1978.

An original holograph version of this appreciation of Narayan's work is to be found in the author's abandoned, early attempt at autobiography included in the *Graham Greene Collection* at the University of Louisville, Kentucky. The relevant section of this holograph is untitled and undated.

B90 *DEAR DAVID, DEAR GRAHAM*

The full title of the book is *Dear David, Dear Graham: A Bibliographic Conversation.*

PART C

CONTRIBUTIONS BY GRAHAM GREENE TO NEWSPAPERS, JOURNALS AND MAGAZINES

C1 'The Tick of the Clock'. A clock speaks words of comfort to a dying woman telling her she has led a blameless life.

C2 'The Poetry of Modern Life'. The writer's vision of a medieval knight tells him that the rumour that poetry and romance are dead is not true as long as heroic and chivalric deeds are still enacted.

C3 'The Tyranny of Realism'. A small boy brought before a king, who has a maiden at his feet, is told to release whatever is restraining him. When the boy complies, he realizes the king's face is the face of a god who then kisses the maiden who is revealed as 'fantasie'.

C5 'An Epic Fragment from "The Dish Pioneers". Canto I: Sarah Beeton and Angels on Horseback. Attributed to A-f-d-N-y-s'.
Written for a competition in the *Weekly Westminster Gazette* in July 1922.
A-f-d N-y-s is Alfred Noyes.

C7 The poem 'Stepping Stones' was written for a competition.

C14 'A Pauper's Wealth'. The same poem is entitled 'Stupidity' both in *Babbling April* (Volume 1, **A1**) and in *Decachord* (Volume 1, **C75**).

C16 The short story 'The New House' was written for a *Weekly Westminster Gazette* competition.

C19 This is not the first publication of 'Apologia'. See also Volume 1, **B1**. The poem also appeared in the *Golden Hind* II/6 in January 1924. However, this version is the only one to carry the dedication 'For V.M.S.', whose identity is not known, although, as a nineteen-year-old, the theme of unrequited love was probably relevant to the poet at the time.

C22 Book review. The review was titled 'The Educational Outlook'. It was a review of the journal *Education Outlook*.

C26 'In the Occupied Area. An Oxford Undergraduate's Impressions'. The article is introduced with a quotation by Thomas Hardy.

C38 This was the first of Greene's works to be published abroad. *The Literary Digest* was a New York general interest weekly magazine.

C43 The full title is 'Eating a Lyons Chop in 1930', not '1930'. It is referred to in *A Sort of Life*.

C44 The full title is 'Sonnet: All things belong to youth; all these I hate'. The poem later appeared as 'Sonnet' (Poem 33) in *Babbling April*. It had earlier appeared with a different title and first line. (See **B4** and **C11** in this volume.)

C45 The book review is signed H.G.G.

C46 The book review is signed H.G.G.

C47 The poem 'The Godly Distance' was published in the *Weekly Westminster*, not the *Weekly Westminster Gazette*.

C55 Greene wrote, 'It is because I am a great admirer of Mr. Acton's poetry that I say without hesitation that his first volume, "Aquarium" was astonishingly bad.'

C64 The book review 'Mr. Priestley in Search of the Comic' was published in the *Weekly Westminster*, not the *Weekly Westminster Gazette*.

C66 The review of *The Life of Henri Brulard* was published in the *Weekly Westminster*, not the *Weekly Westminster Gazette*.

C72 The poem 'First Love' was signed H. Graham. It was published in the *Saturday Review*, not the *New Statesman*. It won a prize.

C74 The entry 'A Walk on the Sussex Downs' is chronologically in the wrong place. It should follow Volume 1, **C75** (see below for redating of **C76**, **C77**, **C78**, **C79**).

C75 The poem 'Stupidity' was published first in the *Oxford Chronicle* under the title 'A Pauper's Wealth' before being renamed 'Stupidity' in *Babbling April*. The publication in *Decachord* was a later reprint, but was published there in March–April 1928, not 1927.

C76 The article 'The Province of the Film: Past Mistakes and Future Hopes' was signed 'From a Correspondent'. It was dated 9 April 1928, not 1927.

C77 The article 'A Film Technique: Rhythms of Space and Time' was dated 12 June 1928, not 1927.

C78 The article 'A Film Principle: Sound and Silence' was dated 10 July 1928, not 1927.

C79 The article 'Barrel-organing' was published in *The Times* on 27 December 1928, not 1927.

C84 'Oberammergau' should be classified as an 'Essay' rather than a 'Play Review'.

C146 The book review 'After Strange Gods' was unsigned.

C162 The correct title of this essay is 'The Seed Cake and the Love Lady', not 'The Lovely Lady'.

C168 The essay described flying in Estonia and Lithuania during a trip to the Baltic States in the summer of 1934.

C224 There are considerable textual differences between the *Spectator* article and the version that appears in *Journey Without Maps* concerning Greene's encounter with Elwood Davis. It was only when he returned to England that the writer realized the extent of the atrocities for which Davis was responsible.

C233 These film reviews were reprinted in their entirety in the first issue of *World Film News* in April 1936, under the heading 'Best Criticism of the Month'. In subsequent issues up to March 1937, Greene's *Spectator* film reviews were often quoted in extract as part of the magazine's 'Review of Reviews'.

C337 This book review was brief and unsigned.

C355 The essay 'Ideas in the Cinema' argues that if English-made films could be more 'English' and less international, ideas might survive the 'megalomania' of film magnates.

C362 The essay 'Alfred Tennyson Intervenes' begins as a brief review of the pamphlet *Authors Take Sides on the Spanish Civil War* but is chiefly concerned with the involvement of the Cambridge poets Arthur Hallam and Alfred Tennyson in nineteenth-century Spanish politics.

C379 'The Blind Eye' is an account of Greene's steamer voyage from Vera Cruz to Lisbon. A slightly revised account of this article appears in the epilogue to *The Lawless Roads.*

C380 'In Search of a Miracle' is an account of Greene's experiences in Las Casas, Mexico. A revised account of this article appears in *The Lawless Roads.*

C387 'A Catholic Adventurer and His Mexican Journal' relates to the diary of Dr Fitzpatrick which was discovered by Greene in Villahermosa. A revised account of this article appears in *The Lawless Roads.* A newspaper interview with the daughter of Dr Fitzpatrick was reprinted in *A Sort of Newsletter*, Issue 77, February 2019.

C405 'The Dark Virgin' concerns the miracle and shrine to the Virgin Mary at Guadalupe, Mexico. A revised account of this article appears in *The Lawless Roads.*

C407 'The Escapist' does not concern Greene's travels in Mexico. It is an extract, slightly revised, from the Epilogue to *The Lawless Roads.* Greene, travelling aboard a ship from Vera Cruz to Europe, encounters a drifter named 'K' or 'Kruger' who tells him his life story.

C449 This poem, signed DG, had the title 'The Happy Warrior' and won first prize in the *Spectator* Competition No. 3.

C478 Greene's poem 'The Winter War: Finland' was a winning entry in the *Spectator* Competition No. 24. Signed Hilary Trench.

C481 'The Lieutenant Died Last'. *Collier's* was a US weekly magazine. 'The Lieutenant Died Last' was published in September 1940 in the women's magazine *Britannia and Eve.* There were textual differences made to suit British and American audiences, explained in an article by Cedric Watts in *A Sort of Newsletter*, Issue 85, February 2021. The reprint in *The Last Word and Other Stories* (**A76**) uses the UK version of the text although it rightly acknowledges that the story first appeared in *Collier's.*

C489 'Great Dog of Weimar' cannot be classed as a review of Barbanell's book but is rather a satirical essay concerning psychic communication with pets based on *When Your Animal Dies.*

C490 'Don in Mexico' book review. Professor Trend responded to Greene's review criticisms of his book in the *Spectator* on 29 November, and Greene responded in return in the same issue.

C491 The article 'An Unknown War' was unsigned.

C501 The book reviews were titled 'A Pride in Bombs', not 'A Pride of Bombs'.

C512 Play review. The title of the play should be *No Time for Comedy.*

C536 'Men at Work' was first published in *The Penguin New Writing No. 9*, September 1941. (See Volume 1, **B17**.)

C539 'Nordhal Grieg – A Personal Note'. The publishing date was March/April, not March.

C550 Greene's review of Orwell's *Animal Farm* was reprinted in *A Sort of Newsletter*, Issue 65, August 2015.

C595 'London Diary'. The second sentence of this entry should read, 'Reflections on the controversy caused by Greene's Open Letter …' etc.

C608 'Before the Attack'. This account concerns the Battle of Dien Bien Phu. It is extracted from Greene's diary.

C638 'Lines on the Liberation of Cuba' and 'The Bay of Pigs' are one and the same poem. (See also Volume 1, **A64** and **A75**.)

C643 'Going into Europe'. The article was in support of the UK joining the Common Market. Greene's contribution was reprinted in *A Sort of Newsletter*, Issue 78, May 2019.

C649 This entry should be described simply as an article. Its full title is 'A Third Man Entertainment on Security in Room 51'.

C660 'Doctor Crombie' appeared in the *New Statesman* on 8 October 1965.

C662 'The Invisible Japanese Gentleman' was published in the United States in the *Saturday Evening Post* in September 1965.

C664 'Return of the Novelist' is the English translation of the German Collected Edition of Greene's Introduction to *England Made Me*, published in 1963. (See **B3** in this volume.)

C665 'The Blessing' was published on 25 February 1966. It was also published in the United States in *Harper's* in March 1966.

C666 Book review. This entry should read 'A Review of *Pinorman* by Richard Aldington, a book about Norman Douglas, with an introductory note entitled "Poison Pen" '.

C668 'Chagrin in Three Parts' was published on 28 October 1966. It was also published in the United States in *Cosmopolitan* in August 1967.

C672 'The Secret' was published in *Vogue* on 1 January 1967.

C705 'The Country with Five Frontiers' was published in the *Sunday Telegraph*, 27 March 1977.

C717 The article 'Freedom of Information' was reprinted in *Reflections* (**A75**).

C719 'While Waiting for a War'. Greene's introduction to *The Tenth Man*, published in March 1985 and containing the error of dating (see Volume 1, **A68**), was published earlier rather than later than the *Granta* diary extract.

C724 The incomplete, unnamed story (titled *The Empty Chair* by Professor François Gallix) was published as *La Chaise Vide* (French translation by Gallix) in *La Chaise Vide et Autres Récits Inédits*, selected and edited by François Gallix and Isabelle D. Philippe, published by Robert Laffont, 2011.

PART D

LETTERS WRITTEN BY GRAHAM GREENE

D43 The letter was a call for information about the life of John Wilmot, Second Earl of Rochester. Greene's biography, written in the early 1930s, was not published until 1974. (See Volume 1, **A56**.)

D97 The letter is about religious persecution in Mexico, contradicting a *Times* article on the subject.

D109 The letter concerned war authors, not war artists.

D186 The letter comprises two extracts in English with French translations, taken from a letter on *The Heart of the Matter*. (See Volume 1, **D179**.)

D254 The letter relates to Greene's attempt to find his doppelgänger in India.

D255 The letter also concerns his attempt to find the 'other Graham Greene'.

D265 The letter concerns Evelyn Waugh's libel suit against Rebecca West and the Beaverbrook Press.

D266 The letter entitled 'Where Freedom Stops' concerns Lord Chorley's failure to comment on the imprisonment of a dissident Chinese writer. It was published on 4 June. On Greene's visit to China, see Volume 1, **C718** and **A74**.

D296 The letter was published on 20 February 1959 and was sent from the Congo explaining why Greene could not accept John Gordon's invitation to dinner.

D337 The letter asks for information from readers about a story in the *Chums* Annual, c.1910–14.

PART E

PUBLISHED INTERVIEWS WITH GRAHAM GREENE

E1 Strictly speaking, 'Save Me Only from Dullness' is incorrectly classified as an interview. It is a transcript of an oral account in which Greene speculates about his future having just published his first novel.
The article was the eighth in a series, commissioned by the *Evening News*, 'in which clever young men and women are revealing, "What I Expect from Life"'. (See **C63** in this volume.)

E83 The entry in Volume 1 is incorrect in several respects. The interview with Greene, which took place on 1 October 1990, was first published in a much shortened version in the *Toronto Globe & Mail*, not the *Progressive Magazine*, on 19 January 1991. Greene's interviewer John R. MacArthur wrote reflections on his experience of interviewing Greene, using hitherto unpublished material, in articles which appeared subsequently in the *Globe and Mail* and the *Progressive Magazine*. (See **E3** in this volume.)

PART F

FILMS MADE OF GRAHAM GREENE'S FICTION AND FILMS WRITTEN BY GREENE

F2 *THE GREEN COCKATOO*

Bruce Seton's character is Madisson, not Madison.

F7 *WENT THE DAY WELL?* (US title: *FORTY-EIGHT HOURS*)

The UK release date was 7 December 1942, not 13 May 1942. The original UK title was to be *They Come in Khaki.*

F14 *THE THIRD MAN*

The actor is Joseph Cotten, not Cotton.

F18 *LOSER TAKES ALL*

The film is in colour, not black and white.

F19 *SAINT JOAN*

The US release was 8 May 1957, not 5 February 1958. The UK release was in June 1957.

F25 *THE POWER AND THE GLORY*

The running time is 102 minutes, not 90 minutes.

F29 *ENGLAND MADE ME*

The screenplay writer was Desmond Cory, not Corey.

F30 *LA NUIT AMÉRICAINE*, not *AMÈRICAINE*

F31 *SHADES OF GREENE*

UNDER THE GARDEN: cast list should have Vivian, not Vivien, Pickles.

THE OVERNIGHT BAG and ***DREAM OF A STRANGE LAND*** were broadcast on 2 February, not 2 March.

F38 *DR FISCHER OF GENEVA*

The running time is 98 minutes, not 110 minutes.

F39 *MONSIGNOR QUIXOTE*

The running time is 118 minutes, not 135 minutes.

F40 *MAY WE BORROW YOUR HUSBAND?*

The film was broadcast on 23 November 1986. The running time was 102 minutes, not 120 minutes.

F41 *THE TENTH MAN*

The story was found in 1983, not 1984. The running time was 95 minutes, not 120 minutes.

Bibliography of published works on Graham Greene

INTERVIEWS WITH GRAHAM GREENE

Allain, Marie-Françoise (1983), *The Other Man: Conversations with Graham Greene*. London: Bodley Head.
In 1982 The Bodley Head published a limited edition of 225 copies of some answers Greene gave in this interview book.

TRAVEL WRITING

Hogarth, Paul (1986), *Graham Greene Country*. London: Pavilion Books.

FILM BOOKS

Falk, Quentin (2014), *Travels in Greeneland: The Cinema of Graham Greene* (4th edn). Dahlonega: University Press of North Georgia.

BOOKS AND MONOGRAPHS

Adamson, Judith (1990), *Graham Greene: The Dangerous Edge – Where Art and Politics Meet*. London: Macmillan.

Maduale, Jacques (1954), *Graham Greene*. Paris: Editions du Temps Présent.

Watts, C. T. (ed.) (1976), *The English Novel*. London: Sussex. Chapter 8: 'Graham Greene': a discussion by Ian Gregor and David Lodge.

COMPACT DISKS

These disks are no longer available. However, some audio recordings of talks at the annual Graham Greene International Festival can be accessed at www.grahamgreenebt.org.

Section 1b NEW ENTRIES

PART B

CONTRIBUTIONS BY GRAHAM GREENE TO BOOKS

B1 1946
Essay
***THE WINDMILL* Vol. 1 No. 3**
Edited by Reginald Moore and Edward Lane, London, Heinemann. Greene contributes 'An English View of François Mauriac'. First publication in English.

B2 1963
Introduction
THE POWER AND THE GLORY
Published by Heinemann Educational Books Ltd, London. The volume was part of Heinemann's 'Modern Novel Series', aimed at advanced school students. Greene's Introduction, written in 'London, June 1962', is the first English publication of the introduction to the book of the French/German Collected Edition of his novels. It is also the first of any of these introductions, on which the UK Collected Edition introductions were based a decade later, to be published in English.

B3 1966
Introduction
***ADAM INTERNATIONAL REVIEW* Nos 304–36**
Edited by Miron Grindea, London, Curwen Press. Greene contributes 'Return of the Novelist', the first English publication of the Introduction to *England Made Me* of the French/German Collected Edition of Graham Greene's novels. This was the second and last of the introductions, on which the UK Collected Edition introductions were based, to be published in English. (See Volume 1, **C664**, which this entry replaces.)

B4 1972
Introduction
COSÌ CAPRI
By Luciano D'Alessandro, Milan, Editphoto. Greene contributes an Introduction to this book of photographs. It is published in four languages, including English.

B5 1983
Foreword
BRIDGING THE GULF
By Canon J. R. Fox, Oxford, Amate Press. Greene contributes the Foreword.

B6 1989

Preface
THE SOUTH AMERICAN HANDBOOK 1989
Edited by John Brooks, London, Trade and Travels Publications, 1989. Greene contributes the Preface.

PART C

CONTRIBUTIONS BY GRAHAM GREENE TO NEWSPAPERS, JOURNALS AND MAGAZINES

C1 1921
Short story
THE BERKHAMSTEDIAN, December
'Castles in the Air' (unsigned). A dishevelled hunchback arrives at a fair promising to enliven proceedings by playing his pipe. When he does, the adults are transfixed and start dreaming of romance and chivalry. The story received Berkhamsted School's 'First Award' for 'An Essay of Imaginative or Descriptive writing, 1921'. It is alluded to in *A Sort of Life*.

C2 1923
Poetry
OXFORD CHRONICLE, 26 April
'A Pauper's Wealth', retitled 'Stupidity' in *Babbling April* and *Decachord*. (See Volume 1, **A1**, **C75**.)

C3 1924
Article/non-fiction
OXFORD CHRONICLE, March
'The Undergraduate Standpoint', signed GG.

C4 1924
Book review
EDUCATION OUTLOOK, May
An untitled review of *Walter de la Mare: A Biographical and Critical Sketch* by R. L. Mégroz. Signed HGG. (See **D1** in this volume.)

C5 1924
Poetry
WEEKLY WESTMINSTER, May
'The Old Clipper', signed HGG. This was a prize-winning poem.

C6 1924
Book review
EDUCATION OUTLOOK, June
An untitled review of *Byron: The Last Journey 1823–1824* by Harold Nicolson. Signed HGG.

C7 1924
Book review
EDUCATION OUTLOOK, June
An untitled review of *The Chilswell Book of English Poetry*, compiled by Robert Bridges. Signed HGG.

C8 1924
Book review
EDUCATION OUTLOOK, July
An untitled review of *An Historical Atlas of Modern European History* by C. Grant Robertson. Signed HGG.

C9 1924
Book review
EDUCATION OUTLOOK, July
An untitled review of *Tendencies of English Modern Drama* by A. E. Morgan. Signed HGG.

C10 1924
Book review
EDUCATION OUTLOOK, August
An untitled review of *Modern European History: A Sketch 1492–1924* by W. F. Reddaway. Signed HGG.

C11 1924
Poetry
WEEKLY WESTMINSTER, 6 September
'A Tramp Finds Himself inspected by an Owl'. A prize-winning poem, signed HGG.
See **A1** and **B4** in Volume 3, above.

C12 1924
Book review
EDUCATION OUTLOOK, September
An untitled review of *Studies in Mid-Victorian Imperialism* by C. A. Bodelsen. Signed HGG.

C13 1924
Article/non-fiction
EDUCATION OUTLOOK, October
'Poetry in the Schools – A Personal View'. Signed H. Graham Greene.

C14 1924
Book review
EDUCATION OUTLOOK, November
An untitled review of *Selections from Matthew Arnold's Poetry*, compiled by R. E. C. Houghton. Signed HGG.

C15 1924
Book review
CHERWELL, November 15
An untitled review of *The Rivet in Grandfather's Neck* by James Branch Cabell. Signed HGG.

C16 1924
Book review
EDUCATION OUTLOOK, November
An untitled review of *An 18th Century Anthology*, introduced by Alfred Austin. Signed HGG.

C17 1924
Book review
EDUCATION OUTLOOK, November
'Two Anthologies': reviews of *A Book of English Poems Graded for Use in Schools* by J. H. Jagger and *A Boy's Book of Verse* by Allan M. Phillips. Signed HGG.

C18 1924
Book review
EDUCATION OUTLOOK, November
An untitled review of *Peacock Pie* by Walter de la Mare. Signed HGG.

C19 1924
Book review
EDUCATION OUTLOOK, December
An untitled review of *On the Art of Reading* by Sir Arthur Quiller-Couch. Signed HGG.

C20 1924
Book review
ISIS, December
An untitled review of *Parents or Pedagogues: A Guide for Parents to The Early Education of Their Children* by Esmé Wingfield-Stratford.

C21 1925
Poetry
OXFORD CHRONICLE, January 23
'The Posthumous Poet'.

__C22__ 1925
Poetry
OXFORD OUTLOOK, January 23
'The Dial'. Signed HGG.

__C23__ 1925
Book reviews
EDUCATION OUTLOOK, January
Untitled reviews of *Two Anthologies: English Satires*, introduced by O. Smeaton, and *The Bond of Poetry: A Book of Verse*, edited by J. J. Bond. Signed HGG.

__C24__ 1925
Book review
EDUCATION OUTLOOK, January
An untitled review of *The Garden of Happiness* by Stella Mead. Signed HGG.

__C25__ 1925
Book review
EDUCATION OUTLOOK, January
An untitled review of *The Brownings, Dickens and Thackeray, Shelley, Sir Walter Scott, Matthew Arnold, Wordsworth* by Oliver Elton. Signed HGG.

__C26__ 1925
Play review
ISIS, 12 February
An untitled review of *The Beaux' Stratagem* by George Farquahar. Signed HGG. Performed by St. Hugh's Amateur Dramatic Society.

__C27__ 1925
Poetry
OXFORD CHRONICLE, 27 February
'It is not that'.

__C28__ 1925
Book review
OXFORD OUTLOOK, February
An untitled review of *Verse in Bloom* by Norman Gale. Signed Hilary Trench.

__C29__ 1925
Book review
EDUCATION OUTLOOK, March
An untitled review of *Alfred de Vigny's Chatterton*, edited with notes by A. Watson Bain. Signed HGG.

__C30__ 1925
Book review
EDUCATION OUTLOOK, March
'A Note on Tennyson'. A review of *Tennyson: Selected Poems*, edited by S. G. Dunn. Signed HGG.

__C31__ 1925
Book review
EDUCATION OUTLOOK, March
An untitled review of *A Boy's Book of Prose*, compiled by W. H. L. Signed HGG.

__C32__ 1925
Book review
EDUCATION OUTLOOK, March
An untitled review of *The Way of History Bk. IV 1815–Present Day* by Kenneth Bell. Signed HGG.
Kenneth Bell was Greene's tutor at Balliol.

__C33__ 1925
Book review
EDUCATION OUTLOOK, April
An untitled review of *Browning's Ring and the Book of Imaginative Literature 1890–1914* by Alexander Haddow. Signed HGG.

C34 1925
Book review
EDUCATION OUTLOOK, April
An untitled review of *Modern English Writers: Being a Study of Imaginative Literature 1890–1914* by Harold Williams. Signed HGG.

C35 1925
Book review
EDUCATION OUTLOOK, April
'Two School Anthologies': reviews of *A Bible Anthology* by Treble and Vallins and *The Golden Book of Narrative Verse* by Frank Jones. Signed HGG.

C36 1925
Book review
EDUCATION OUTLOOK, June
'Matthew Arnold', a review of *Sorab and Rustum, The Scholar Gypsy Thyris* edited by G. E. Hollingsworth. Signed HGG.

C37 1925
Book review
EDUCATION OUTLOOK, June
An untitled review of *An Eton Poetry Book* edited by Cyril Abington and George Lyttleton. Signed HGG.

C38 1925
Book review
EDUCATION OUTLOOK, July
An untitled review of *Hours with English Authors* edited by E. T. Campagnac. Signed HGG.

C39 1925
Book review
EDUCATION OUTLOOK, July
An untitled review of *A Medley of Occasional Verse* by Charles Swynnerton. Signed HGG.

C40 1925
Book reviews
WEEKLY WESTMINSTER, 18 July
'Leeds to Quetta', a review of *By Car to India* by Major F. A. C. Forbes-Leith and an untitled review of *The Political Career of Lord Byron* by Miss D. N. Raymond. Both signed G.G.

C41 1925
Book review
EDUCATION OUTLOOK, August
An untitled review of *The Best Poems of 1924*, selected by Thomas Moult. Signed HGG.

C42 1925
Book review
WEEKLY WESTMINSTER, 24 October
'Gissing on Dickens', a review of *The Immortal Dickens* by George Gissing. Signed G.G.

C43 1925
Book review
WEEKLY WESTMINSTER, 31 October
'A Dilettante as Historian', a review of *The Pleasure Haunts of England* by E. Beresford Chancellor. Signed G.G.

C44 1925
Book review
WEEKLY WESTMINSTER, 7 November
'A Life of Cary', a review of *The Translator of Dante: The Life, Work and Friendships of Henry Francis Cary* by R. W. King. Signed G.G.

C45 1925
Book review
WEEKLY WESTMINSTER, 5 December
'The Medici Guides', a review of the Medici Society's Picture Guides. Signed G.G.

C46 1925
Book review
WEEKLY WESTMINSTER, 12 December
'Written in Blood', a review of *The Idle Hours of a Victorian Invalid* by Lane Crauford. Signed G.G.

C47 1925
Book review
WEEKLY WESTMINSTER, 19 December
'Pompadour', a review of *Madame de Pompadour* by Marcelle Tinayre. Signed G.G.

C48 1926
Essay
THE TIMES, 13 March
'Mothering Sunday'. Unsigned.

C49 1926
Book review
GLASGOW HERALD, 8 April
An untitled review of *The Charwoman's Shadow* by Lord Dunsany. Unsigned. (Referred to in a letter by Greene to his mother, March 1926.)

C50 1926
Book review
GLASGOW HERALD, 8 April
An untitled review of *Thunder on the Left* by Christopher Morley. Unsigned.

C51 1926
Book reviews
GLASGOW HERALD, 10 June
'Mr. De La Mare': reviews of *The Connoisseur*, *Memoirs of a Midget* and *Henry Brocken* by Walter de la Mare. Unsigned.

C52 1926
Book review
EDUCATION OUTLOOK, July
An untitled review of *The Warden* by Anthony Trollope.

C53 1926
Book review
GLASGOW HERALD, 12 August
An untitled review of *The Lunatic in Charge* by J. Storer Clouston. Unsigned. (Referred to in a letter from Greene to his mother, 8 October 1932.)

C54 1926
Essay
EDUCATION OUTLOOK, September
'The Popular Song and Ernest Dowson'. Signed HGG.

C55 1926
Book reviews
EDUCATION OUTLOOK, September
'Some Anthologies': reviews of *The Poet's Highway* edited by Elizabeth D'Oyley, *The First Book of Lyrical Poetry* edited by Treble and Vallins and *The Golden Book of Modern English Poetry* edited by Thomas Caldwell. Signed HGG.

C56 1926
Book review
EDUCATION REVIEW, September

'Pope', a review of *Homer's Iliad Books XXII, XXIV*, ed. F. H. Colson. Signed HGG.

C57 1926
Book review
EDUCATION REVIEW, September
An untitled review of *The Little White Gate* by Florence Hoatson. Signed HGG.

C58 1926
Book reviews
GLASGOW HERALD, 28 September
'News of the Devil – a Modern Satire': reviews of *News of the Devil* by Humbert Wolfe, *Time and Chance* by Stella Gibbons and *Many Mansions* by Lord Gorell. Unsigned.

C59 1926
Book reviews
GLASGOW HERALD, 28 October
'Three Poets': reviews of *Adam* by John Gould Fletcher and *Questings* by A. Phelps Clawson. Unsigned.

C60 1927
Book review
GLASGOW HERALD, 6 January
'Men and Fairies', a review of *Goodbye Stranger* by Stella Benson. Unsigned.

C61 1927
Essay
GLASGOW HERALD, 13 January
'Books and Bookmen', an essay opposing Wordsworth's views on eighteenth-century poetry. Unsigned.

C62 1927
Article/non-fiction
THE TIMES, 17 November
'Ashridge Park "That Goodly Place" ', an article about the park near Berkhamsted. Unsigned.

C63 1930
Article/non-fiction
EVENING NEWS, 23 January
'Save Me Only from Dullness', an article 'in which clever young men and women are revealing, "What I expect of life" '. (See Volume 1, **E1**.)

C64 1931
Book reviews
OXFORD MAGAZINE, June
'Poetry and Verse': reviews of four recent books of poems.

C65 1931
Book reviews
OXFORD MAGAZINE, 31 October
'Poets and Academicians': reviews of a number of recent poetry anthologies.

C66 1931
Short story
MANCHESTER GUARDIAN, 24 December
'Proof Positive'.

C67 1932
Short story
MANCHESTER GUARDIAN, 9 September
'I Spy'.

C68 1933
Book reviews
JOHN O'LONDON WEEKLY, 1 July

'New Books at a Glance': reviews of *Mr Jiggins of Jigginstown* by Lady C. Langford; *Yet in My Flesh* by M. E. Mitchell and *Pound Foolish* by Renée Shann.

C69 1933
Book reviews
JOHN O'LONDON WEEKLY, 22 July
'Looking for Leaders': reviews of *The Prince of Captivity* by John Buchan; *In Scarlet and Plain Clothes* by T. Morris Longstreth; and *Violence* by Joseph Stamper.

C70 1933
Book review
SPECTATOR, 17 November
An untitled review of *The Poems of Charles Churchill*. Signed GG.

C71 1935
Short story
NEWS CHRONICLE, May/June
'The Basement Room', published as a five-day serial.

C72 1936
Short story
THE PASSING SHOW, 21 March
'Crazy Elopement', renamed 'A Drive in the Country' when published in *Nineteen Stories*. (See Volume 1, **A19**, and later collections of short stories.)

C73 1936
Manifesto
WORLD FILM NEWS, April
'Broadcasting and Television Manifesto' by Alberto Cavalcanti, Cedric Belfrage, Thorold Dickinson, John Grierson and Graham Greene. A proposed way forward for the new medium of television, in relation to film. 'Part 1: The Use of Film' was included here. 'Part 2: The Psychology of the Audience' was promised for the May issue but never appeared. In the June issue, a further manifesto, 'Television Must Contact the Individual', was published but with no authors listed.

C74 1936
Book review
OBSERVER, 30 August
'Desert Adventure', a review of *The Paradise of Fools* by Michael Mason.

C75 1936
Book review
OBSERVER, 15 November
'A Dane in Africa', a review of *Desert Encounter* by Knud Holmboe.

C76 1936
Book review
LISTENER, 2 December
An untitled review of *Myself, My Two Countries* by X. M. Boulestin. Signed Graham Greene.

C77 1937
Article/non-fiction
NEW VERSE, November
'Sixteen', about Auden's poetry.

C78 1938
Book review
LISTENER, 11 August
An untitled review of *The Thought-Reading Machine* by André Maurois. Unsigned.

C79 1938
Novel serialization

EVENING STANDARD, September
Serialization of *Brighton Rock*.

C80 1938
Book review
LISTENER, 1 September
An untitled review of *It's Draughty in Front* by Herbert Hodge. Unsigned.

C81 1938
Short story
BRITANNIA AND EVE, September
'Across the Bridge'.

C82 1938
Book review
LISTENER, 22 December
An untitled review of *Edgar Wallace* by Margaret Lane. Unsigned. The review was reprinted in *A Sort of Newsletter*, Issue 80, November 2019. Greene later wrote an introduction to a revised edition of the biography. (See Volume 1, **B54**.)

C83 1939
Book review
LISTENER, 6 April
An untitled review of *A Flying Start* by René MacColl. Unsigned.

C84 1939
Book review
LISTENER, 13 April
An untitled review of *My Father Was a Gentleman* by Robert Holmes. Unsigned.

C85 1939
Book review
SPECTATOR, 28 April
'Prometheus', a review of *What Rough Beast* by 'Mark Benny' (Henry Ernest Degras). Signed GG

C86 1939
Competition entry
SPECTATOR, 29 September
Untitled. Greene's entry for the *Spectator* Competition No. 1, signed Hilary Trench. The entry won first prize. Greene's entry took the form of a letter to a Divisional Petroleum Controller claiming a supplementary ration of petrol. It was composed in the epistolary style of Henry James.

C87 1939
Book review
LISTENER, 19 October
An untitled review of *It's Too Late Now* by A. A. Milne. Unsigned.

C88 1939
Book review
LISTENER, 23 November
An untitled review of *New Writing: Christmas, 1939*, Hogarth Anthology. Unsigned. The review was reprinted in *A Sort of Newsletter*, Issue 80, November 2019.

C89 1939
Article on literature/competition entry
SPECTATOR, 24 November
'An Acute Analysis of the Unattractive Qualities of Thoreau', a prize-winning critique of Henry Thoreau's memoir *Walden*. Signed Hilary Trench. Greene's winning entry for the *Spectator* Competition No. 9.

C90 1940
Book review
TABLET, 20 January
'Old and Mild', a review of *The Local* by

C91 1940
Book review
LISTENER, 8 February
An untitled review of *Portrait of a Young Man* by Franklin Lushington. Unsigned.

C92 1940
Book review
LISTENER, 14 March
'The Last Decade', a review of *The Thirties 1930–1940 in Great Britain* by Malcolm Muggeridge. Signed Graham Greene.

C93 1940
Book review
LISTENER, 30 March
'Invisible Ignorance', a review of *My Life* by Havelock Ellis.

C94 1940
Book review
LISTENER, 1 May
An untitled review of *The Story of J.M.* by Denis McKail, about J. M. Barrie. Unsigned.

C95 1940
Short story
STAR WEEKLY (Toronto), 13 July
'The Case for the Defence'. (See Volume 1, **A19**.)

C96 1940
Book review
LISTENER, 25 July
An untitled review of *East End My Cradle* by Willy Goldman. Unsigned.

C97 1940
Article/non-fiction
SPECTATOR, 1 August
'Bloomsbury Lighthouse', an article concerning the blackout, written on behalf of the Ministry of Information. Signed Holborn Warden.

C98 1940
Article/non-fiction
SPECTATOR, 9 August
An anonymous article titled 'Ministry of Information' in which Greene condemns the government department he worked for at the time for its overstaffing and its pointless activities.

C99 1940
Book review
SPECTATOR, October
An untitled review of *Animal, Vegetable and South Kensington – A Book of Drawings* by Nicholas Bentley.

C100 1941
Book review
SPECTATOR, 3 January
An untitled review of *A London Family between the Wars* by M. Vivian Hughes. Unsigned.

C101 1941
Book review
SPECTATOR, 24 January
An untitled review of '*You Have Been Listening to …*' by Commander A. B. Campbell RN. Unsigned.

C102 1941
Book reviews
SPECTATOR, 31 January
Untitled reviews of *How to Read a Book: A Guide to Self Education* by Mortimer J. Adler and *Forever Freedom*

by Josiah C. Wedgwood and Allan Nevens. Unsigned.

C103 1941
Book review
SPECTATOR, 14 February
An untitled review of *The Book of Margery Kemp Vol. 1* edited by Professor Sanford Brown Meech. Unsigned.

C104 1941
Book review
SPECTATOR, 9 May
An untitled review of *Haunted England* by Christina Hale. Unsigned.

C105 1941
Book reviews
SPECTATOR, 23 May
Untitled reviews of *Estonia* by J. Hampden Jackson and *Outside Information* by Naomi Boyde-Smith. Unsigned.

C106 1941
Book review
SPECTATOR, 18 July
An untitled review of *The Bible for Today* edited by John Stirling. Unsigned.

C107 1941
Article/non-fiction
WORLD REVIEW, November
'The Man's Case', one of a series of articles on justice between the sexes.

C108 1945
Play reviews
BRITAIN TODAY, January
'The Theatre': reviews of *Hamlet* and *Richard III.*

C109 1950
Article
NEW YORK TIMES, 19 March
'The Third Man as a Story and a Film'. First publication of what became the preface to the novella.

C110 1952
Book review
SUNDAY TIMES, 15 June
'Goodbye to Capri', a review of *Footnote on Capri* by Norman Douglas. This entry also amends the statement about the review in Volume 1, **B34**.

C111 1952
Book review
OBSERVER, 28 September
'Just So So', a review of *A Choice of Kipling's Prose*, selected and introduced by W. Somerset Maugham.

C112 1952
Book review
OBSERVER, 14 December
'Durable Colours', a review of *Portraits* by Sir Joshua Reynolds.

C113 1955
Travel writing/reportage
SUNDAY TIMES, 24 April
'The Drama of Indo-China: The Dilemma of the South', the first instalment of a three-part series of articles about the First Indo-China War. The second and third parts are Volume 1, **C618** and **C619**.

C114 1955
Extract/novel
LISTENER, 15 September

'A Memory of Indo-China', an extract from *The Quiet American*, as broadcast on the BBC Third Programme.

C115 1955
Novel serialization
PICTURE POST, 10 December 1955–14 January 1956
Abridged five-part serialization of *The Quiet American.*

C116 1955
Book reviews
SUNDAY TIMES, 25 December
Books of the Year. A brief review of *Lolita* by Vladimir Nabokov.
The review of *Lolita* was the prelude to the John Gordon correspondence caused by the *Sunday Express* editor's vehement opposition to Greene's support of Nabokov's novel. This in turn led to the creation of the John Gordon Society founded by Greene and his friend John Sutro.
Greene contributed regularly to this annual *Sunday Times* feature, each contribution written by what were described as 'Eminent Contemporaries'. As they are little more than brief recommendations the reviews have not been otherwise included. This one is an exception owing to the reference to *Lolita* which precipitated the ongoing controversy.

C117 1957
Book review
OBSERVER, 16 June
'Monster or Genius', a review of *Desert Love* by Henry de Monthelat.

C118 1959
Book review
OBSERVER, 11 October
'Portrait of a Priest', a review of *The Life of Ronald Knox* by Evelyn Waugh.

C119 1959
Book review
OBSERVER, 29 October
'The Victor and the Victim', a review of *Days with Albert Schweitzer* by Frederick Franck. Reprinted in *Collected Essays* (Volume 1, **A48**). (See also Volume 1, **B49**.)

C120 1961
Short story
SUNDAY TIMES, 1 January
'Upended: A Macabre Meditation'. The story was reprinted in *A Sort of Newsletter*, Issue 55, August 2013.

C121 1961
Preface
SUNDAY TELEGRAPH, 17 September
'Novelist in the Theatre', the Preface to *Three Plays*. (See Volume 1, **A40**.)

C122 1961
Extracts
OBSERVER, 22 October
'In Search of a Character'. Extracts from 'Congo Journal'. (See Volume 1, **A39**.)

C123 1963
Article/non-fiction
SUNDAY TIMES, 29 December
'Delightful Age', an article on the editing of *The Bodley Head Ford Madox Ford.* (See Volume 1, **B51**.)

C124 1964
Introduction
SUNDAY TIMES, 15 November
'Edgar Wallace Revalued', Greene's Introduction to *Edgar Wallace: Biography of a Phenomenon* by Margaret Lane. (See Volume 1, **B54**.) Greene had reviewed the book when it was first published in 1938. (See **C82** in this volume.)

C125 1965
Extracts
SUNDAY TIMES, 24 January
'The Comedians'. Three extracts from the novel; also on 31 January and 7 February 1965.

C126 1965
Book review
SUNDAY TIMES, 7 March
'Eighty Years on the Barrack Square', a review of *Journal of a Soul: Diary of Pope John XXIII*. The review was included in *Collected Essays* (Volume 1, **A48**).

C127 1968
Book reviews
OBSERVER, 18 February
'Our Man in Moscow': reviews of *Philby: The Spy Who Betrayed a Generation* by Bruce Page, Phillip Knightley and David Leitch, and *The Third Man* by E. H. Cookridge.

C128 1968
Text of speech
ENCOUNTER, 28 March
Transcript of a brief address to the P.E.N. meeting in London regarding the Daniel/Sinyavsky Trial.

C129 1969
Article
SPECTATOR, 8 November
'Regina vs Sir James Barrie', a mock indictment for obscenity of James Barrie's *The Little White Bird*.

C130 1971
Extract/autobiography
SUNDAY TIMES, 15 August
'The Boy with a Gun', the first of three extracts from *A Sort of Life*; continued 22 and 29 August 1971.
Commonweal, *Esquire*, *Critic* (Chicago) magazines also published extracts from *A Sort of Life*, September–December 1971. The *Critic* extract had minor textual changes.

C131 1972
Article/non-fiction
OBSERVER MAGAZINE, 9 January
'Can the New Chile Survive?'

C132 1972
Introduction/film reviews
DAILY TELEGRAPH MAGAZINE, 27 October
'Last Days of the Pleasure Dome', the Introduction to *The Pleasure-Dome: The Collected Film Criticism 1935–1940*. (See Volume 1, **A52**.) The article also includes nine of Greene's film reviews.

C133 1973
Introduction
OBSERVER MAGAZINE, 1 July
'My Adventures as a Bookhunter', the Introduction to *With All Faults* by David Low. (See Volume 1, **B65** and **A75**.) Contains some textual changes from **B65**.

C134 1973
Memoir
TRAVEL AND LEISURE, October/November
'To Indochina with Love', a memoir of Greene's first visits to Vietnam.

C135 1974
Extracts/biography
THE TIMES SATURDAY REVIEW, 31 August
'Something of the Angel yet Undefac'd', extracts from *Lord Rochester's Monkey.* (See Volume 1, **A56**.)

C136 1974
Book review
OBSERVER, 10 November
'The Ghost of R.L.S.', a review of *Robert Louis Stevenson* by James Pope-Hennessy.
See **D23** in this volume. See Volume 2, p. 145, for an account of Greene's plans to write a biography of his distant cousin to coincide with the centenary of Stevenson's birth in 1950.

C137 1975
Preface
DAILY TELEGRAPH MAGAZINE, 12 September
'Survivor', the Preface to *An Impossible Woman: The Memoirs of Dottoressa Moor of Capri.* (See Volume 1, **B67**.)

C138 1976
Introduction/literature
DAILY TELEGRAPH MAGAZINE, 20 February
'A Young Man's Fancy', the Introduction to The Bodley Head Collected Edition of *The Man Within.*

C139 1976
Introduction/literature
DAILY TELEGRAPH MAGAZINE, 27 February
'Tales from a Vienna War', the Introduction to The Bodley Head Collected Edition of *The Third Man.*

C140 1976
Introduction/literature
DAILY TELEGRAPH MAGAZINE, 5 March
'Vagaries of Fortune', the Introduction to The Bodley Head Collected Edition of *Loser Takes All.*

C141 1976
Introduction/literature
DAILY TELEGRAPH MAGAZINE, 12 March
'Black Humour in Haiti', the Introduction to The Bodley Head Collected Edition of *The Comedians.*

C142 1976
Article
SUNDAY TIMES, 6 June
'On the Train from Belfast to Dublin'.

C143 1976
Book review
BOOKS AND BOOKMEN, October
'Both Dross and Gold', a review of *The Diaries of Evelyn Waugh*, edited by Michael Davie.

C144 1978
Extract/novel
PLAYBOY, February
'The Human Factor', an extract from the novel.

C145 1978
Introduction
THE TIMES, October 28
'R.K. Narayan – An Introduction', a new introduction for the reissue of *Bachelor of Arts*. (See Volume 1, **B73** and **A75**.)

C146 1980
Extract/novel
THE TIMES, 29 March
'The Porridge Party', Chapter 9 of *Doctor Fischer of Geneva*.

C147 1980
Song lyric
SUNDAY TIMES, 22 June
'World War Three', written for composer, pianist and former school friend Russell Landale. Landale was an ex-pupil of Berkhamsted School, and by 1980 he had retired from his career as a diplomat and was a neighbour of Greene's in Antibes. Following trouble in the New Hebrides (now Vanuatu) there was a (successful) call on 8 June 1980 for French and British troops to intervene. Greene's anti-war song lyric was a response to this call.

C148 1980
Extract/autobiography
SPECTATOR, 27 September
'Any Robberies? Any Murders?', an extract from *Ways of Escape* on the origins of *The Honorary Consul*.

C149 1980
Extract/film reviews
THE TIMES, 4 October
'Mornings in the Dark', an extract from *Ways of Escape* about Greene's time as a film critic.

C150 1980
Extract/autobiography
SPECTATOR, 4 October
'Invention and Prediction', an extract from *Ways of Escape* on the origins of *The Human Factor*.

C151 1980
Extract/autobiography
SPECTATOR, 11 October
'Learning by Imitation', an extract from *Ways of Escape* on Greene's suppressed novels *The Name of Action* and *Rumour at Nightfall*.

C152 1981
Extracts/autobiography
COMMONWEAL, 16 January
'The Labyrinthine Ways', extracts from three chapters of *Ways of Escape*.

C153 1981
Fiction/competition entry
SPECTATOR, 3 January
Spectator Competition No. 1145, entry signed Michael Willett.
An imaginary message of an extraterrestrial intelligence jamming of the Queen's Christmas broadcast. The entry won runner-up prize in the Christmas Competition. Greene wrote to the editor, Alexander Chancellor, 10 January 1981, claiming to be the 'ghost writer' for the 'eminent author Mr. Michael Willet' (*sic*) who had authorized him to collect the prize money. By that time Chancellor was wise to Greene's various aliases as a reply, dated 26 January, suggests.

C154 1982
Memoir

***CULTURES*, Vol. 8 No. 2**
A brief memoir of Victoria Ocampo, the Argentine editor of the literary journal *Sur* and the translator of some of Greene's work. Ocampo was a close, personal friend of Greene.

C155 1982
Article/non-fiction
SUNDAY TIMES, 9 May
'J'Accuse'. Subtitled 'A Famous novelist's bitter attack on Riviera corruption'. (See Volume 1, **A62**.)

C156 1984
Memoir
TIME AND TIDE, Autumn
'The Last Decade'.
For more information about this short memoir, see Volume 2, pp. 215–17. There are several significant textual revisions made between the original manuscript (1964) and the published version.

C157 1985
Short story
TIME AND TIDE, Summer
'An Impossibly Bad Hotel'. Original title: 'A Really Impossibly Bad Hotel'. Uncollected.

C158 1987
Memoir
INDEPENDENT, 21 September
'A Constant Question Mark'.
This brief memoir concerning dreams and a belief in telepathy was prompted by Greene reading Brian Inglis's book *The Unknown Guest*.

C159 1988
Book review
WEEKEND TELEGRAPH, 7 May
Untitled review of *The Missionaries* by Norman Lewis.

C160 1989
Article/non-fiction
IRISH INDEPENDENT, 1 July
Title unknown. Greene claimed that in 1924 he had written to the Free State government in Dublin, offering to cross the border and report on military deployment from inside Ulster.

PART D

LETTERS WRITTEN BY GRAHAM GREENE

None of these letters has been reprinted.

D1 1924
EDUCATION OUTLOOK, June
'Two Protests: Walter de la Mare', replying to R. L. Mégroz's complaint about Greene's review in the May issue. Signed HGG. (See **C4** in this volume.)

D2 1928
SATURDAY REVIEW OF LITERATURE, 28 April
'The Oxford Outlook', regarding the periodical Greene had edited in 1924–25.

D3 1931
TIMES LITERARY SUPPLEMENT, 16 April
'Otway & Mrs Barry', concerning the seventeenth-century romance between the dramatist and the actress. Written in response to a review.

D4 1931
OXFORD MAGAZINE, 18 June
Untitled. Agreeing with Pinchbeck Lyre's assessment of Humbert Wolfe as 'the most pretentious poetaster'.

D5 1934
SPECTATOR, 26 January
'Sense and Poetry', adding further errors he had noted in John Sparrow's book *Sense and Poetry*.

D6 1934
SPECTATOR, 9 February
'Sense and Poetry', replying to John Sparrow's letter.

D7 1934
DAILY TELEGRAPH, 2 August
'The Old School at Work', objecting to a review of *The Old School*, edited by Greene. (See Volume 1, **B9**.)

D8 1934
SPECTATOR, 31 August
Untitled. Replying to readers who had criticized Greene's review of *Blind Men Crossing the Bridge* by Susan Miles.

D9 1935
SPECTATOR, 20 September
'A Restoration Fantasia', correcting an error in a review of *Rochester* by Charles Williams.

D10 1936
TIME AND TIDE, 23 May
'Journey Without Maps', replying to Geoffrey Gorer's review of Greene's travel book. Greene had reviewed Gorer's book ... Dahomey and Senegal in 1935. (See Volume 1, **C174**.)

D11 1938
TABLET, 18 June
'Bombing from the Air', protesting about the journal's editorial of 11 June regarding the Spanish Civil War.

D12 1939
TIMES LITERARY SUPPLEMENT, 19 August
'Doll Caudel', a hoax letter about a fictitious character, signed Henry Ash.

D13 1940
SPECTATOR, 29 November
'Don in Mexico', replying to a letter from J. B. Trend concerning Greene's review of his book *Don in Mexico: A New Spin with Old Friends*.

D14 1941
SPECTATOR, 21 March
'Escape', replying to a letter concerning Greene's review of *Escape* by F. L. Griggs.

D15 1941
SPECTATOR, 25 July
'The Chestertons', apologizing for a misprint in a recent review of Mrs Chesterton's book.

D16 1943
HORIZON, May
Untitled, concerning Evelyn Waugh.

D17 1943
SPECTATOR, 22 October
'The Poker Face', correcting typographical errors in ...

D18 1945
NEW STATESMAN AND NATION, 3 November
Untitled. Protesting about an inequality in the Labour government's income tax policy.

D19 1946
SPECTATOR, 22 March
'Parcels from America', a hoax letter signed Henry Wedderburn concerning statistics he had kept on parcels he had received during the war from America and how many had been tampered with. He cites his friend Mrs Henry Montgomery, using another of Greene's pseudonyms.

D20 1946
SPECTATOR, 5 April
'Parcels from America', a hoax letter, signed (Mrs) K. Montgomery, disowning knowledge of Henry Wedderburn. Two other letters, written the same month, one to *Time and Tide* magazine signed M. E. Wimbush (another pseudonym), may well not have been written by Greene.

D21 1946
SPECTATOR, 15 November
'First Class Travel', protesting about rail travel conditions.

D22 1948
DAILY MIRROR, 9 January
'Razor-Slasher Film', written in defence of the film of *Brighton Rock*. See Volume 1, **F12**.

D23 1949
TIMES LITERARY SUPPLEMENT, 24 June
'R.L. Stevenson', requesting materials for a forthcoming biography Greene intended to write about his relative but later abandoned. See **C136** in this volume.

D24 1953
NEW STATESMAN AND NATION, 10 January
'The Red Tape Curtain', concerning Communist hysteria in the United States.

D25 1953
NEW STATESMAN AND NATION, 17 January
'Tito and Stepinac', concerning the lack of religious tolerance in Yugoslavia.

D26 1953
NEW STATESMAN AND NATION, 31 January
'Tito and Stepinac', replying to a critical response to Greene's letter concerning Yugoslavia.

D27 1953
NEW STATESMAN AND NATION, 14 February
'Tito and Stepinac', a further letter on the subject of Yugoslavia, adding to the evidence about Tito's intolerance of religious freedom.

D28 1953
SUNDAY TIMES, 19 April
'The Angry Man Within', correcting details about an interview published in the paper earlier in the month entitled 'The Angry Man Within'. (See Volume 1, **E11**.)

D29 1953
NEW STATESMAN AND NATION, 19 August
'First Reading', on the use of the word 'don' in a dispute about poetry reading at the BBC.

D30 1954
SPECTATOR, 29 January
'Death of the Topes', concerning the survival of the topee as a symbol of class in North Vietnam.

D31 1955
SUNDAY TIMES, 8 May
'Indo-China', concerning the relation of the Hoa Haos to Buddhism.

D32 1956
NEW STATESMAN AND NATION, 11 February
'Catholic Confessional', questioning a report about Catholic election coercion in Malta.

D33 1956
SPECTATOR, 13 July
'A Coward's Way', defending an author's right to live abroad.

D34 1957
SPECTATOR, 8 March
'Not Surprising', concerning naïve assumptions made by drama critics.

D35 1957
DAILY TELEGRAPH, 10 June
'Lord Chorley and Mr. Greene – the end of the affair', on the contradictions in Lord Chorley's letter concerning Greene's criticisms of the peer's views on the dissident Chinese writer Hu Feng. Greene's views on the Chinese Government's treatment of the writer differed sharply from those of the Labour peer. Their disagreement surfaced during their trip to China in 1957, described by Greene in his essay 'A Weed Among the Flowers', and was followed up in letters to the press. (See Volume 1, **A74**, **C718** and **D266**.)

D36 1958
NEW STATESMAN, 15 February
'The Potting Shed', concerning the textual differences between the UK and US productions.

D37 1958
THE STAGE, 5 June
'A House of Reputation', a denial by Greene of an announcement in an earlier edition of the newspaper that he had written a play of that name and that it would appear on Broadway the following autumn.

D38 1958
THE TIMES, 27 October
'A Meeting in 1983 – how to assess a day's work', a satirical letter visualizing a businessman assessing a novelist's output in 1983.

D39 1958
TIME, 10 November
'Our Man on pgs. 29–41', replying to criticisms of his creation of a dumb US businessman in *Our Man in Havana*.

D40 1959
SPECTATOR, 23 January
'John Gordon', requesting materials

unauthorised'. There were responses from Gordon himself and John Osborne. Subsequently, Frederic Warburg offered to publish the biography.

D41 1959
SPECTATOR, 10 September
'West End Look', replying to the clichéd pieties of the critic Colm Brogan.

D42 1960
SUNDAY TIMES, 8 December
'Worst Seller', defending *Nemo's Almanac.*

D43 1961
SPECTATOR, 6 October
'Lord Home on TV', on a bad TV habit of the foreign secretary.

D44 1962
SPECTATOR, 27 July
'Macmillan Expects', criticizing the composition of the new cabinet.

D45 1962
SPECTATOR, 30 November
'Boothby and Empire', defending Robert Boothby against a 'journalistic smear'.

D46 1964
TIMES LITERARY SUPPLEMENT, 26 March
'Cuban Itch', disputing a reviewer's assertion that Castro 'has dispatched' the Catholic Church in Cuba.

D47 1965
NEW STATESMAN, 19 March
'Was Oswald Guilty?', replying to Lord Devlin's review of the Warren Report on the assassination of President Kennedy.

D48 1965
TIMES LITERARY SUPPLEMENT, 16 September
'Last Post', on Bodley Head's publishing Ford Madox Ford's *Parade's End* as a trilogy, omitting *Last Post.*

D49 1965
TIMES LITERARY SUPPLEMENT, 30 September
'Last Post?', responding to a letter dated 23 September, with Greene defending the right of authors to have their wishes on their books respected.

D50 1966
OBSERVER, 13 February
'The Comedians', replying to Kingsley Amis's review of Greene's novel.

D51 1966
SPECTATOR, 10 June
'The Heart of the Matter', concerning journalistic reticence about using 'I'.

D52 1966
TIMES LITERARY SUPPLEMENT, 28 July
'Gordon', on Africa, the Victorian death wish and General Gordon of Khartoum.

D53 1967
NEW STATESMAN, 5 May
'Vietnam', differing with Kingsley Amis on American policy in Vietnam.

D54 1968
THE TIMES, 22 March
'Violent Protest', concerning student protest in London against the Vietnam War.

D55 1968
THE TIMES, 25 March
'Mistaken Identity', on Greene's mistake in attributing a London editorial on student protest to a Warsaw newspaper.

D56 1969
OBSERVER, 2 November
'Haig at a Funeral', apologizing for an error in his review of V. S. Naipaul's novel.

D57 1969
NEW STATESMAN, 28 November
'Travels with My Aunt', concerning a review of Greene's novel.

D58 1970
THE TIMES, 5 April
Statement to Press supporting Fr Raúl Oscar Marturet, a member of the 'Third World Movement' of priests, for doing great work.

D59 1970
SPECTATOR, 19 September
'Pop Generation', concerning American involvement in Vietnam.

D60 1971
COMMONWEAL, 26 November
'Greene on Greene', correcting an error about *The Fugitive* in Ralph McInerney's article titled 'The Greene-ing of America'.

D61 1972
NEW YORK REVIEW OF BOOKS, 31 August
'Greene's Meaning', recalling a dreadful lunch in a Soho restaurant with a critic who did not trust Greene.

D62 1973
TIMES EDUCATIONAL SUPPLEMENT, 16 November
'English Style', recommending Herbert Read's *English Prose Style* and Lubbock's *Craft of Fiction* as guides on accuracy of written style.

D63 1973
DAILY TELEGRAPH, 31 December
'Philby and Sikorski', on speculation about connections between Philby and the death of General Sikorski.

D64 1974
BOOKS AND BOOKMEN, June
Untitled, on Kenneth Tynan's criticism of *The Living Room*.

D65 1975
TIMES LITERARY SUPPLEMENT, 20 June
'Ms.', on the pronunciation of the new abbreviation.

D66 1975
NEW YORK REVIEW OF BOOKS, 18 September
'Odd Sound', questioning the sense of a passage in the novel *Shardik* by Richard Adams.

D67 1976
SPECTATOR, 13 March
'Marxianity', on a meeting between Pope John XXIII and Khrushchev's son-in-law, as reported to Greene in Havana. The letter is in reply to an article by Stuart Reid on the actions of the Pope and the World Council of Churches towards Communism.

D68 1976
BOOKS AND BOOKMEN, June
Untitled, on Auberon Waugh's review of *The First Cuckoo*, a selection of letters to *The Times*, and Greene's own job there as assistant letters editor.

D69 1976
NEW STATESMAN, 16 July
'Cary's Writing Habits', correcting an error in Paul Theroux's article on the writer Joyce Cary.

D70 1976
NEW STATESMAN, 5 November
'Not My Style', complaining about the poor quality of the winning entry in a competition to write a pastiche of Greene.

D71 1977
TIMES EDUCATIONAL SUPPLEMENT, 4 February
'Parade's End', defending the publication of Ford Madox Ford's *Parade's End* as a trilogy against criticism by Anthony Burgess. (See **D48** and **D49** in this volume.)

D72 1977
NEW STATESMAN, 11 February
'Oxford's 19th century Ghost', concerning the Oxford Union.

D73 1977
SPECTATOR, 26 February
'WHS', questioning Kingsley Amis's critique of W. H. Smith bookshops.

D74 1977
SUNDAY TELEGRAPH, 27 February
'Greek Fire'.

D75 1977
BOOKS AND BOOKMEN, February
'Untitled', regarding Enoch Powell's misquotation of 'Boy Campbell'.

D76 1977
SUNDAY TELEGRAPH, 6 March
'Timon of Menton', a reply to Francis King.

D77 1977
NEW YORK REVIEW OF BOOKS, 14 April
'Danger Zone?', replying to criticism of his article 'The Country with Five Frontiers'. (See Volume 1, **C705**.)

D78 1978
SUNDAY TIMES, 9 April
'Flies ... Not Fly-Buttons', concerning the novel *The Human Factor.* (See Volume 1, **D548**.)

D79 1978
SPECTATOR, 13 May
'F.R. Leavis', crediting Sir Herbert Grierson with the revival in metaphysical poetry in the 1920s.

D80 1978
THE TIMES, 3 August
'Mary Fairfax', concerning the Duke of Buckingham's wife.

D81 1979
DAILY TELEGRAPH, 11 June
'Headless Coin'. Extracts from a letter to the Paris Mint, rejecting its proposal that Greene's head should be depicted on a coin. This proposal may have been in connection with Greene being awarded

France's highest award *Chevalier de la Légion d'Honneur* in 1969.

D82 1979
NEW YORK REVIEW OF BOOKS, 27 September
'Information wanted', asking for information from readers about Frederic Stimson, the author of *The Crime of Henry Vane*.

D83 1979
NEW YORK REVIEW OF BOOKS, 8 November
'You're Welcome', thanking readers for answering a call for information about J.S. of Dale.

D84 1980
SPECTATOR, 22 March
'Sound Thinking, But …', concerning the 1980 US presidential elections.

D85 1980
TIMES LITERARY SUPPLEMENT, 30 May
'Somerset Maugham', correcting an earlier letter from Constantine Fitzgibbon about a film version of Norman Douglas's *South Wind.* Greene wrote that in order to generate rights income for Douglas, he had tried but failed to write a treatment for a film, to be directed by Mario Soldati.

D86 1980
SPECTATOR, 7 June
'Notebook … Graham Greene, so it is said'. The editor, Alexander Chancellor, identified two winners, so it is said, of Competition No. 111 as Greene's siblings Hugh Greene and Elisabeth Dennys and published the 'unsuccessful attempt'
Colin Bates at imitating a Greene novel. Graham, who had submitted the opening paragraph of what became the novel *The Captain and the Enemy*, commented, 'Yes but in fact it was not written for the competition but was a piece out of an unfinished story.'

D87 1980
SUNDAY TIMES, 6 July
'Wrong Tack', responding to a letter about Greene's lyrics in 'World War Three' (see **C147** in this volume), suggesting they lacked relevance in the less threatening world of the 1980s than they would have had in the 1950s.

D88 1981
DAILY TELEGRAPH, 21 April
'Greene and Hollis', a response to an article by Maier Asher.

D89 1981
SPECTATOR, 25 April
'Ladies of Detection', correcting a reviewer's comment about the earliest female detective writer.

D90 1981
TIMES LITERARY SUPPLEMENT, 29 May
'Herbert Padilla', criticizing the review of a book about Cuba.

D91 1981
SPECTATOR, 17 October
'Land So Unbenighted', correcting a review of Barbara Greene's book *A Land Benighted* about the cousins' journey through Liberia in 1935. (See Volume 1, A18.)

D92 1982
NEW YORK REVIEW OF BOOKS, 12 August
'The FBI and Pearl Harbor', on the attempt by double agent Dusko Popov to warn J. Edgar Hoover of the Japanese attack.

D93 1983
NEW YORK REVIEW OF BOOKS, 21 July
'The Chestertons', regarding a recent discussion of the Chestertons in the journal.

D94 1984
SPECTATOR, 21 April
Disputing another correspondent's views on the political situation in Nicaragua.

D95 1987
INDEPENDENT, 24 September
'A Painful reminder of Argentina's recent past', concerning the case of Senõr Juan Gelman.

D96 1988
SPECTATOR, 16 January
Further letter in a sequence on the behaviour of the Sandinista government in Nicaragua.

D97 1989
IRISH INDEPENDENT, 1 July
Title unknown. Concerning Greene's visit to Dublin in the early 1920s.

PART E

PUBLISHED INTERVIEWS WITH GRAHAM GREENE

E1 1952
NEW YORK HERALD TRIBUNE, 15 February
'Graham Greene Says U.S. Lives in Red-Obsessed "State of Fear" '.

E2 1975
DAILY MAIL, 26 May
'Graham Greene Today', an interview with David Lewin.

E3 2019
GRAHAM GREENE: THE LAST INTERVIEW AND OTHER CONVERSATIONS
(BROOKLYN AND LONDON, MELVILLE HOUSE PUBLISHING)
Edited with an Introduction by John R. MacArthur.
The volume consists of four interviews with Greene, all undertaken during the 1980s: 'God, Literature and So Forth', with Anthony Burgess (1980) (see Volume 1, **E57**); 'Graham Greene at Eighty', with Martin Amis (1984) (see **E70**); 'I'm An Angry Old Man, You See', with John Mortimer (1986) (see **E74**); and 'The Last Interview', with John R. MacArthur (1990) (see **E83**).
John R. MacArthur's interview is published, unabridged, for the first time.

Bibliography of Published Works on Graham Greene

Bibliography and Historiography

Wise, Jon and Hill, Mike (2012), *The Works of Graham Greene: A Reader's Bibliography and Guide*. London: Continuum.

Wise, Jon and Hill, Mike (2015), *The Works of Graham Greene Volume 2: A Guide to the Graham Greene Archives*. London: Bloomsbury.

Biography

Greene, Richard (2020), *Russian Roulette: The Life and Times of Graham Greene*. London: Little, Brown. (North American title: *The Unquiet Englishman: A Life of Graham Greene*. New York: W.W. Norton & Company Ltd, 2021.)

Memoirs and Personal Reminiscences

Diederich, Bernard (2012), *Seeds of Fiction: Graham Greene's Adventures in Haiti and Central America 1954–1983*. London: Peter Owen.

Interviews with Graham Greene

MacArthur, John R. (ed.) (2019), *Graham Greene: The Last Interview and Other Conversations*. Brooklyn: Melville House.

Film Books

Hand, Richard and Purssell, Andrew (2014), *Adapting Graham Greene*. Basingstoke: Palgrave Macmillan.

Henrey, Robert (2013), *Through Grown-up Eyes: Living with Childhood Fame*. Clifton-upon-Theme, Worcestershire: Polperro Heritage. (Henrey was the child actor in *The Fallen Idol*.)

Books and Monographs

Brennan, Michael (2010), 'Graham Greene's *Monsignor Quixote*: A Pilgrimage of Doubt and Reason towards Faith and Belief', in Reichardt, Mary R. (ed.), *Between Human and Divine: The Catholic Vision of Contemporary Literature*. Washington, DC: Catholic University of America Press, 154–70.

Brennan, Michael (2016), *Graham Greene: Political Writer*. Basingstoke: Palgrave Macmillan.

Fiegel, Lara (2013), *The Love Charm of Bombs: Restless Lives in the Second World War*. London: Bloomsbury.

Fromental, Jean-Luc and Hyman, Miles (2018), *The Prague Coup*. London: Titan.

Goetz-Sota, Germaine (2012), *Manic-Depressive Dynamics and Dramaturgy in the Life of Graham Greene*. New York: Mellen.

Hepburn, Allan (2005), *Sewers: Fantasies of Death and Disgust in* The Third Man in *Intrigue, Espionage and Culture* London: Yale University Press, 110–13.

Hull, Christopher (2019), *Our Man Down in Havana: The Story Behind Graham Greene's Cold War Spy Novel*. New York: Pegasus.

Iyer, Pico (2012), *The Man Within My Head: Graham Greene, My Father and*

Levya, Monica (2015), *Graham Greene's Narrative in Spain: Criticism, Translations and Censorship (1939–1975)*. Newcastle: Cambridge Scholars.

Mikkonen, Kai (2015), 'The Rhetoric of the Mad African Forest in Joseph Conrad, Louis Ferdinand Céline and Graham Greene', in Phelan, James, Rabinowitz, Peter J. and Warhol, Robyn (eds), *Narrative Paths: African Travel in Modern Fiction and Non-fiction*. Columbus: Ohio State University Press, 69–87.

Piette, Adam (2009), *The Sacrificial Logic of the Asian Cold War: Greene's* The Quiet American *and McCarthy's* The Seventeenth Degree in *The Literary Cold War, 1945 to Vietnam*. Edinburgh: Edinburgh University Press, 152–208.

Rainsford, Sarah (2018), *Our Woman in Havana: Reporting Castro's Cuba*. London: Oneworld.

Salvan, Paula (2015), *The Language of Ethics and Community in Graham Greene's Fiction*. Basingstoke: Palgrave Macmillan.

Sampson, Martyn (2021), *Between Form and Faith: Graham Greene and the Catholic Novel*. New York: Fordham University Press.

Schwartz, Adam (2005), 'The Heart of the Matter: Mapping Graham Greene's Religious Journey', in *The Third Spring: GK Chesterton, Graham Greene, Christopher Dawson and David Jones*. Washington, DC: Catholic University of America, 110–201.

Schweizer, Bernard (2001), 'Graham Greene', in *Radicals on the Road: The Politics of English Travel Writing in the 1930s*. Charlottesville: University of Virginia Press, 61–79.

Smolik, Pierre (2013), *Graham Greene: The Swiss Chapter*. Vevey, Geneva: Call Me Eduoard.

Spanos, William (2006), 'Who Killed Alden Pyle?: The Oversight of Oversight in Graham Greene's *The Quiet American*', in Tong, Q. S., Shouren, Wang and Kerr, Douglas (eds), *Critical Zone 2: A Forum of Chinese and Western Knowledge*. Hong Long: Hong Kong University Press, 11–46.

Villar Flor, Carlos (2022), *The Real Monsignor Quixote: Graham Greene's Travels around Spain and Portugal*. Oxford: Oxford University Press.

Webster, Harvey (1970), 'Graham Greene: Stoical Catholic', in *After the Trauma: Representative British Novelists since 1920*. Lexington: University of Kentucky, 97–123.

Journal Articles

Adamson, Judith (2017), Reflections'. *Graham Greene Studies*, 1, 1–7.

Adamson, Judith (2021), 'Graham Greene as Publisher'. *Graham Greene Studies*, 2, 1–12.

Assa, Frances Peltz (2021), ' "Quite a Good Spy": The Emergent Graham Greene'. *Graham Greene Studies*, 2, 13–39.

Bosco, Mark (2017), 'Shades of Greene in Catholic Literary Modernism'. *Graham Greene Studies*, 1, 8–23.

Davis, Robert (2017), 'Figures in Graham Greene's Carpet: "The Power and the Glory" to "Monsignor Quixote"'. *Graham Greene Studies*, 1, 24–38.

Gallix, François (2017), 'Graham Greene's Children's Books'. *Graham Greene Studies*, 1, 39–45.

Halper, Thomas (2021), 'Graham Greene and Bridges across Cultures'. *Graham Greene Studies*, 2, 40–58.

Hanson, Johanne (2021), 'Nordahl Grieg's Friendship with Graham Greene'. *Graham Greene Studies*, 2, 59–70.

Hollyfield, Jerod R. (2021), 'Catholic Adaptation, Irish Conversion: The Postcolonial Graham Greene in Neil Jordan's *The End of the Affair*'. *Graham Greene Studies*, 2, 71–89.

Hoskins, Robert (2012), 'Greene's Alchemical Novel: Brighton Rock'. *CEA Critic*, 74 (2/3), 133–43.

Kemp, Emma and Hormbrey, Philip (2021), 'The Shadow Within: Solving the Mystery of *A Day Saved*'. *Graham Greene Studies*, 2, 90–7.

Lechat, Michel (2017), 'Graham Greene and The Congo, 1959: Personal Memories and Background of "A Burnt-Out Case"'. *Graham Greene Studies*, 1, 46–55.

McCormack, Frances (2017), ' "Memory Cheats": Deception, Recollection and the Problem of Reading in "The Captain and the Enemy"'. *Graham Greene* Studies, 1, 82–96.

McCormack, Frances (2021), 'A Hint of the Eucharist: Desecration, Morality, and Faith in "The Hint of an Explanation" '. *Graham Greene Studies*, 2, 98–103.

Meeuwis, Michael (2017), 'The Furthest Escape of All: Darkness and Refuge in The Belgian Congo'. *Graham Greene Studies*, 1, 56–81.

Meeuwis, Michael (2021), 'Graham Greene's Congo Journal: A Critical Edition'. *Graham Greene Studies*, 2, 104–238.

Pursell, A. M. (2009), 'Of Other Spaces: Conrad, Graham Greene and Tourism'. *Conradian*, 34 (2), 21–34.

Ruane, Kevin (2012), 'The Hidden History of Graham Greene's Vietnam War: Fact, Fiction and "The Quiet American"'. *History*, 97 (3), 431–52.

Ruane, Kevin (2017), 'Graham Greene in Love and War: French Indo-China and the Making of "The Quiet American" '. *Graham Greene Studies*, 1, 97–109.

Sato, Motonori (2017), '"The Invisible Japanese Gentleman": Graham Greene's Literary Influence in Japan'. *Graham Greene Studies*, 1, 110–21.

Sinyard, Neil (2004), 'The Strange Case of Alfred Hitchcock and Graham Greene'. *Strand Magazine*, XII, 6–20.

Sinyard, Neil (2017), '"All Writers Are Equal but Some Writers Are More Equal Than Others": Some Reflections on Links and Contrasts between Graham Greene and George Orwell'. *Graham Greene Studies*, 1, 122–32..

Snyder, Robert (2010), '"Shadow of Abandonment": Graham Greene's *The Confidential Agent*'. *Texas Studies in Literature and Language*, 52 (2), 203–26.

Steigman, Karen (2012), 'Rereading Graham Greene in an Age of Security'. *College Literature*, 39 (1), 1–26.

Stollery, Martin (2012), 'Scarred a Cheated Ending/Not Suitable for Audiences in this Colony: The Film Adaptation of Graham Greene's "The Heart of the Matter" in Metropolitan and Colonial Contexts'. *Literature/Film Quarterly*, 40 (3), 133–43.

Walton, Katherine (2021), 'Rose and the Modern "Religious Sense" in Graham Greene's *Brighton Rock*'. *Graham Greene Studies*, 2, 239–54.

Watts, Cedric (2017), 'Darkest Greeneland: "Brighton Rock"'. *Graham Greene Studies*, 1, 133–44.

Doctoral Theses

Bahrawl, Nazry (2013), 'Sacred Impulses, Sacrilegious Works: Postsecular Intimations in Graham Greene and Naguib Mahfouz'. University of Warwick.

Bell, Martha, Frances (1966), 'Graham Greene and the Idea of Childhood'. University of North Texas.

Kazanova, Yuliya (2017), 'Tragic Irony in Selected Works by Graham Greene'. University of Leeds.

Korn, Frederick (2000), '"Condemned to Consequences": A Study of Tragic Process in Three Works by Joseph Conrad and Graham Greene'. University of Illinois.

Pursell, Andrew Martin (2011), 'Space and Empire in the Fiction of Joseph Conrad and Graham Greene'. Royal Holloway College, University of London.

Reeve-Tucker, Alice (2012), 'Evelyn Waugh, Graham Greene and Catholicism 1928–1939'. University of Birmingham.

Wangui, Dorcas (2018), 'Visual Theologies in Graham Greene's "Heart of Faith"'. Lancaster University.

Section 2

The Works of Graham Greene Volume 2: A Guide to the Graham Greene Archives

Section 2a ADDITIONAL MATERIAL

p. 43: Volume 2 of Greene's 1986–7 diary includes entries relating to one of his visits to Spain and Portugal (3–12 August 1987) in the company of Fr Leopoldo Durán. It was the only time that Greene recorded his thoughts and opinions on his Spanish sojourns, and as such it constitutes an important counterbalance to Durán's extensive recollections of this near annual event.

p. 123: Greene's next book (not novel) was his autobiography *A Sort of Life* which was published by Simon and Schuster.

pp. 134, col. 1, line 17 and 355, col. 1, line 15: Nicholas 'Scheetz' not 'Sheetz'.

pp. 144 and 244: Michael Richey Correspondence. It is thought that Greene first made the acquaintance of Michael Richey in 1940 although there is evidence that they met through Tom Burns 'after the war'. It appears that any early correspondence (before 1954) is missing.

p. 149: Francis Greene attended Dragon School, Oxford, and later Ampleforth College, North Yorkshire, and not Berkhamsted School.

p. 265: Balliol College Archive. Greene gave the typescript copy of *The Great Jowett* to the College in 1980, not 1990.

p. 280: 29/1 Book Reviews (undated): 'Judgement on Deltchev', not 'by Deltchev'.

p. 319: Sub-series K: Poetry. 58/3–5 Poetry: should read '1922–83', not '1924–83'; 'An Epic Fragment From "The Dish Pioneers" Attributed to A-F-D-N-Y-S', add (1922).

Section 2b NEW ENTRIES

PART 1 CONTEXT AND ANALYSIS

ARCHIVES IN THE UNITED KINGDOM

Berkhamsted, Hertfordshire

BERKHAMSTED SCHOOL ARCHIVE

Graham Greene's school possesses a complete set of copies of the school magazine *The Berkhamstedian.* These include Greene's contributions published in the period 1920–2, identified in Volume 1 of this guide as **C1**, **C2**, **C3**, **C5** and the previously unidentified short story 'Castles in the Air' (**C1** in this volume). It was Greene's specific wish that these short stories and poems would not be republished. Therefore, the location of copies of his earliest published works are mentioned here simply for 'completeness' and owing to their extreme rarity.

Manchester

MANCHESTER METROPOLITAN UNIVERSITY

PAUL HOGARTH ARCHIVE

Paul Hogarth (1917–2001) was an artist and illustrator whose work included watercolours which made striking covers for Penguin editions of Greene's works from the 1960s onwards. In 1986 Hogarth published *Graham Greene Country*, with illustrations of locations associated with Greene's books in the UK and around the world. The book also had extracts from Hogarth's travel diaries, extracts from Greene's works and a foreword by Greene and his brief commentaries on the books covered (see Volume 1, **B85**).

The archive's correspondence between the two men, which is not complete, begins in 1969 and runs to 1991. In October 1969, Greene wrote that 'I much admire your work and have one of your Far Eastern drawings – of a bird-fisher – hanging on my wall [in Paris]'. Greene also wrote in 1970 about some of Hogarth's Penguin covers – 'I like PH's drawings very much as a rule' – but asking why there is a rat on the cover of

Collected Essays and complaining about the cover of *England Made Me*.

By August 1984, Hogarth was writing to propose what became *Graham Greene Country*, arguing its appropriateness because of his Penguin covers and his life as an 'artist-traveller'. Greene wrote in enthusiastic support in September, giving examples of locations for specific books, including this for 'Under the Garden' from the short story collection *A Sense of Reality*: 'It would be pleasant if you would do Harston House, Harston, nr. Cambridge which was the actual scene where I used to spend my childhood. It's a very pleasant looking house primarily Queen Anne with additions. I think you would even find the pond there!' Hogarth was soon making plans for his globetrotting itinerary and asking for further information on locations and possible contacts; Greene continued to respond to the queries, including in February 1985 a recommendation that for Spain Hogarth should contact 'a great friend of mine', Father Durán. (Later, Greene's sister and secretary Elisabeth Dennys wrote to Hogarth about Durán, 'you will love him – everyone does'.) In April 1985 Greene advised in relation to *The Tenth Man*, 'Brinac does not exist even under another name.' Hogarth suggested that the book might contain extracts from his own travel notes, and Greene responded enthusiastically, commenting, 'I found your diary excellent.' In November 1985, on returning from Zaire, Hogarth commented, 'Your visit there is recalled like an Irish folk tale,' and Greene wrote in response, 'I hope you won't come out with leprosy in ten years' time. Edith Sitwell was afraid to kiss me when I came back.' In February 1986, Greene commented that Castle's house in *The Human Factor* was 'based on a house owned by an aunt of mine not by my sister'.

By March 1986 Hogarth's travels were complete, and Greene wrote to correct some of his diary entries: 'I never made any notes during the period I lived in Nottingham'; in relation to *The End of the Affair*, 'Nor have I any abhorrence of cremation. In fact it would be the form of burial which I would prefer'; and Greene reported that Yvonne Cloetta was happy to be mentioned but that as a description of her they both preferred 'lively' to 'vivacious' ('horrid word'). As the finished book was published, Greene refused a request to do a television interview but attended a launch party in October 1986.

The two men continued to correspond, and Hogarth sent Greene a watercolour of the 'Chez Felix' restaurant in Antibes. In March 1989, Greene responded to a query about the USSR with 'Yes, I've been to Russia (including Georgia, Ukraine and Siberia) 5 times in the last three years and believe completely in G[orbachev]'. The last letter in the collection, by Hogarth to Elisabeth Dennys after Greene's death, gives a final insight into the relationship, commenting that he had lost a very dear friend and recalling that the two men had met around twelve times while working on his book.

The remainder of the *Graham Greene Country* archive contains no further original material by Greene, but much else of interest on the book, including Hogarth's travel sketch books and travel diaries, and photographs of Greene and

Hogarth in Antibes. Elsewhere in the Hogarth archive are Penguin book cover designs and other artwork relating to *Graham Greene Country.*

Oxford, Oxfordshire

OXFORD UNIVERSITY BALLIOL COLLEGE LIBRARY: ARCHIVES AND MANUSCRIPTS

PAPERS OF MARIE BICHE RELATING TO GRAHAM GREENE

The Biche archive is a rich, extensive and important resource for Greene scholars, giving a detailed insight into Greene's career, feelings and opinions over a very long period of his life as a writer. Despite the title of this collection, the papers include Greene's correspondence with Denyse Clairouin from the 1930s in addition, much more substantially, to that with Marie Biche from 1946 to 1991. Though letters tend to be in chronological runs, the papers are in catalogue numerical order but not, overall, chronological order.

Frenchwoman Denyse Clairouin was Graham Greene's first translator and then his agent in France, and the thirty-four items in the archive run from 1931 to 1939. (Clairouin, a brave and heroic member of the French Resistance movement in the Second World War, died in Mauthausen concentration camp in March 1945.) Greene's letters are mostly handwritten and begin with 'Dear Mlle Clairouin', becoming 'Dear Denyse – May I?' in 1934. Early letters concern the cutting out by editor Jacques Maritain of some sexual references from the French edition of *The Man Within* (*L'homme et lui-même*); for a time Greene insisted on an author's note in the book to the effect that certain passages had been omitted with his 'consent' not 'approval'. Receiving a copy of the French edition of the novel in April 1931, Greene commented that he liked the cover and, indeed, preferred the book in French. Greene was grateful for Clairouin's (unsuccessful) efforts in trying to get *The Name of Action* published in France, and by the end of 1931 he made her his agent in France; indeed by 1936 he trusted her sufficiently to ask her if she could possibly take on German and Scandinavian rights issues. In 1933 he wrote wishing her well in getting *Stamboul Train* accepted in France, but interestingly commented, 'But how I wish it was *Rumour at Nightfall*, which obstinately and in spite of publishers & public I so much prefer.' Greene and Clairouin met socially in London, and in 1934 she drove him around Paris to report on any trouble in the General Strike there; he wrote in March to thank her for her help and mentioned the article on the business for the *Spectator.* Later that year he wrote her a wide-ranging letter announcing his forthcoming trek across Liberia, appreciating the irony of censorship of him in France and commenting on how pessimistic he felt about the situation in Germany ('that nice, sentimental, abysmally stupid race'). Further letters concern the publication of some of Greene's short stories, his continuing output of novels and of the travel books *Journey Without Maps* and *The Lawless*

he was getting into the 'film racket', doing a picture with Basil Dean; 'All this may prove more profitable than writing books,' he commented. Further visits to Paris are mentioned and a proposed one to Bilbao during the Spanish Civil War. In the last letter in the archive, in January 1939, Greene expressed sadness that Clairouin has been so ill and sent news of a dramatized version of *Brighton Rock*.

After Denyse Clairouin's death, her business associate Marie Schebeko (after her marriage in 1951, Biche) became Greene's French agent. The Balliol archive has well over nine hundred letters, telegrams and postcards from Greene to Biche spanning a period of forty-plus years, making it one of the most extensive collections of his correspondence to a single person in any archive. Her language skills and knowledge of the publishing industry made her indispensable to Greene, and they became very close friends, her efforts on his behalf going well beyond purely business matters. They met on many occasions, usually in Paris.

A great many of Greene's letters to Biche are handwritten, and around three-quarters of them date from the 1950s and 1960s. A number of the letters to the Bureau Denyse Clairouin in Paris from 1946 and 1947 are to Mme A. Renaud de Saint Georges (who retired in 1947), but Greene first wrote to Marie Schebeko at the Bureau in July 1946, and she soon became his sole correspondent there, addressing her as 'Dear Marie'. Over the years Biche dealt with a great many issues concerned with French translations, adaptations and royalties, with Greene coming to rely on her energy and judgement.

Since much of the correspondence deals with Greene's writing, the letters give a kind of continuous narrative of his career over a period of almost half a century. Greene kept Biche informed of the progress of his current writing projects, commenting at one point in 1965 that he had five books on the go at once. Publishing opportunities and possibilities were explored. Greene was very particular, and sometimes critical, about the quality of the French translations of his books, and from the 1960s he involved his companion Yvonne Cloetta in helping with translations, and she became a very influential figure. (In a letter of January 1979 Biche herself made the suggestion to Greene that Cloetta might take over Verdant business in Paris, because of Biche's 'pottyness'. Verdant SA was a company set up in the early 1960s to handle Greene's publishing and business interests.). Greene also included in his letters comments on the covers of his books, again sometimes critically. He showed himself keen to promote and protect his output as a writer – in February 1970 he wrote of the newly published *Travels with My Aunt*, 'In Antibes there's no sign that the book has been published – no copy in any of the 5 bookshops! I hope they've done better in Paris'; while in August 1968 he commented, 'I noticed in Buenos Aires an awful pocket book edition of The Man Within. I suppose we know all about that?' He came to rely heavily on Biche promoting and protecting his interests and showed his gratitude, but he could be critical of her, too. In January 1956 he wrote to her of the terrible introduction by François Mauriac to the newly published *The Quiet American*, with accompanying appalling illustrations: 'I do think you might have let me see these. It's no good trying to protect your author!' And in August 1964 he expressed his anger at her for talking to journalists. Sometimes he wrote in the heat of the moment, then relented and apologized.

Scattered through the correspondence are interesting comments by Greene which give insights into his views on his work, either in retrospect or as the work in hand evolved. On 7 March 1946 he wrote, 'The short story has never attracted me very much and I am not very good at the form.' On *The Name of Action* and *Rumour at Nightfall* Greene commented, 'They are very bad books which I wish forgotten' (7 July 1948). Once again looking back, he referred to *The Ministry of Fear* as 'my best entertainment' (October 1964). Before the first rehearsal of the stage version of *The Heart of the Matter* in February 1950, Greene wrote, 'I'm beginning to feel a faint interest – though no optimism.' He showed a continuing dissatisfaction with *The End of the Affair* – 'The book's finished, but I think it's lousy' (19 August 1950); 'the end needs to be more or less completely re-written' (20 September 1950); and 'it's still not right, & I know what's wrong, but the book's finished & I can't bring myself to write new scenes' (25 December 1950). In 1954 Greene declared, rather surprisingly, 'I seem to write nothing but funny stories now.' He professed a low opinion of *Our Man in Havana*: 'I've been astonished at the English reviews [illegible] for the book as you know' (27 October 1958). The strain of writing is often in evidence. When he had completed the first draft of the play *Carving a Statue* he commented on his sense of release: 'I don't mind a bit if it's bad – it's finished and I can think of something else' (13 December 1963). On *The Comedians* he declared himself 'impatient to get rid of this bloody book' (25 March 1965), while on writing *The Honorary Consul* he commented, 'Finished 70,000 – only another 20 at most!' (31 July 1971).

There are too in Greene's letters to Biche a number of other scattered comments which are of interest. He had things to say on those who write for a living. 'Gatherings of writers are a little like masturbation,' he wrote on 5 April [1951?], while on 27 April 1959 he declared, 'I want to be confirmed in my detestation of journalists and misrepresentations!' His relationships sometimes featured in these letters. On Alexander Korda's death he commented, 'Luckily we had made it all up a month before and had two very friendly and affectionate meetings. I loved the old boy' (30 January 1956). On his holiday in Tahiti Greene commented, 'My companion Michael Meyer was a bit restive and dissatisfied so that in the end I brought the trip to a close earlier than I had intended' (16 February 1960). His political attitudes sometimes surfaced, too. During a British general election, he reported on going to London to 'record my protest vote – alas! There is no Communist standing for Westminster!' (13 October 1964). And on 9 November 1964 Greene wrote, 'My jury duty starts they know the anarchist who comes to the jury room. Last time – at another place – 12 years ago we found everyone innocent!'

Marie Biche went well beyond her official role as Greene's French agent. In the correspondence there is news of health issues, of Greene's developing relationship with Catherine Walston and later with Yvonne Cloetta, mixed in with details of royalties and translations. Biche's work in dealing with the royalties on Greene's French publications merged into more general advice and action on money and taxation. In the mid-1960s Greene's letters became much concerned with financial matters, a reflection of the impact of the Thomas Roe affair, in which a financial advisor swindled Greene out of much of his money: in August 1965 he wrote to her, 'Bad news about Roe. Cling to any money and don't transfer it for the time being.' Marie Biche also often acted as a social secretary – helping, for instance, with Greene's visit to Paris in July 1949 with Catherine Walston. She became indispensable in making travel and accommodation arrangements for him and booked play tickets. In September 1955 Greene asked her to provide introductions to people in Tours when Rodney Dennys went there. In February 1960 he enquired about acquiring an apartment in Paris, and in later letters he involved her in problems he was having at the flat with heating, the bath and windows; the same later happened with the electric boiler and radiators in his flat in Antibes. In October 1965, as he contemplated moving permanently to France, he asked Biche about domicile in France and what French nationality would involve. Sometimes his requests were cryptic: 'Could you let me have a double dose of the usual when I see you?' (28 April 1964). Greene was suitably grateful for all her help, and presents, sometimes quite expensive ones, were a regular feature of their correspondence. 'The trouble is you spoil me,' he wrote in April 1964.

The correspondence therefore reflects a very close and long-lasting relationship, one which combined business with genuine friendship. The letters give a detailed insight into Graham Greene's middle and later years.

THE CHERRY RECORD COLLECTION OF JOSEPHINE REID'S PAPERS AND BOOKS RELATING TO GRAHAM GREENE (from 1959)

Note: This entry expands on the collection detailed briefly in Volume 2, pp. 265–6.

Josephine Reid was Greene's secretary from 1958 to 1975 after which she gave up her secretarial duties but continued to type his literary manuscripts until 1992, the year after his death. Her archive, consisting of correspondence, documents, books and ephemera, provides a rich source of fresh information about the writer's working practices as well as some aspects of his personal life. The degree to which Greene valued his secretary's efficiency, loyalty and utmost discretion can be appreciated in the warm and sincere dedications to be found in many of the presentation copies of his work which form an important part of this collection.

The archive is divided into fifteen 'Series'. Although the majority of the items relate to the period when Reid was in Greene's employment, Series 10 and 11 provide glimpses of his reclusive secretary's private life prior to working for Greene, in the form of letters and photographs. Correspondence addressed to Josephine Reid in Series 1 and the considerable collection of letters, newspaper cuttings and other material in Series 5–9 testify to her enduring personal interest in his work and its critical reception together with her indefatigable loyalty and discretion shown both during their professional partnership and after his death.

Reid steadfastly refused to discuss her employer publicly. In October 1991 she wrote politely to Donald Sturrock at the BBC, 'I am sorry I am not prepared to talk to you about Mr Greene … I only wish I could say this to you in a more friendly and polite way. But there it is.' She appeared fiercely protective of the writer's reputation. In an address book listing personal and business acquaintances of Greene she had written details relating to Anthony Mockler, one of his biographers, to which she had added, 'bastard'. Her obvious affection for the author is summed up in a note on a Christmas card from Greene in 1970 which enclosed a cheque in gratitude for her years of service. Reid's note reads, 'Given to me by Mr Greene at the end of a lovely day in Brighton on 19/12/70.'

Arguably the most significant papers in this archive are located in Series 3, 4 and 10. Series 3 and 4 consist of a collection of around two hundred letters

using the audio 'Dictabelt' system. This method was favoured by Greene as a way of circumventing the problem of living in Antibes and using the services of Josephine Reid in Minehead, UK. They cover a three-year period at the end of his life between September 1987 and September 1990. Sadly, none of the original Dictabelt recordings survived as his secretary, following her employer's instructions to the letter, destroyed each one after use.

The transcriptions comprise pages of drafts of letters and notes, on various but mostly unrelated topics, frequently written in reply to mail which had accumulated at Greene's home after one of his trips abroad. A typical page includes some suggestions to the scriptwriter Christopher Neame regarding an adaptation of *A Burnt-Out Case*, an answer to a copyright matter raised by his Swiss lawyer Jean-Félix Paschoud and short note to Judith Adamson asking her to exclude the text of a speech he had made from his forthcoming book of essays *Reflections* as he wanted to use 'a little anecdote at the end of the speech I am now planning to turn possibly into a short novel'.

Series 10 includes over seventy letters, cards and notes from Greene to Reid, written over a thirty-year period from 1959 onwards. From the start, the writer sent letters from various parts of the world the content of which consisted mostly of instructions and requests but were interspersed with glimpses of the places he was visiting or his mood at the time. In February 1959, less than three months after Reid started working for on 5 February, 'Terribly hot yesterday and humidity 100%. The air broke on one's cheek like tiny drops of rain.' He went on to describe how he found relief in such oppressive conditions, 'I love my two strolls a day, early morning and evening, to the Congo to read a book on the deck of an old rusting tin boat.'

That quite tranquil description contrasts with his mood of frustration when he wrote from Mexico City in July 1963 having been delayed there for several days following the non-arrival of a connecting plane,

> I don't like Mexico even after 25 years, but it's better to be stuck here than Kingston [Jamaica] which is the worst spot of all. I had all my loose cash – about 100 dollars and 20 pounds – lifted out of my pockets at Mexico airport at midnight by a cunning kid who left behind on purpose a book of traveller's cheques.

By the late 1960s, practically a decade after Reid started working for him, Greene's letters had become warmer and the content more 'chatty', at least by his standards. The tone of the opening of a letter dated 25 July 1968, written from the home near Buenos Aires of his friend and South American publisher Victoria Ocampo, illustrates this developing familiarity, 'Dear Josephine, A hasty line. Victoria is a dear and I am very comfortable in her house, but she has made me jump in the ring with press conferences, parties, author's clubs and all.' Greene goes on to divulge, 'The time has not been wasted … I've had time to gain ideas for the book which had been rather stagnant.' Whether the 'ideas for the book' referred to *Travels with My Aunt*, which was to be published the following year, or to its successor *The Honorary Consul* is unclear. Nevertheless, in a letter to Reid the following month from Asunción, Greene was able to claim that in the Paraguayan capital he had found 'quite the place for Aunt Augusta's final home'.

Josephine Reid continued to work for Greene following her retirement in 1975, as mentioned above. A letter in 1979, as well as asking her to type the manuscript of a 'nouvelle', *Doctor Fischer of Geneva or The Bomb Party*, contained a further request. It is clear from the tentative tone that Greene adopts that he is sensitive about intruding too much on what were meant to be Reid's retirement years. The extract from this letter also provides an insight into his working practices.

> Another thing I should like to have done if you could undertake it is a typing out of the various cuttings of my travel articles and reportage which I propose to revise and publish under some title like 'The Troubled Places'. I find it almost impossible to work on these articles in the form of photographed cuttings. It would be much easier to work on them as typescripts. This affair would be almost book length and I would like to have some part of it anyway ready for me to work on whilst I was in Capri.

The book never materialized.

Greene's penultimate letter to Reid was written in his own hand in June 1988 as his sister Elisabeth Dennys, by then his secretary, had recently suffered a stroke. The handwriting is shaky and the writer clearly exhausted. He confessed that he was working on two books and was 'longing for Anacapri'. He told Reid that he was not going to Russia for the anniversary celebrations – 'too tired and too many people'.

Amongst the other correspondence addressed to Josephine Reid in Series 10 is a lengthy letter from Elisabeth Dennys written in 1979. The content is 'gossipy' with news and not always flattering remarks about several of her brother's acquaintances, including Jeanne Stonor, Jocelyn Rickards, the Sutros and Marie Biche. The most intriguing paragraph concerns the whereabouts of the original manuscripts of *The End of the Affair* and *The Quiet American*. Dennys remarked that her brother had 'a faint memory' of Heinemann borrowing the manuscript of *The Quiet American*, perhaps for an exhibition, while 'Catharine [*sic*] had the "heavily corrected typescript"'. Greene thought he had lent the manuscript of *The End of the Affair* for a Festival of Britain exhibition. Dennys concluded, 'Stolen I expect.' The whereabouts of both of these important original manuscripts remain unresolved. This passage in his sister's letter suggests either that Greene had little regard at the time for the importance for posterity of the original drafts of his own work or else his rather hazy recollections are indicative of his emotionally troubled state of mind in the early 1950s. Perhaps the truth lies somewhere in between.

GRAHAM GREENE, PERSONAL DOSSIER

The 'Old Member' dossier (1922–2004) consists of chiefly administrative correspondence to and from Balliol, including seventeen original letters by Graham Greene. The existence of this archive is to a large extent serendipitous; there was no specific decision taken to compile dossiers on notable alumni such as this writer. Fortunately, Greene generated more paperwork than some others, and it survived in a better state. The dossier is important for two reasons. Firstly, the earliest dated documents provide a unique insight into the writer's character and intellectual capabilities as others perceived him both at the beginning and at the end of his time at Balliol. Secondly, the correspondence between Greene and successive Masters of the College reveals a warm relationship which grew from the 1960s onwards and which contrasts with the accepted view that he had little to do with the establishment during his lifetime. The recent formation of this archive is testament to Balliol's stated commitment to make the college 'the most important gathering of material relating to Greene in the UK'.

The earliest letter in the archive, from Greene's father Charles, is dated 13 June 1922 and enquires of the Balliol admissions tutor Cyril Bailey whether it would be possible to admit his son in October of that year. He adds that he had entered the 'late Balliol scholarship' and that Kenneth Bell had promised to speak to Bailey on Graham's behalf. Bell's reply to Bailey's request for a reference produced a brief but astute pen-portrait of the young Greene. Bell writes, 'He seems to me to be a very clever boy, not very robust in health, and rather above possibilities.' A more detailed, academic assessment was given in a further letter in which Bell revealed that in Greene's earlier failed scholarship exam his marks had varied between alpha minus and gamma plus. He adds that 'some of us thought very well of it, others the reverse'. He and two colleagues were 'inclined to the alpha view because it was highly imaginative stuff, sometimes thin and fantastic but with real power over words. The boy had only done History for six weeks before coming in and his efforts to disguise his ignorance, though not very convincing, were extremely ingenious'.

In May 1925, shortly before Greene took his final exams at Balliol, Francis Urquhart, the dean of the college, wrote to Geoffrey Dawson, editor of *The Times*, recommending Greene who was seeking work at the paper. Urquhart remarked that although he did not know him well he was nevertheless aware that Greene was 'an able fellow' with 'a very distinct power of writing'. He thought that he would be able 'to write quickly and effectively'. Greene started work for *The Times* the following year after gaining journalistic experience in Glasgow and Nottingham.

Apart from a letter of acceptance from Greene for a dinner at the college in 1937 there are no other communications in the archive until 1963 when the master, David Lindsay Kerr, wrote to him with the news of a unanimous college meeting resolution inviting him to accept an honorary fellowship. Balliol College Honorary Fellowships are conferred only rarely. Robert Browning, who Greene greatly admired, was the first recipient. He replied, 'I can think of nothing which would give me more pleasure and more vanity.' Three years later, in a handwritten letter to Kerr's successor as master J. E. C. Hill, Greene clearly demonstrated his feelings about his old college, 'And thank you too for enabling me to feel part of Balliol – as I never felt with Smith or Lindsay' (masters 1916–24 and 1924–49, respectively).

The good relations continued throughout the 1960s and 1970s during which time Greene sent copies of his latest books to the college and in 1980 the manuscript of his 1939 radio play *The Great Jowett*, about the life of the Victorian master of Balliol, Benjamin Jowett. Anthony Kenny, the current master, took the opportunity to enquire politely whether Greene had already made arrangements to dispose of his other manuscripts. Greene's reply on 31 October 1980 is intriguing. After admitting that he had sold his manuscripts to the University of Texas, 'like so many others', he remarked, 'I believe however that there are a collection of letters and an unpublished novel earmarked for you by an old friend who had died but I'm afraid they won't come to you until the death of her husband.' It can be deduced that the 'friend' referred to was Catherine Walston. Greene clearly changed his mind as during the 1980s he recommended Harry Walston, Catherine's husband, to sell her letters to Georgetown University Library. The 'unpublished novel' was most likely the heavily corrected typescript of *The Quiet American* referred to by Elisabeth Dennys in her letter to Josephine Reid the previous year (see the Josephine Reed, Cherry Record Collection above).

In 1982 the dean and archivist of Balliol John Jones enquired of Greene regarding the location of his rooms at the college. Despite the passage of time Greene was able to recall that it was 'in a small modern block close to the back door on St. Giles and facing a half-timbered building. I was on the first floor I think and my room next to that of Rev. M.R. Ridley.'

There was regular correspondence between Greene and Anthony Kenny throughout most of the 1980s although the master never succeeded in enticing Greene to accept an invitation to a formal dinner at which he would have been the principal guest. When he was awarded the Order of Merit in 1986 he replied to Kenny's invitation declining the suggestion of a public event in his honour, 'A quiet celebratory drink with you would another matter. I feel this award has an oddly melancholy effect like writing FINIS at the end of an M.S.'.

ARCHIVE IN SWEDEN

Stockholm

NATIONAL LIBRARY OF SWEDEN

RAGNAR SVANSTRÖM ARCHIVE

Ragnar Svanström was literary adviser to Norstedts Förlag, Sweden's oldest book publishing company. Greene met him having been introduced to the Anglo-Swedish Literary Foundation, a fund for the development of cultural relations between the UK and Sweden. Svanström and Greene became friends in addition to being connected through publishing. Later, Max Reinhardt, the owner of Bodley Head, developed a publishing arrangement with Norstedts. He and Svanström were fellow members of the Savile Club in London.

The archive covers correspondence dated February 1952–May 1977 and comprises fifty-three separate communications, principally letters or extracts from letters from Greene to Svanström. They cover business matters almost exclusively and are copy-typed in English – presumably being intended as aides-memoire for the publisher in his daily work. The archive provides valuable insights into Greene's then current 'work in progress' on several novels and plays such as *The Quiet American*, *A Burnt-Out Case* and *The Living Room*.

In April 1952 Greene first broached the subject of the expected date for the premiere of his play *The Living Room*. He hoped that there would be a Swedish production at some point. Svanström replied later the same month that Greene's theatrical agent Jan van Loewen had already posted a copy to Karl Gierow, director of the Royal Dramatic Theatre in Stockholm. A further letter from Svanström followed on 21 July to say that it had been agreed that the play would be performed in Stockholm in October of that year. Greene replied that 'it might be fun to come over for the first night' adding that the first performance in the UK of *The Living Room* had had to be postponed until the following spring. Notes dictated by that Greene had just completed a week-long visit to Stockholm. Greene had told him that *The Quiet American* might be finished by summer 1954 and that he rated it equally with *The Power and the Glory*, *The End of the Affair* and *England Made Me* as his best works to date. By October, however, Greene was clearly struggling with the novel, writing that he was off to Indo-China again in the hope that he would find inspiration as *The Quiet American* 'has not progressed at all'.

The visit to Indo-China appeared to work and the following year, 1955, there were exchanges regarding publication dates. Svanström appeared to 'steal a march' on Heinemann when, on hearing that the UK publisher was intending to bring the novel out in January 1956, asked if Norstedts could publish before Christmas, otherwise the book would have to be delayed until the following autumn. Greene reported that A. S. Frere, Heinemann's Chairman, had acquiesced but had urged Svanström to find a good translator.

Greene and Svanström continued to correspond over the next five years regarding *Our Man in Havana* and the plays *The Potting Shed* and *The Complaisant Lover*. In March 1960 the writer advised Svanström that he had finished the first draft of *A Burnt-Out Case* and unless he consigned it to the wastepaper basket he should be able to send him the manuscript in a couple of months' time. In the event, *Utbränd*, the Swedish edition of the novel, was published in Sweden the following November ahead of the UK edition in January 1961. It has been argued that there was a connection between publicity in Sweden for the novel and Greene's candidacy for the Nobel Prize for Literature. But that appeared not to be the case when Greene wrote his March letter: 'I don't know whether Frere is going to stick to his idea of publishing in the first week in January as an experiment or whether he'll change his mind,' adding that, as things stood, the chairman had no objections to the novel appearing in Sweden first. Later in August Greene appeared to confirm what he had written claiming that Frere thought that the early Swedish edition would not attract the attention of the press as few people in England spoke Swedish. After the novel was published it was given an unfavourable review in a prominent Stockholm newspaper. Greene commented that no one yet seemed to suspect that it might have been 'a farewell to Catholicism', adding somewhat enigmatically, 'though the farewell is a friendly one!'

By the next year, what was to become *The Comedians* was beginning to take shape. He wrote to Svanström that he had written seven thousand words, but until he had completed twenty thousand he would not know if the work would 'march or not'. If it was to be an entertainment, he would call it 'The Word Pterodactyl', and if a novel, 'A Man of Extremes' (please refer to Volume 2, pp. 89–90, for further details of these manuscripts). Svanström was supplied with regular 'bulletins' over the next two years about the progress of *The Comedians* before Greene wrote from Paris in August 1965 with his familiar gloomy outlook on completion, 'The book has dragged on a long time and I am not at all happy with it.' The writer still had doubts about it seven years later when, on having just completed *The Honorary Consul*, he told Svanström's successor Lasse Bergström that he preferred it to *The Comedians*, 'which I didn't think really quite came off'.

There are precious few glimpses in the archive of the personal relationship between the two men, but Svanström does mention in a note in August 1969 that he spent a few days on holiday in Finland with Greene. He recalls that while in Helsinki the writer had received a cable from Viking in New York suggesting a title change for his new book *Travels with My Aunt*, 'This made Greene so angry he decided to change his American publisher and join Schuster and Schuster.' We later learn that Greene's initial rage subsided and the move was put off, albeit temporarily. The next year he wrote from Paris that his autobiography would be published in America in 1971 by Simon and Schuster.

Greene and Svanström's final professional exchanges, before the latter retired, concerned *The Honorary Consul*. Greene, thanking his friend for his positive comments about the novel, wrote that he thought Clara was the least successful character, 'rather as Phuong was in *The Quiet American*'.

The archive principally comprises the exchanges between the two men but also includes a few written communications from Bergström and Greene's secretary Josephine Reid.

PART 2 LISTINGS

Note: These listings include those discussed in 'Context and Analysis' earlier and other brief listings not dealt with there

ARCHIVES IN THE UNITED KINGDOM

Aberystwyth, Dyfed

NATIONAL LIBRARY OF WALES: ARCHIVES AND MANUSCRIPTS
www.library.wales/NLW
CLEDWYN HUGHES PAPERS: Letter to Cledwyn Hughes, 1945.

Berkshire, Eton College

Diana Cooper Correspondence Box IV: Eight letters and two cards to Diana Cooper.
Literacy Society Collection Vol. 1: Two letters to Ben Whitaker, 1952.
Hayward Memorial File: Essay and covering letter to John Carter.
Horner 1: Letter to Osbert Sitwell, 1950.

Bristol

UNIVERSITY OF BRISTOL LIBRARY: SPECIAL COLLECTIONS
www.bristol.ac.uk/library/
DM1679: Two letters to Michael Rubenstein, 1960.

Cambridge, Cambridgeshire

CAMBRIDGE UNIVERSITY ST JOHN'S COLLEGE LIBRARY SPECIAL COLLECTIONS
www.sjcarchives.org.
Beaton/A/A1/223: Letter to Cecil Beaton, 25 June 1953, typed, signed

Durham

DURHAM UNIVERSITY LIBRARY: ARCHIVES AND SPECIAL COLLECTIONS
www.dur.ac.uk/library/
PLOMER COLLECTION
PLD/252: Two letters to Zelda Friedlander, 1965.

Exeter, Devon

UNIVERSITY OF EXETER LIBRARY: SPECIALCOLLECTIONS: ARCHIVES AND MANUSCRIPTS
www.exeter.ac.uk/library/
GB29 EUL MS423: Correspondence with Elwin Malcolm.

Leeds, West Yorkshire

LEEDS UNIVERSITY LIBRARY: BROTHERTON SPECIAL COLLECTIONS
www.library.leeds.ac.uk/
Typed letter to Jeffrey Young, dated August 1989, held with a copy of *Brideshead Revisited* by Evelyn Waugh.

London

THE BRITISH LIBRARY: DEPARTMENT OF WESTERN MANUSCRIPTS
www.bl.uk/
RP 1864: Letter to Patrick Balfour, Lord Kinross.
Ms.Eng.c6859: Letter to Vivien Greene, 1944.
Add.MSS.89295/1 Bryan Forbes & Graham Greene Correspondence, 1970–91. Thirty-one letters from Greene to Bryan Forbes including acknowledgement of receipt and feedback on Forbes's work; discussion about a production of *The Living Room*; a request for Forbes to look at *A House of Reputation* with a view to possible theatre or television production; and some mention of Greene's deteriorating health by the summer of 1990.
Add.MSS.79453, 79454, 79460: Three letters and a note to Reginald Moore, 1943–5.
Add.MSS.87634: Two letters to Dilys Powell, 1989.
Add.MSS.87645: Letter to Leonard Russell, 1954.
Add.MSS.59546: Letter to Evelyn Wrench, 1946.
GB58 Add.MSS.88938/2/3/6: Copy letter to Victor Gollancz Ltd, having read *Empires of the Sun* by James Ballard 'with great interest', and providing the publishers with two appreciative sentences for quotation 'if you like'.

THE NATIONAL ARCHIVES AT KEW
www.nationalarchives.gov.uk
Note: The following files may be useful to researchers as they contain information relating to Graham Greene's life and work but not necessarily, or identifiably, in his own writing.
KV2/634, 635 & 636: William Herbert Greene alias Midorikawa.
KV3/2/70: Headquarters of the SS in Spain.
KV6/120, 121, 122, 123: Ralph Arthur Parker, journalist, 'Times' correspondent, SOE agent.

FO371/18044: Liberia 1934. (Concerning Greene's visit to the country in 1935.)
FO371/184883: Cuban pilots stowaway on 'New Heath'.
FCO7/249: Relations with the United States and the UK – protest over Graham Greene's book and film *The Comedians*.

TATE GALLERY ARCHIVE
www.tate.org.uk
GB70 TGA 200410/1/1/1279: Correspondence with John Piper.

UNIVERSITY COLLEGE, LONDON UNIVERSITY: SPECIAL COLLECTIONS
www.ucl.ac.uk/library

MERVYN PEAKE MANUSCRIPTS
Box VII, iv: Two letters to Mervyn Peake, 1954 and undated.

VICTORIA & ALBERT MUSEUM THEATRE & PERFORMANCE COLLECTIONS
THM/31/3/5/77/1–6: Six letters to Diana Graves and Dick Green.
THM/452/33/66: Three letters to Peter Brook.

Manchester

MANCHESTER METROPOLITAN UNIVERSITY: ALL SAINTS LIBRARY: SPECIAL COLLECTIONS
specialcollections.mmu.ac.uk
PAUL HOGARTH ARCHIVE
Graham Greene Country: HOG/1
HOG1/1 (1969–91): correspondence, mainly between Greene and Hogarth, including twenty-eight by Greene; the great bulk are from 1984–7 and concern work on the book *Graham Greene Country.*
HOG/2: travel sketch books.
HOG/3: locations research (including travel diary).
HOG/4: proof typescripts.
HOG/5: miscellaneous (including photographs).

Oxford, Oxfordshire

OXFORD UNIVERSITY BALLIOL COLLEGE LIBRARY: ARCHIVES AND MANUSCRIPTS
www.balliol.ox.ac/about-balliol/welcome-to-balliol-library

PAPERS OF MARIE BICHE RELATING TO GRAHAM GREENE
GGMB 001-979: 979 letters, postcards and telegrams from Graham Greene to Denyse Clairoiun (GGMB 432-465, 1931–9) and to Marie Schebeko (later Biche) (GGMB 001-431 and 466-979, 1946–91).

THE CHERRY RECORD COLLECTION OF JOSEPHINE REID'S PAPERS AND BOOKS RELATING TO GRAHAM GREENE (from 1959)
GGJR Series 1: Correspondence – 14 letters, cards and so on to Josephine Reid, 1992–2005.
GGJR Series 2: Two administrative notebooks and an address book, 1980s–1990s.
GGJR Series 3: Correspondence–Dictabelt transcripts; 43 A4 pages of transcripts,

GGJR Series 4: Correspondence–Dictabelt transcripts; 43 A4 pages of transcripts, June 1988–September 1990.
GGJR Series 5: Correspondence, assorted press cuttings and articles about Greene, 1980s–2003.
GGJR Series 6: Correspondence and ephemera – regarding the deaths of Graham Greene and Raymond Greene, 1982–2002.
GGJR Series 7: News cuttings – regarding Graham Greene's life and work, 1984–2012.
GGJR Series 8: Assorted material – regarding sale of Graham Greene's archive and library, 1988–97.
GGJR Series 9: Articles etc. – regarding Graham Greene's life and work, 1950s–2006.
GGJR Series 10: Correspondence – 106 letters and cards to Josephine Reid, the majority from Graham Greene, 1946–89.
GGJR Series 11: Photographs – 15 black-and-white and colour photographs of Graham Greene and Josephine Reid, 1940s–1980s.
GGJR Series 12: Cassette tapes – 4 tapes of PEN Writers Day, March 1992, and 1 of Graham Greene's Memorial Service, June 1991, 1991, 1992.
GGJR Series 13: Oil painting – 'Windy Day on Coast', gift from Greene to Reid, 1962.
GGJR Series 14: Insert material removed from Josephine Reid's collection of printed books, letters, newspaper cuttings and so on.
GGJR Series 15: Josephine Reid's personal collection of Greene's works from the 1940s onwards, including approximately 70 presentation copies from Greene; others signed by him and some by other writers.

GRAHAM GREENE PERSONAL DOSSIER

GGBD01-97: Contents of individual Old Member dossier for HG (Graham) Greene, 1904–91, Balliol 1922. Chiefly administrative correspondence to and from the college, including 17 original letters by Graham Greene; 97 items, arranged in chronological order, 1922–2004.

THE BODLEIAN LIBRARY

www.bodleian.ox.ac.uk/bodley
MSS.Berlin 188 and 189: Correspondence with Isaiah Berlin, 1970.
MS.Cary adds. 11, folders 1–5: Five letters to Joyce Cary, 1936–54.
Deps Chandler 57, folders 259 and 75; folder 24; also Dep. Chandler 57, folders 159–60: correspondence with Raymond Chandler, 1958.
Ms.Eng.c.5290, folders 190–1: Two letters to E. J. Thompson, no dates.
Ms.Eng.c.2302, folders 44–6: Correspondence with Ann Thwaite, 1975.
Ms.Eng.c.5290, folders 190–1: Two letters to Walter de la Mare, no dates.

Reading, Berkshire

UNIVERSITY OF READING LIBRARY: SPECIAL COLLECTIONS

www.reading.ac.uk/library/
GB6 RUL MS5118: Three letters to the British Council, 1982–8.
MS1391/8: Letter to Peter Fleming, 1955; viewing by appointment.
MSS2750/610: Letter to Hogarth Press; viewing by appointment.

Swansea

SWANSEA UNIVERSITY: SPECIAL COLLECTIONS
www.swansea.ac.uk/library/archice-and-research-collections
RICHARD BURTON COLLECTION:
GB217 RWB/1/2/2/6/7
Letter to Richard Burton, 20 January 1983, relating to the possibility of Burton acting in a film of *The Quiet American.* Greene writes that he had heard that Peter Petric was trying to persuade Burton to take the part of Fowler in a remake of *The Quiet American.* He had read the script and thought it 'basically good'. He would be delighted if Burton would consider it as the first version was 'a betrayal – both politically and in casting'.

ARCHIVES IN THE UNITED STATES OF AMERICA

Austin, Texas

UNIVERSITY OF TEXAS: HARRY RANSOM CENTER
www.hrc.utexas.edu/

GRAHAM GREENE COLLECTION
Additional material in the collection:
15-07-016-P: Graham Greene's personal annotated copy of *It's a Battlefield* (London: Heinemann, 1934). The author's personal copy with a letter of provenance laid in. Extensively revised throughout for the third edition of 1948.
16-04-011-P: Graham Greene letters to Monica McCall. A small file relating to issues around the 1962 Time-Life republication of Greene's *The Power and the Glory* and the 1966 publication of *The Comedians*, containing five letters from Greene to Monica McCall, his American agent, three typed carbons from McCall to Greene, one signed carbon from Stuart Ostrow to Greene and a signed copy of the 1942 screenwriting contract between Warner Bros Pictures and Greene.
16-06-001-P: Graham Greene typescripts from the office of Monica McCall. Carbon typescripts for 'A Really Impossibly Bad Hotel' (published as 'An Impossibly Bad Hotel'), 'A Birthday in October' and 'An Incident in Sinai', and carbon typescripts of corrections for Greene's introductions to *Our Man in Havana* and *Brighton Rock*.
16-09-027-P: Graham Greene letters. Five letters by Graham Greene to his agent, Mitch Douglas, at ICM.
16-11-003-P: Graham Greene correspondence with his American agent. Eight typed and autographed letters signed from Graham Greene to the office of Monica McCall, Inc, together with McCall outgoing carbons; 1955–65.
17-04-010-P: Graham Greene correspondence from Viking Press editors. Carbons of correspondence from Viking Press editors Marshall A. Best, B. W. Huebsch and Harold K. Guinzburg to Graham Greene, 1938–66. 76 pages.

ERNESTO CARDENAL PAPERS, 1960–2000
Box 1, Folder 34: Correspondence with Ernesto Cardenal.

Baltimore, Maryland

UNIVERSITY OF BALTIMORE: ROBERT L.BOGOMOLNYLIBRARY:SPECIAL COLLECTIONS
library.ubalt.edu/special-collections/
SEYMOUR LAWRENCE PAPERS
Correspondence 1955–80: Letters to Seymour Lawrence.

Bloomington, Indiana

INDIANA UNIVERSITY: LILLY LIBRARY
www.indiana.edu/
Papers of Frank Norman, 1943–70
Correspondence with Frank Norman.

Boston, Massachusetts

BOSTON COLLEGE: JOHN J. BURNS LIBRARY: ARCHIVES AND MANSCRIPTS DEPARTMENT
www.bc.edu/burns
GRAHAM GREENE PAPERS: MS1995.003
The papers were completely recatalogued in February 2016, which consolidated archival holdings and described them together. They now consist of 69.5 linear feet in 104 boxes. As a result of the recataloguing, the following GRAHAM GREENE PAPERS have been included in the main collection and are no longer catalogued separately: MS 04-61, MS 1986-69, MS 1996-05 and MS 1997-06.
The GRAHAM GREENE PAPERS are now arranged in eleven series (with rearranged sub-series) as follows:
I:Art, artifacts and ephemera
II:Auction and manuscript sales
III:Correspondence
IV:Legal records
V:Literary works
VI:Loose materials removed from books
VII:Memberships and honors
VIII:Photographs
IX:Subject files
X:Travel
XI:Writings by others
Full details of each of these series can be found in the College's Finding Aid: https://library.bc.edu/finding-aids/MS1995-003-finding-aid.pdf.
New material included in the recatalogued archive consists of some correspondence from Graham Greene and typescripts of 'The Last Word', 'The Man who Stole the Eiffel Tower' and 'Regina vs Sir James Barrie'.
Boston College continues also to have Graham Greene's Library, the FATHER PHILIP CARAMAN S.J. PAPERS MS 1998-030 and the GERALD C. WALLING – GRAHAM GREENE PAPERS MS 1993-07.

Cambridge, Massachusetts

HARVARD UNIVERSITY: SCHLESINGER LIBRARY, RADCLIFFE INSTITUTE
www.radcliffe.harvard.edu/schlesinger-library
Papers of Mary Bancroft
Letters to Mary Bancroft concerning articles in the *Manhattan East* journal, 1961–75.

Evanston, Illinois

NORTHWESTERN UNIVERSITY: CHARLES DEERING MCCORMICK LIBRARY OF SPECIAL COLLECTIONS
www.librarynorthwestern.edu/libraries-collections/mccormick-library/index.html
HARVEY BREIT CORRESPONDENCE
Box 1, Folder 29: One letter to Harvey Breit, 1952.

Philadelphia, Pennsylvania

UNIVERSITY OF PENNSYLVANIA
franklin.library.upen.edu
ARCHIBALD MACLEISH COLLECTION
Letter 1965 to Lewis Mumford.

Princeton, New Jersey

PRINCETON UNIVERSITY LIBRARY
library.princeton.edu/
JUAN GELMAN PAPERS
Box B-000726, Folder 34: Correspondence with Juan Gelman, 1987.

San Francisco, California

UNIVERSITY OF SAN FRANCISCO: GLEESON LIBRARY
www.usfca.edu.library
MARY PRITCHETT COLLECTION,
1932–75
Correspondence with Mary Pritchett.

Stanford, California

STANFORD UNIVERSITY: HOOVER INSTITUTION LIBRARY & ARCHIVES
www.hoover.org/library-archives/collections

JOSEF ŠKVORECKÝ PAPERS
Box 30, Folder 18: Correspondence with Josef Škvorecký.

YVGENY YEVTUSHENKO PAPERS
Box 2, Folder 10: Correspondence, two typed, signed letters to Yvgeny Yevtushenko.

Washington, DC

LIBRARY OF CONGRESS RARE BOOK AND SPECIAL COLLECTIONS DIVISION
www.loc.gov/rr/rarebook/
THE SYLVESTER AND ORPHANOS ARCHIVE COLLECTION
Publications 1976–2008.
Box 5 *How Father Quixote Became a Monsignor* (1980)
Correspondence 1979–80, 18 items; page proofs, 10 items.
Box 20 *A Quick Look Behind: Footnotes to an Autobiography* (1983)
Correspondence, 1981–3, 40 items; agreement between Sylvester and Orphanos and Greene, April 1981, 2 items; copy of poem 'Cowardice'; holograph manuscript of book; transcribed copy of book by Ralph Sylvester, January 1982, typescripts, galley; page proofs, set up, notes and designs, 11 items.

Box 24 *A Weed Among the Flowers* (1990) Correspondence, 1984–90, 18 items; 2 manuscript copies; 3 page proof; manuscript introduction by Stephen Spender, 2 items; artwork and designs and notes, 11 items; unbound gatherings, 6 items.

UNIVERSITY OF GEORGETOWN: SUZANNE DEAL BOOTH AND DAVID G. BOOTH CENTER FOR SPECIAL COLLECTIONS, JOSEPH MARK LAUINGER MEMORIAL LIBRARY: SPECIAL COLLECTIONS

www.library.georgetown.edu/

YVONNE CLOETTA PAPERS

In addition to the Graham Greene-Yvonne Cloetta Collection is this single box of inserted material transferred from purchased books. It includes letters from editors to Greene, letters to Cloetta, news clippings on Greene and a watercolour by Jacqueline Duheme, inscribed to Greene.

BONTE AND GUSTAVO DURAN PAPERS

One box of material consists of 28 letters, mostly sent from Bonte Duran, sister of Catherine Walston, to her husband Gustavo, with frequent mentions of Graham Greene. Several letters were written by Greene, a few by Catherine Walston. The letters include discussion of the affair between Greene and Walston.

LEOPOLDO DURÁN PAPERS

An additional box has been added to these papers:

5. Other Greene-related material

Box 49: Miscellany – loose items found inserted into books from Durán's library.

SHIRLEY HAZZARD PAPERS

These papers are now organized as follows: 21 boxes of material, in 8 series:

Series 1: Assorted individual correspondents

Series 2: Correspondence with Graham Greene

Series 3: Correspondence with Michael Richey

Series 4: Correspondence with Norman Sherry

Series 5: Correspondence with organizations and publishers

Series 6: Manuscripts, proof copies and publication material relating to Hazzard's book *Greene on Capri*

Series 7: Printed items – books and clippings of news items

Series 8: Photographs and mixed media

ANN G. MCDONALD COLLECTION OF GRAHAM GREENE

McDonald wrote the PhD dissertation 'A Bibliography of the Periodical Contributions of Graham Greene' at George Washington University in 1969. The single box of material includes a typed letter from Greene from March 1967 and a handwritten note by him from May 1969 congratulating her on completing her dissertation. The box also includes printed articles and reviews by Greene and a copy of the dissertation.

B.W. HUEBSCH PAPERS, 1893–1964

Box 11: Correspondence with B.W. Huebsch.

ARCHIVES IN CANADA

Calgary, Alberta

UNIVERSITY OF CALGARY
library.ucalgary-ca/
BRIAN MOORE COLLECTION
Seven letters from Greene to Brian Moore, April 1957–September 1968, on subjects ranging from praise for his latest novel to the award of a Guggenheim Fellowship.

OTHER ARCHIVES

Republic of Singapore

NATIONAL LIBRARY BOARD, SINGAPORE
www.nlb.gov.sg/
Autograph letter to Fr C. C. Martindale, 1951. Letter includes graphic descriptions of scenes Greene had witnessed during the Malayan Emergency.

Stockholm, Sweden

NATIONAL LIBRARY OF SWEDEN
https://archiverdict.fandom.com/wiki/National_Library_of_Sweden
ERNST RAGNAR SVANSTRÖM ARCHIVE
KB1/L205 26.2.52–6.5.77
Thirty-eight typed copies of extracts from letters from Greene to Svanström. Six copies of extracts of letters from Svanström to Greene. A copy of extract from a letter from Svanström to Josephine Reid and two letters by Reid to Svanström. Three relevant notes by Svanström pertaining to communications with Greene. Two letters by Greene to Lasse Bergström.

Bern, Switzerland

SWISS LITERARY ARCHIVES
ead.nb.admin.ch/highsmith.html
PATRICIA HIGHSMITH (NACHLASS) PAPERS
B-02-GREGR: 22 letters to Patricia Highsmith, 1966–90, sent from Paris and Antibes.

Section 3

Essays

Vivat Bristowa: Graham Greene, Berkhamsted and the unfinished novel *Lucius*

Mike Hill

In the 1950s, as a therapy suggested by the psychiatrist Eric Strauss, Graham Greene began writing about what he remembered of his childhood.[1] In the late 1960s, in what he took to be his 'last decade',[2] Greene built on this writing and settled to write about his early life. The resultant 'fragment of autobiography' was published as *A Sort of Life* in 1971. It is a fascinating book, combining honest disclosure with discreet omission. It only goes up to 1932, and more than half the book concerns his life growing up in Berkhamsted, opening with the famous sentence 'If I had known it, the whole future must have lain all the time along those Berkhamsted streets.'[3]

It is striking just how often Greene included Berkhamsted in his fictional writings. It runs like a vein through the decades. While at Oxford he wrote a novel called *Anthony Sant*, never published, which is set in a school, recognizably Berkhamsted, though never named as such.[4] In 1927 he began an unfinished novel *Fanatic Arabia*, where Berkhamsted is 'Boxstead'.[5] The 1934 novel *It's a Battlefield* has a scene set in Berkhamsted. Greene started another novel around 1936–7 which he never completed, but which was later published as the short story 'The Other Side of the Border'; there Berkhamsted is 'Denton'. Around the same time Greene wrote the short story 'The Innocent', with Berkhamsted now called 'Bishop's Hendron'. Then, towards the end of his life, Greene published two novels featuring Berkhamsted: *The Human Factor* (1978), with Berkhamsted at last given its own name; and *The Captain and the Enemy* (1988), where Berkhamsted is unnamed but unmistakable to anyone who knows the town.

I think I first came across Berkhamsted as a place when I read *The Human Factor* in the late 1970s. A few years later I read *A Sort of Life*, and for the first time I started to know a little of Graham Greene the man, in his own words. I learnt of his childhood,

This essay is an amended version of a talk given at the Graham Greene International Festival in Berkhamsted on 24 September 2017.

1 Richard Greene, *Russian Roulette: The Life and Times of Graham Greene* (London: Little, Brown, 2020), pp. 195–6.

2 See Jon Wise and Mike Hill, *The Works of Graham Greene Volume 2: A Guide to the Graham Greene Archives* (London: Bloomsbury, 2015), pp. 215–17.

3 Graham Greene, *A Sort of Life* (London: Penguin, 1988), p. 9.

4 The typescript of the novel is at the Harry Ransom Center, University of Texas at Austin, Graham Greene Collection (HRC), Box 27, Folder 7.

his memories of his family, the town and Berkhamsted School and his unhappiness in adolescence, particularly the eight terms he spent as a boarder in St John's House in the school. I also remember being struck by a short passage about novels Greene had started and then abandoned. Here I was reading his works for the first time, and I became aware, and interested in the fact, that there were other unfinished and unpublished works – it might have been the first stirrings of the bibliographer in me. Among these unfinished stories Greene referred to 'a school novel of a timid boy's blackmail of the housemaster who had protected him'.[6] The reference meant nothing to me at the time, and as I read further books by and about Greene, I never came across anything to explain the enigmatic reference.

Cut now to 2014. Jon Wise and I had by then produced a guide to Greene's published writings and had embarked on a second volume to cover the riches of material in Greene archives, much of it never published. As part of our research, we travelled to Austin, Texas, to examine the Greene archive there – all ninety-six boxes and forty linear feet of it. In advance, we used the archive catalogue to divide up the material between us, and once there, we set to work. By chance, I was allocated a mixed bunch of material beginning with the letter 'L', in Box 21, Folder 1. And so it fell to me to examine *Lucius*, an unfinished piece of fiction never mentioned in anything I had read about Greene.[7] It consisted of around fifty foolscap sheets in Greene's mature handwriting, very difficult to read – clearly an unfinished novel of, I estimated, about twenty-three thousand words.[8] The manuscript is not dated, but evidence allowed us eventually to date it reasonably firmly – Greene seems to have written it in the interval between finishing *Our Man in Havana* in June 1958 and setting off for the Belgian Congo in January 1959.[9] So this was *Lucius*, a substantial but unfinished story written in the late 1950s. As I read it, I realized that here was the 'school novel of a timid boy's blackmail of the housemaster who had protected him'.

It soon became clear that the novel was set in Berkhamsted, that the school in question was Berkhamsted School and that, in essence, the story is based heavily on Graham Greene's own time at the school. To give some context to that, a brief outline of the unfinished story will help. It begins with a prologue, with the British foreign secretary, Sir Luke Winter, returning to his old school for the first time since he had left there, to give a speech at a prize-giving. The question arises as to what happened to one of Winter's old teachers, a man called Stonier, and it transpires that he left the school and later killed himself. Winter meets his old school matron, who was involved in the whole business, and she bitterly asks him, 'Do you still betray your friends?'

6 Greene, *A Sort of Life*, p. 132.

7 More recently, *Lucius* has been mentioned in Greene, *Russian Roulette*, p. 301.

8 HRC, Box 21, Folder 1. All subsequent quotations from *Lucius* come from this holograph, transcribed by Mike Hill.

9 See Wise and Hill, *The Works of Graham Greene Volume 2: A Guide to the Graham Greene Archives*, pp. 86–7. Additionally, in a footnote to *A Sort of Life* referred to at the end of this essay Greene writes of having started his school novel around 1958, before going to the Congo in January 1959.

The story then switches back perhaps forty years to the first term at the school as a boarder in Collier's House for Winter, whose real name, we learn, is Lucius Darling, and proceeds to unravel the backstory. We see Lucius's overbearing mother, an actress who wears a silly hat, dropping him off as a new boy at the school. We read of a shy boy being unhappy at the school – at the lack of privacy, at the physical conditions in the dormitories, at being bullied by two other boys, despite attempts by the sympathetic assistant housemaster Stonier to protect him. We also become aware of a developing secret relationship between Stonier – a married man, we learn – and Miss Wilson, the house matron. And crucially Lucius himself also sees evidence of this relationship, dimly aware that something furtive is afoot. The story finishes, incomplete, at the end of Lucius's first, unhappy term at school, with Christmas approaching.

That this story is set in Berkhamsted is evident from the very beginning – here is the opening paragraph:

> The little town had grown since Winter's day, but the smell of coal dust and canal and tired brick were about the same. The memory came in through his nose of something deeply forgotten: he couldn't have told whether the memory was of happiness or unhappiness, he only knew that here had been his beginning. He put the documents back into the red despatch box and handed the box into the hands of his private secretary; the King's Arms, the Town Hall, the road that led uphill between the brick villas to …

All of these references are familiar to anyone who knows Berkhamsted. Later on the secretary gives Winter some notes on the place, to work into his speech at prize-giving, and again Berkhamsted is evoked, this time in its history – '"Crusader's helmet in parish church." "… Castle besieged by foreign enemy – French in time of King John." "Simon de Montfort, founder of Parliament, passed through on way to London."' Later still we read of the railway station near the canal, and Greene remembers the Castle Street of his childhood:

> Stonier turned and went back towards the school: up from the canal bank by the little humpbacked bridge and the public house that called itself a hotel as though some meaning lay in the water under the windows, where a card advertised accommodation for cyclists: past the fish and chip shop on his left and the junk shop on the right with two china dogs inside, a soup tureen, some steel rimmed spectacles, two sets of false teeth and a Colonial Library edition of Bulwer Lytton's *Rising*: the almshouses that had been built by a philanthropist called Salmon in 1849: then round a corner the gable and brickwork, the gravel and stained glass.

This is Berkhamsted, here given the name 'Bristow' by Greene – and even here there may be a veiled reference to Berkhamsted and its school. The late David Pearce, a there was an Elizabethan usher (schoolmaster) at the school, John Bristowe – a man who was murdered in 1597. David Pearce reckoned that Graham Greene would have known the story and the name.[10] So calling Berkhamsted Bristow becomes a sort of in-joke for Old Berkhamstedians, perhaps, in a story where names are significant.

It is clear that Greene is writing about his alma mater when he describes Bristow School. Here Winter arrives at the school through its lychgate:

> The car swung down the hill and the red brick buildings stood like beefeaters on either side of the road. Boys clustered under the arch and walked through the quad.

And here, Winter looks at the walls around him, clearly in the school's Old Hall:

> Winter looked at one headmaster's portrait after another: beards gave place to side whiskers, side whiskers to moustaches, the clean shaven came last, but no growth of hair destroyed the common likeness: an air of conscious probity, of stern kindliness: if you sought eccentricity it could be found only in such details as the artist's treatment of the M.A. gown.

There is even a sly bit of autobiography in Greene's description of the prize-giving ceremony, as the headmaster announces the award of a Domus Exhibition in Modern History at Balliol – rather of the kind awarded to Greene himself.

Greene's most vivid descriptions of the school in the story *Lucius* are those parts he remembered from when he was a pupil at Berkhamsted. A bit of biography will help here: Greene entered St John's House as a boarder in September 1918, when he was just short of his fourteenth birthday, and was there for eight terms, until April 1921, when he was sixteen. Then, because he was so unhappy at St John's, he was allowed to move back to School House, where his family lived. In *A Sort of Life*, Greene refers to 'that hated brick barracks called St John's'[11] and remembers the physical details of life as an adolescent boarder there:

> There was a schoolroom with ink-stained nibbled desks insufficiently warmed by one cast-iron stove, a changing-room smelling of sweat and stale clothes, stone stairs, worn by generations of feet, leading to a dormitory divided by pitch-pine partitions that gave inadequate privacy – no moment of the night was free from noise, a cough, a snore, a fart.[12]

And here, for comparison, is Greene's description of the physical realities of Collier's House at Bristow School:

> Outside the open door the stone stairs, painted checked like children's bricks, led up to the lower dormitory …

10 Information from David Pearce in emails on 14 March 2016.

11 Greene, *A Sort of Life*, p. 77.

12 Ibid., p. 54.

> Afterwards [Stonier] went down the long narrow passage to the schoolroom. The hacked and inky desks stood in rows on iron legs facing the black stove with its cast-iron lilies surrounding the maker's name, Pannier's of Coventry: beside it the master's desk that contained the only drawers with a lock. One door opened on the dining room: the tables already laid for breakfast: a second on the gymnasium now unnaturally tidy; a third on the changing room which would soon smell of steam and stale clothes and soap.
>
> Stonier went up the back way to the dormitories. Nothing was ever quiet on these floors: the communal breathing sounded like a deep whisper and always there was someone who turned or spoke in a dream or coughed. With his door open it was like trying to sleep with a large dog in the room.

Graham Greene clearly had vivid memories of St John's House at his old school, and they find expression in his depiction of Collier's House in the story *Lucius*.

Greene's descriptions of life at Bristow School are interesting. There is humour in his depiction of prize-giving day, particularly in the Bishop of Crewe, who preaches the sermon – a malicious and gossipy cleric described as having a face 'like an early map of an ill-explored continent: large and white and indeterminate along the coastline, only the two brown eyes were definitely placed like the sites of known cities'. And as the masters in black gowns and white ermine hoods process across the quad, the school song is sung, a sporty refrain betokening perhaps a place of stiff upper lipism, a song written, of course, by Greene:

> When your hat trick is over and the over's over,
> You mustn't show your success:
> When you have to convert and the ball goes under
> You mustn't show your distress.
> The game's a game but the school stands there:
> The players pass, but their sons declare,
> *Vivat Bristowa*

When the story switches back to Lucius's time at Bristow as a boy, there is a lot of acute observation of school life. He describes a lesson in which the hapless master is side-tracked from his intended plan by diversionary talk from smart-aleck pupils, with a subtle recognition that the bored teacher welcomes the diversion. There is also a wonderful passage set in the master's common room during a break. Here is how it begins:

> The master's common room too had a cast-iron stove made by Pannier's of Coventry. There were lockers and hooks for gowns. Only the absence of desks seemed to distinguish it from the schoolroom … Notices hung on a green baize board like the notices on the gym door

> distinguished by the absence of boys, for the boys were there: they had suffered a sea-change, that was all, the flesh had bloated or fallen from the bones, the hair turned another colour, lines like the erosion of water had been worn in their cheeks.

So the masters are really just grown-up boys, and the scene that follows portrays a range of teaching types, including the old-timer who complains that someone has pinched the condensed milk, the young and enthusiastic teacher still with a sense of vocation, the science master who as a young man 'had decided to take up "Stinks" and had wasted many a class manufacturing pear drops'. Graham Greene, not just a former pupil at an independent boys' school but the son of the headmaster there, shows an acute awareness of the lives of pupils and masters alike.

It is worth emphasizing that Greene's depiction of school life at Bristow is not remorselessly unsympathetic. In *Lucius* he pokes gentle fun at some of its characters and practices: he describes with an unblinking eye the unattractive physical conditions of the life of a boarder, and of course, the core of his story is about the terrible bullying of a timid boy. But there is no sense of Greene condemning the school as a whole or the system it is part of. In this sense, we do through *Lucius* get a feel for Greene's attitude towards not just Bristow but also Berkhamsted School – a willingness to describe it, warts and all, but not in a savage or unsympathetic way. I remember in this respect a letter Graham Greene wrote in January 1986 to his nephew James, the son of Graham's younger brother Hugh: 'Whatever induced Hugh to send you to Eton? I realise what a civilised school Berkhamsted was by contrast and Hugh was happy at Berkhamsted.'[13] Greene was bullied at Berkhamsted and was very unhappy for part of his time there, but still he regarded it as a civilized place; and that is how he depicts Bristow School.

However, there is one particular aspect of the regime at Bristow School that produces unhappiness for Lucius – the requirement for boys to sign up for walks on Sundays in groups of three. A new boy at school and with no real friends, Lucius is always the one not chosen by the others – as Greene comments, 'it would have been absurd to expect anyone to consort publicly with the known victim'. So Lucius is humiliated in not being wanted, and even when he sets out on walks with others, they soon deliberately lose him. This was clearly an important part of Graham Greene's own unhappiness in St John's House at Berkhamsted School: in the 1934 book *The Old School* which he edited, Greene's most sustained criticism of his old school was this:

> Solitary walks … were forbidden. Each Sunday a notice was pinned on the gymnasium door giving the names of the boys walking together. On the first evening of term one went round filling up a kind of dance programme of walks for the term. The mental agony of a boy with a limited number of friends who failed to book all his walks was, of course, extreme. He would not be allowed to walk by himself and would have to

13 Lauinger Library, University of Georgetown, Washington, DC: James Greene Papers, Correspondence.

> impose himself or be imposed on others. What the house-master gained by this is difficult to understand, except a comforting illusion that he knew who everyone was with. In practice it was perfectly easy to arrange with another boy to start out together and then separate. A foolish rule.[14]

Greene repeats this criticism in *A Sort of Life*, and it was an issue that clearly caused him much anguish. He tells us there that 'after a term or two of purgatory, I received permission from my parents to spend Sunday afternoons at home'.[15] No doubt before then he had also used the escape route used by the boy Lucius in Greene's story – he absconds from the system by pretending to have letters to post, then finds his way to a ditch by a hedge where no one can find him. (Greene in *A Sort of Life* refers to 'my truancies, those peaceful hours hidden in the hedge'.[16]) Lucius imagines the search parties looking for him on Cold Harbour Common and in the Boxhill Woods in a passage so extended and detailed that it is clear that Greene is reliving his own experience of Sunday at school. And in his hiding place the bullied young boy daydreams of revenge on his torturers.

Much of the sympathetic depiction of Bristow School comes through the central adult character Stonier, the master who tries to help the unhappy Lucius. Stonier tells Lucius at one point that 'I hated school myself … I suppose I still hate it' and admits that at school 'I didn't have many friends'. As Lucius's assistant housemaster in Collier's House he recognizes the boy's vulnerability immediately. He sees the overbearing nature of Lucius's mother and the effect that has had on him. He is aware that the boy's name will be a red rag to a bully and advises him to adopt a different one at school – Luke rather than Lucius. Stonier sees the boy's tears on his first night in the dormitory and thinks, 'Poor little bastard.' He spots the first sign of Lucius as victim when the boy is sent the wrong way to his next lesson by other pupils. So Stonier does what he can to befriend and protect Lucius, trying to encourage him to develop some interests, enquiring about his preferred reading, inviting him to tea on Sunday as an alternative to a walk with other boys and sacking the house prefect who fails to intervene when Lucius is being bullied (and replaces him by another boy, called Carter, the name of one of Greene's tormentors at Berkhamsted – a macabre in-joke by Greene). It is Stonier more than anyone else who tries to humanize the school for Lucius.

Did Stonier have a real-life equivalent when Graham Greene was at Berkhamsted? When the late David Pearce read the story, his suggestion was a teacher called Dale, nicknamed Dicker Dale by the boys – David's email refers to 'the unfulfilled and directionless housemaster' of the story and adds, 'It suggests the sort of relationship that Greene had with Dicker Dale to whom he gave copies of early novels.'[17] A reading

14 Graham Greene (ed.), *The Old School* (Oxford: Oxford University Press, 1985), p. 232.

15 Greene, *A Sort of Life*, p. 59.

16 Ibid., p. 64.

17 [illegible]

of Greene's sympathetic portrayal of Dale in *A Sort of Life* confirms David's guess. 'Dicker', Greene writes there, 'was a youngish man in those days (though, of course, to me middle-aged) with a bald head and gold-rimmed glasses and a drawl which sometimes became a slight stutter; a difficulty of communication, one would have said, and yet to those willing to listen he communicated more than any other master, except perhaps my father.'[18] Dicker Dale had a best friend on the staff, comically enough called Hill, and the two compiled crosswords together, just as Stonier helps his housemaster Dolland to do at Bristow School. Moreover, Greene adds, 'some of Dale's kindness must have rubbed off on Hill, for I remember how I was once invited to tea by him and how two hours of anchovy-toast and tea-cakes and adult conversation atoned for a week of misery and postponed again the final breakdown'.[19] Here, of course, is the origin of Stonier's invitation to tea to Lucius. That word 'kindness' as applied to Dicker Dale is echoed elsewhere, for in talking about his school matron in *A Sort of Life*, Greene writes, '[Her] kindness stood out by its rarity in that world, and perhaps because of its rarity two gentle people were drawn together and the assistant housemaster, Mr Dale … married the matron.'[20] And so in the compost of his imagination, Dicker Dale marrying the matron at Berkhamsted became Stonier having an illicit affair with the matron at Bristow, a liaison Lucius will in due course betray.

The character at the centre of the story is Lucius. The name is important, since names have significance in the story. We do not know what title Graham Greene would eventually have adopted for the novel had he finished it, but in its unfinished state there the title is 'LUCIUS', in capital letters on the first page of the manuscript. What a very un-Greene-like title it is. We are used to the resonant titles that have come to have a life of their own beyond the books – *The End of the Affair* and *Brighton Rock* and *Travels with My Aunt* and *The Heart of the Matter*. There is not a one-word title anywhere among Greene's novels and only *Doctor Fischer* and *Monsignor Quixote* containing a character's name. *Lucius* as a title gives central prominence to one person and to the name itself. The story gives a particular emphasis to the name. The boy's real name, we learn, is actually Lucius Darling, a silly name in both parts. 'Darling' is a name which might invite laughter, indeed ridicule, while the Latinate sound of 'Lucius' is also comical. Actually, the silliness goes further, for we hear the explanation for the name given by Lucius's mother, an actress, in the story: 'He was born, you know,' she says, 'just after I had finished Portia. Julius Caesar not the Merchant. I wanted to call him Brutus, but my husband objected, so we compromised.' So poor Lucius has been given a silly second-best name after a marital tiff, named after a character in Shakespeare; perhaps Greene even intended a further in-joke based on the nature of that character in *Julius Caesar*. The ultimate irony is that poor Lucius Darling becomes Sir Luke Winter – Luke to avoid being bullied at school, Winter because in later life he adopts

[18] Greene, *A Sort of Life*, p. 63.
[19] Ibid., pp. 63–4.
[20] Ibid., p. 63.

his mother's maiden name. At the beginning of Greene's tale we are presented with the knight of the realm, foreign secretary and possible future prime minister, only to learn later that his names are not the real ones. He has hidden his former self, the timid schoolboy hiding behind the assertive politician. What's in a name?

Graham Greene knew that a name is a weapon for a bully – as he says of his fellow pupil and tormentor Carter in *A Sort of Life*: 'The sneering nicknames were inserted like splinters under the nails.'[21] The boys who bully Lucius, who are called Morley and Roberts, know how to use a name. They first identify Lucius as a victim when they happen to overhear his mother's words of parting on the first day of term, at the railway station: 'Dearest, goodbye,' she says. 'Write to me *every* [original emphasis] week. You know your father isn't really interested in all your doings, but I am.' Later Greene writes, '[Stonier] heard Roberts's voice repeating, "Dearest." Morley said, "Did you see the dove [in her hat]?" "I saw everything," Roberts said. "Everything."' They have their victim, and the combination of 'Dearest' and 'Darling' is irresistible to them in their bullying.

From his experiences at Berkhamsted, Greene knew all about the psychology of bullying and anatomizes it in a later incident in the story. It is Sunday in Collier's House at Bristow, and Lucius is trying to write a letter home when he hears Roberts's voice:

> 'Who are you writing to, Darling?' When they called him by his own name it was like the offer of a truce, and at first he had been quick to respond until he discovered that always behind the white flag the ambush was laid. So now he was careful not to answer: he wouldn't give them the satisfaction of deceiving him.
>
> 'What's the matter, Darling? Why don't you want us to know?' Morley joined the game.
>
> 'Dearest's writing to his tart.'
>
> 'His mother's a tart.'
>
> 'Dearest is your mother a tart?'
>
> 'She's only an actress,' Morley said, taking up his spurious role of prisoner's friend (the first time that one too had deceived Lucius).
>
> 'My dear Morley all actresses are tarts. That's how they get work. You don't pay them you give them a job.'
>
> 'Is she a good actress, Darling?'
>
> 'Haven't you seen her, Morley? At the Windmill without any clothes on. She doesn't act. She has to stand still by the Lord Chamberlain's orders.'

Here are all the ingredients of the kind of bullying Lucius endured: two against one, with the rest looking on; an apparent offer of truce, designed to ambush; conversations between the bullies, their cruel words intended to be heard by the victim and to wound;

21 Ibid., p. [illegible]

and the use of names. The torments meted out to Lucius are psychological rather than physical, as they had been for Graham Greene – he says in *A Sort of Life*, 'Though children can be abominably cruel, no physical torments were inflicted on me.'[22] Greene emphasizes the randomness of the choice of victim, as Roberts and Morley chance to overhear Lucius's mother's words on parting from him. But Roberts and Morley can spot a potential victim a mile off – a new boy at the school, a timid boy, a boy with a silly name and a rude and overbearing mother.

Lucius suffers much of the cruelty suffered by Greene before him and shares some of Greene's own characteristics – including an admiration for the adventures of Rider Haggard's Quatermain, and, more significantly, a sharp eye for things – Lucius is a quiet but acute observer, which allows him to pick up on the relationship between Stonier and the matron, just as Greene had the novelist's eye for detail and 'the splinter of ice'[23] in his writer's heart. But Lucius is not of course an exact representation of Greene. One of the elements of the bullying he suffered at Berkhamsted, as he makes clear in *A Sort of Life*, was the fact that he was the headmaster's son, an authority figure at one remove, a boy whose loyalties could be seen as divided. Lucius has none of this background, merely a loud and exotic mother and an absent father. But like the schoolboy Greene he is shy and timid and lonely and finds the lack of privacy and the physical conditions of life as a boarder intolerable. And so, like Greene, he is bullied.

What of Lucius's tormentors? The boys who made Greene's life a misery were called Carter and Wheeler, and Greene says a little about them in *A Sort of Life* (where Wheeler is given the name Watson). Lucius's equivalents are Morley and Roberts, and here is Greene's description of these two:

> Morley was an undersized boy of fifteen, meagre, insignificant, with wrists of extraordinary strength. Where others fought with fists or feet he had perfected a technique of fighting with wrists. You were deceived and trapped by his weak and flapping hands, boneless like gloves, but suddenly the wrist would turn and lock like a handcuff. Roberts for his part never fought except with his tongue. He was tall and gangling and a little knock-kneed, and his face was spotted with the eruptions of a premature adolescence. He had a way of sucking his lips as though they enclosed a lollipop, but what they actually enclosed was some choice and wounding word. Morley and Roberts were not popular, but they had won a kind of respect by their singleness of aim. They were not feared except by their victim, for they were careful to concentrate on one victim at a time (two might have resisted and three might have defeated them).

22 Ibid., p. 55.
23 Ibid., p. 134.

We must allow something for Greene's creative imagination and not assume that pen portraits are drawn from life, but some of these details are so specific one cannot help but wonder whether we have here descriptions of Carter and Wheeler.

In his battle against his tormentors, Lucius begins to develop some strategies, which have some effect. He starts to ignore them when he can; on one occasion he gets one up on them in a conversation; and once he even brandishes a penknife and lets out a scream, which alerts Stonier to the extent of his misery. There is also the clear suggestion that Lucius's experiences are forming the future man – at one point Greene writes this:

> Despair produces pride, a pearl that forms itself from pain. When Lucius was alone he discovered a capacity to dream. In his dreams he had power, he tortured his torturers. The slow movements, the pasty face, the expressionless brown eyes held a tyrant. Ambition was born: one day he would show the world …

Of course, as we know from the prologue, Lucius will grow up to be a successful politician – foreign secretary, no less. In parallel, in *A Sort of Life*, Greene wrote of his own career: 'I wondered … if I would ever have written a book had it not been for Watson and the dead Carter, if those years of humiliation had not given me an excessive desire to prove that I was good at something, however long the effort might prove.'[24]

At the end of term, during pre-Christmas charades in the schoolhouse, Lucius proves himself very adept at mime and acting – a shy boy adopting a confident persona, as he will later do as a politician. But all these developments come from within the thoughtful boy. Crucially and tragically for the story to come, Lucius does not respond to Stonier's attempts to befriend and help him. Stonier's afternoon tea on Sunday is regarded by Lucius as merely a teacher doing his professional job, not an indication of genuine concern. So when Lucius witnesses growing evidence of a relationship between Stonier and Stella Wilson, the house matron, he does so with a hardened heart. He overhears one of their furtive conversations; he arrives at the school sports pavilion just after the two have had sex over a table; and later, snooping in Stonier's room, he finds a photograph of a semi-naked Stella Wilson being used as a bookmark in Stonier's book and steals it. The ground is laid for what Greene in *A Sort of Life* refers to as Lucius's 'blackmail' of the schoolmaster, and then for Stonier's leaving the school under a cloud and subsequent suicide.

We never get to the denouement of the story, so we will never know just how Greene would have completed this tale of betrayal and blackmail. So let me speculate for a moment. I hope that Greene would at some stage have reintroduced the imperious mother, perhaps returning to the school in response to Lucius's distress – she is much too good a character to be given merely a cameo role. We might have heard more of Lucius's absentee father and of Stonier's absent wife. Perhaps Lucius might be seen developing further his coping strategies in dealing with the bullies, or perhaps he might sink further into the abyss.

[24] Ibid., p. 61.

Reading *Lucius* I also got the impression that the whole plot might well unravel during the course of a single school year; after the prologue, what we have of the story occupies a single term, and a three-act drama might fit very well. I originally had some inkling that the pavilion sex around November might have resulted in any increasingly obvious pregnancy in the house matron Miss Wilson, but if so Stonier might have been exposed by other means than blackmail by Lucius. Since we are told in the prologue that Sir Luke had never heard of Stonier leaving the school, let alone his subsequent suicide, perhaps what happens in the remainder of the school year climaxes with Lucius himself leaving the school for another before its end, followed by Stonier's resignation or dismissal in the wake of the revelation of his affair with the matron by Lucius himself. But of course Lucius not only betrays Stonier – this is the matron's word in the prologue – but also blackmails him – Greene's word in *A Sort of Life*; so perhaps Lucius is so desperate to get out of Collier's House that he tells Stonier he will reveal all about his relationship unless he arranges a switch to another school house for Lucius, away from Morley and Roberts. Greene, of course, finally persuaded his own parents at Berkhamsted to move him out of St John's House to end his misery there. If that is Lucius's attempt at blackmail, then perhaps Stonier does not or cannot give way to it, and Lucius is removed from the school but before Stonier's relationship becomes public knowledge. But who knows if this was the future arc of the story? Greene abandoned it early in 1959, and all else is now guesswork.

So, in the end, what should we make of *Lucius*? Is it just another of Greene's unfinished novels, a mere curiosity for bibliographers? I think not. For one thing, it is a very substantial piece of work – at twenty-three thousand words it is not a great deal shorter than, say, *Doctor Fischer of Geneva*. Moreover, it is not a juvenile work, not an early attempt to ape someone else's style – as Greene's 1920s detective story *The Empty Chair* is, for instance.[25] This is the mature Greene, who has found his own voice and style, writing in the same decade in which he also produced *The End of the Affair*, *The Quiet American* and *Our Man in Havana* and was being spoken about as a possible winner of the Nobel Prize. Because the book was never finished, it was not fully polished and revised to Greene's usual standard, and there are less accomplished passages in some parts of the writing. But there are some very fine ones too, including the prologue and the scene in the masters' common room. The story does grip. And of course, the work has special significance in telling us so much more, in fictional form, about Greene's school experiences. In that respect, I have found it an imaginative expansion of what Greene tells us in *A Sort of Life*. *Lucius*, it seems to me, should see the light of day as a published work, unfinished as it is.[26]

In *A Sort of Life* Greene tells us of his chance meeting in 1951 in Kuala Lumpur with one of his old tormentors, Wheeler. He remembers what an anticlimax the meeting was, and how quickly he forgot him afterwards. 'Perhaps, unconsciously,' Greene wrote,

[25] Greene's attempt at a 'whodunnit', *The Empty Chair* is an unfinished novel written in the mid-1920s. Its five chapters were eventually published in *Strand Magazine* in 2009–11.

[26] The Prologue of *Lucius* has recently been published in Donna A. Gessell and Jon Wise (eds), *Graham Greene Studies* 2 (Dahlonga: University of North Georgia Press, 2021), pp. 295–303.

'that was my revenge – to have forgotten him so easily. Now that I had raised the stone again, I knew that nothing lived beneath it.'[27] Well, perhaps. But that passage from *A Sort of Life* has a sort of relevance to my final question about *Lucius* – why did he never finish it? Elsewhere in *A Sort of Life* Greene wrote this about unfinished stories: 'Even today, until I have passed a quarter of the course, I am uncertain whether I will be able to reach the end.'[28] With *Lucius* he got as far as twenty-three thousand words, and given that he never wrote very long novels, it is hard to believe that he had not already passed his 'quarter of the course' with it. So why did he give up? Was it simply, I wondered, that he could not work out where the story should go next? Did he feel that characters like Stonier and Lucius had failed to come alive? Did he just lose interest in his own story? As I pondered these possibilities, I came across a footnote in *A Sort of Life* which reveals all. There, writing in 1970 or 1971, Greene remembers going back to St John's House at Berkhamsted School around 1958:

> Memory often exaggerates, but some twelve years ago, because I had started a novel about a school, I revisited the scene and found no change. I abandoned the novel – I couldn't bear mentally living again for several years in these surroundings. A leper colony in the Congo was preferable so I went to Yonda in search of a burnt-out case.[29]

So *Lucius* was never finished because Greene simply could not cope with the unhappy memories. Writing the story proved to be not therapy but renewed torture. Graham Greene may have believed that he had got over Carter and Wheeler, but he never got over his eight terms at St John's House in Berkhamsted.

27 Greene, *A Sort of Life*, p. 62.
28 Ibid., p. 132.
29 Ibid., p. 54.

Graham Greene's *The Virtue of Disloyalty*: Origins, context and significance

Jon Wise

When Graham Greene accepted the 'Shakespeare-Preise' for 1968 from the University of Hamburg on 6 June 1969, he became just the second British post-war recipient following the director Peter Hall in 1967. The prize recognized outstanding achievement in writing or performance by a British citizen. He received DM 25,000, a 90-gramme gold medal and a year-long scholarship at the university, which he subsequently donated to a student.[1]

The writer did not enjoy the occasion. He told Catherine Walston later that he found the Germans pompous, the sherry bad, the lunch interminable – although he conceded that the Moselle wine was very good. To make matters worse, he was suffering from a debilitating attack of piles. When it came to his acceptance speech, following a fulsome 'laudatio' by a German professor, Greene delivered a provocative speech criticizing his country's most celebrated playwright in whose name the prize had been created.

Greene made comparatively few public speeches, famously avoided television appearances and reputedly even disliked the sound of his own voice in radio broadcasts.[2] The texts of his speeches are therefore quite elusive for the researcher. *The Virtue of Disloyalty* is an exception; it was published twice in his lifetime, thus making it reasonably accessible.[3]

It was clear from his opening remarks that the selected audience at Hamburg University was not going to listen to a speech gently extolling the Bard's virtues or his subliminal influences on the author's work. In his first sentence, Greene describes Shakespeare as the 'supreme poet of conservatism'. He suggests that the reader might even tire of the endings of the great tragedies where the beauty of the verse 'takes

This essay has been adapted from a paper presented at the Graham Greene International Festival, Berkhamsted, September 2018.

1 The prize was first presented in 1937 as a counter to international tension. It was awarded only twice before the outbreak of the Second World War – to composer Ralph Vaughan Williams and poet John Masefield. The giving of the award resumed in 1967, and the last time it was awarded was in 2006.

2 In 1934 Greene turned down an opportunity to read his first story accepted for radio broadcast, 'A Day Saved'. BBC Written Archives Centre, Reading, UK, General Correspondence and Memos File, 8 August 1934.

3 The speech was published in Philip Stratford (ed.). *The Portable* [illegible]

away the sting' and re-establishes the status quo, thus allowing this 'bourgeois poet' to achieve his 'house at Stratford and his coat of arms'.[4]

Greene is then quick to draw attention to the concerns of the present day to those he describes as 'we who live in times just as troubled as his' and lists a number of contemporary protestors who had suffered for their beliefs. Shakespeare, in his opinion, does not merit featuring in that role of honour although he admits he might have done had he lived longer. He would then have joined the likes of Zola, Dostoevsky, Dante and, less obviously perhaps, the poet Robert Southwell. 'If only Shakespeare had shared his disloyalty,' he claims, 'we would have loved him better as a man.'[5]

Greene argues that it is the writer's responsibility to take the opposing view, to argue on behalf of those who do not comply with accepted opinion, those who rebel against authority, those 'who lie outside the boundaries of State approval'. He goes further, even challenging the very notion of consistency or loyalty to a particular cause. Greene asserts that if the writer can convey to the reader a wider, looser perspective, it constitutes a service to society. He states that it is a 'genuine duty … to be a piece of grit in the State machinery'. Greene brings his argument to a climax by stating that although the then current Soviet state might approve of classical Russian literature, in the end it would be the embedded themes of non-conformity in those works which would exercise a greater influence than loyalty to the Party. Greene ends by claiming that in his eyes Dietrich Bonhoeffer, the German theologian, who was hanged for his beliefs and for his opposition to Nazi dictatorship, was a greater hero than Shakespeare.[6]

Those with prior knowledge of Greene's views would have recognized several of the sentiments expressed in this short speech, including his assertion that it is the duty of the writer to be disloyal to the state and to advocate the opposing view. Twenty years earlier he had been a participant in a three-way 'exchange' with fellow writers V. S. Pritchett and Elizabeth Bowen. The result was a series of seven letters passed between the three writers. These were collated, edited and later broadcast as a programme entitled 'The Artist in Society' on the BBC's 'Third Programme', a radio station devoted to the dissemination of the arts.[7]

4 Greene, *Reflections*, pp. 266 and 267.

5 Ibid., p. 268. Although not mentioned specifically by Greene, the inclusion of the lesser-known Robert Southwell as an example of a writer/martyr may well have been influenced by the fact that the Jesuit priest was one of the Forty Martyrs of England and Wales who were going through the process leading to canonization during the 1960s and therefore in the public eye.

6 Ibid., pp. 269–70.

7 The 'Third Programme' had first broadcast two years earlier in 1946. It was deliberately 'highbrow' in tone and frequently dealt with obscure subject matter.

Victor Pritchett had suggested the idea for the correspondence in 1946, and the written exchange had commenced in 1947. Pritchett had worked for the BBC during the Second World War, which probably accounts for the fact that it was thought that the idea for the programme made suitable material for the new radio station. The three writers were roughly the same age; Pritchett had established his reputation in the interwar period, particularly with a short story collection *The Spanish Virgin and Other Stories* (1932), while Elizabeth Bowen had written two highly acclaimed evocations of life in wartime Britain – *The Demon Lover and Other Stories* (1945) and *The Heat of the Day* (1948). Thus far, Greene's intellectual reputation probably rested on *The Power and the Glory* (1940) which had sold 12,398 copies in its first

Greene contributes twice to this exchange. He broaches the matter of a writer's 'disloyalty' in his letter to Elizabeth Bowen. He perceives disloyalty as a 'privilege' which, as a Catholic, saved him as a writer. He compares himself with François Mauriac, a writer he greatly admired: 'If my conscience were as acute as M. Mauriac's showed itself in his essay God and Mammon, I could not write a line.' By the time of his Hamburg speech, this privilege had become more or less an expectation: 'Isn't it the story-teller's task to act as the devil's advocate,' he demands.[8]

Greene's reply to V. S. Pritchett's letter uses phrases, even entire passages, which reappear twenty years later. He employs the exact phrase 'the virtue of disloyalty' and draws attention to the dangers of becoming over-loyal to, and thus constrained by, 'some invented ideology of their own'. Later, he reintroduces the 'piece of grit in the State machinery' argument as well as the entire passage about Russian classical literature mentioned earlier.[9]

The writer returned to the exact same theme in 1963 in an essay entitled 'La misión del escritor en la sociedad actual' (The writer's mission in contemporary society). This piece was intended originally to be delivered as a speech at the P.E.N. Club meeting in Buenos Aires in October 1962. Greene failed to attend the event, but his speech was later published in *Sur*, a leading Latin American literary magazine.[10] It has never been officially published in English.

On this occasion, he avows that it is the 'duty' of the writer to be disloyal to the state. He repeats the statement that he would be unable to write at all if his Catholic conscience had been as acute as that of Mauriac. He quotes from Robert Browning's 'Bishop Blougram's Apology' to show how, as a writer, he must have the freedom to argue from the opposing

UK printing. This figure was shortly to be dwarfed by the 89,783 copies sold of *The Heart of the Matter* published in 1948.

The exchange of letters was published in book form in Elizabeth Bowen, Graham Greene and V. S. Pritchett, *Why Do I Write? An Exchange of Views between Elizabeth Bowen, Graham Greene and V.S. Pritchett* (London: Percival Marshall, 1948). The scripts for the 'Third Programme' broadcast were later published in John Morris (ed.), *From the Third Programme: A Ten Years' Anthology* (London: Nonesuch, 1956). The writers took part in the broadcast.

8 Bowen et al., *Why Do I Write?*, p. 31; Greene, *Reflections*, p. 268. Greene's admiration for Mauriac the novelist is apparent in his then recent essay 'An English View of Francois Mauriac', in Moore, Reginald and Lane, Andrew (eds), *The Windmill* (London: William Heinemann, 1946), pp. 80–3.

Greene's comparative freedom of conscience had enabled him to explore the extremes of human behaviour in the face of Catholic doctrine in *Brighton Rock* (1938) and *The Power and the Glory* (1940). He was to do so again in *The Heart of the Matter* (1948), *The End of the Affair* (1951) and *The Potting Shed* (1958).

9 Bowen et al., *Why Do I Write?*, pp. 47 and 48–9; Greene, *Reflections*, pp. 269–70.

10 Graham Greene, 'La misión del escritor en la sociedad actual', *Sur*, no. 280, Buenos Aires, Argentina, 1963 (translated into Spanish by Miguel Olivera). (I am indebted to Paul Juckes for translating 'La misión del escritor en la sociedad actual' back into English for me.)

Victoria Ocampo, the founder of *Sur* and a prominent Argentinean intellectual, had tried for several years to persuade Greene to visit and meet the Buenos Aires literary circle. The P.E.N. Club meeting in late 1962 provided the ideal opportunity. He finally, and belatedly, used the excuse of pressure of work to cancel his trip. Three reasons lay behind this decision: his avowed dislike of public speaking; his dislike of mixing with certain members of the P.E.N. fraternity; and his experiences of attending a P.E.N. Club conference in Rio de Janeiro in 1960 which he wrote about amusingly in an unpublished short story, 'Mr. Conway's Congress'. See Harvard University, Houghton Library, Papers of *Victoria Ocampo 1908-1979*. A holograph and a typescript of this story are present in the University [illegible]

viewpoint, 'la duda y aún la negacion deben tener su oportunidad de expresarse' (doubt and even negation must have the opportunity to be expressed).[11] This notion is expressed more concisely in *The Virtue of Disloyalty* where he claims that writers should have the licence 'to roam through any human mind'. Although Shakespeare is mentioned only in passing, there is an indirect reference to the person who was to become the target of Greene's opprobrium six years later. He states that by being true to the doctrine of disloyalty one can avoid one's integrity being undermined through honours, state protection and the like.[12]

It is harder, but not impossible, to find examples of Greene's negative views about Shakespeare prior to 1969. Norman Sherry notes that as an 'immature twenty-two-year-old' he had written to Vivien about 'that nasty Shakespeare's sonnets' of which at least two-thirds were seemingly addressed to a young man. Sherry assumes that Greene's prudish stance was intended to curry favour with his future wife.[13]

He reviewed three films of Shakespeare's plays for the *Spectator* in the 1930s. In his account of *A Midsummer Night's Dream* (1935) he confesses to having 'little affection for the play' because 'it seems to me to have been written with a grim determination on Shakespeare's part to earn for once a Universal Certificate'. This personal aside, implying that the playwright's mercenary aims took precedence, finds echoes in *The Virtue of Disloyalty* in Greene's comments about the 'bourgeois poet' wanting his house in Stratford and his coat of arms. At the end of what amounts to a eulogy on John Webster in *British Dramatists*, he claims that the playwright's ability to express in words 'the night-side of life' exceeded that of Shakespeare. The allusion to the dramatist's emotional detachment, he suggests, adversely affected the actual quality of his writing: 'That enormous genius must be allowed his limitations; even in his darkest period he was too sane, too conscious of his art, to express madness convincingly.'[14]

There is a further example to be found, this time a more overt criticism of Shakespeare's skill in presenting the full range and depth of human emotion. Greene wrote the introduction to *The Autobiography of an Elizabethan*, published in 1951. John Gerard was a Jesuit priest who had been arrested and tortured in the Tower of London before managing to escape and

11 Greene, 'La misión', p. 3.

12 Greene, *Reflections*, p. 269; Greene, 'La misión', p. 3. Greene ends the essay by reusing his passage about classical Russian literature. Clearly he was happy with the wording to use it three times.

His reference to Browning's poem is well known. A more extensive version of the influence of 'Bishop Blougram's Apology' on his own philosophy is to be found in Graham Greene, *A Sort of Life* (London: Bodley Head, 1971), pp. 114–17. Perhaps unexpectedly this reference is not used in *The Virtue of Disloyalty*. By mid-1969 his autobiography was nearly complete and Greene may not have wanted to be accused of unnecessary duplication.

13 Norman Sherry, *The Life of Graham Greene, Volume 1: 1904–1939* (London: Jonathan Cape, 1989), p. 483.

14 William Shakespeare, 'A Midsummer Night's Dream', in *The Pleasure Dome: The Collected Film Criticism 1935–40*, edited by John Russell Taylor (London: Secker & Warburg, 1972), pp. 28–9; Graham Greene, *British Dramatists* (London: William Collins, 1942), pp. 24–5.

Greene's depiction of Shakespeare being driven by mercenary ambitions is a little unfair. For example, James Shapiro asserts that the playwright might have been tempted to write masques which were highly popular at the time and typically earned the writer more than eight times the rate a dramatist earned from a single play. See James Shapiro, *1606: Shakespeare and the Year of Lear* (London: Faber & Faber, 2016), p. 5.

later write his memoir. One of Gerard's torturers was Francis Bacon. In his introduction, Greene invites the reader to indulge in a flight of fancy, to 'imagine oneself a follower of the Baconian heresy' and place Shakespeare in the role of the persecutor:

> If Shakespeare had sat where Bacon had sat and given the orders for the torture, one wonders whether into the great plays which present on the inner side, however much on the outer Lear may rave or Antony lust, so smooth and ambiguous a surface, there would have crept a more profound doubt than Hamlet's, a sense of a love deeper than Romeo's.[15]

Thus, much of the thinking contained in the 1968 speech had evolved over the years and had been used in other writings. Even the title *The Virtue of Disloyalty* is not original. It had been borrowed from another source. During a protest march against British rule in India in 1930, Mahatma Gandhi had written an article advocating that the path to 'swaraj' (home rule) lay through 'satyagraha' (passive political resistance). In order to attain this goal, Indians needed to understand their political obligations: 'It is the duty of those who have realised the awful evil of the system of Indian Government to be disloyal to it and actively and openly to preach disloyalty. Indeed, loyalty to a State so corrupt is a sin, disloyalty a virtue.'[16]

Gandhi himself admitted that in advocating this course of action, he owed a debt to the American Henry David Thoreau, a lifelong abolitionist, who in his essay 'Civil Disobedience' had argued in favour of protest and resistance in order to attain a more just form of government.[17]

But why did Graham Greene chose this particular occasion to make this deliberately provocative speech? He leaves clues in a short preface which, typically perhaps, was intended to be read only by a limited audience. Although the central text of the speech was later published twice, in 1973 and 1990, neither publication carries this preface. It appears in book form only in a limited edition of three hundred copies which were published in November 1972. This formed a private publication for friends of the author and his publisher to be presented as a seasonal gift.[18]

15 Greene, *Reflections*, pp. 123–8. The 'Baconian heresy' refers to the theory that it was Francis Bacon who wrote Shakespeare's plays.

Gerard's autobiography had been translated from the Latin by Fr Philip Caraman SJ. Greene was very friendly with Caraman for many years, and it was the Jesuit priest who identified the figure of Francis Bacon in Gerard's torture chamber.

In his introduction, Greene comments on the notable absence of Christian religious themes in Shakespeare's plays and particularly the lack of references to martyrdom, which is a central component of *The Virtue of Disloyalty*.

16 M. K. Gandhi, *Non-violent Resistance (Satyagraha)* (New York: Courier Dover, 2001).

17 Thoreau is also said to have influenced Martin Luther King Jr who was assassinated in 1968, the year before Greene gave his speech.

In common with his contrary nature, Greene had written a bitingly satirical and condemnatory essay about Thoreau's most famous book *Walden* in 1939 under his pseudonym Hilary Trench as a *Spectator* Magazine Competition entry. Hilary Trench, 'An Acute Analysis of the Unattractive Qualities of Thoreau', *Spectator*, 24 November 1939.

18 The University of Hamburg marked the presentation of the 1968 and 1969 [illegible]

In the preface, Greene relates how the theme of disloyalty had been an obsession since youth and how it had appeared 'like a tiresome and persistent weed' in many of his novels. He admits that he did not understand why he had been awarded the Shakespeare Prize but felt that his theme was a suitable subject for a German audience composed mainly of students who were not born when Hitler was alive and older professors with memories of the Nazi regime who might well have been disquieted by the references to divided loyalties.

In the final paragraph of the preface, he makes it clear that his admiration for Shakespeare is qualified: 'The suspicion of something cold and prudent in the poet's nature that at times makes the blank verse, however free and rugged, seem to be smoother than the alexandrines of Racine.' Perhaps Michael Shelden is correct in concluding that in Greene's world, when writers become 'grit in the State machinery', no one is safe, even when accepting a prize dedicated to the very person you are about to criticize. If someone is truly a great literary figure, he or she will be able to survive. However, Shelden notes that 'the pretentious, the humourless, the dogmatic, the corrupt, will suffer', adding that 'the enemy is "the pretending part of the proud world" – that part which recognises no wisdom but its own'.[19]

Significantly, Greene states that the whole speech 'should be taken with a grain of salt' and that it 'masks a different offensive'.[20] One is left to speculate on quite what the writer meant by this 'different offensive'. It is tempting to single out a specific incident. The previous year, the spy Kim Philby's autobiography *My Silent War* had been published. Greene had written a controversial foreword, siding with the notorious traitor to his country. In places his admiration borders on adulation: he praises his leadership, loyalty to those who worked for him, wit, skill and intelligence. Above all, he admired Philby for his unwavering devotion to the Communist cause, even though that meant betraying his fellow countrymen and being indirectly responsible for the deaths of an unknown number of people. His outright honesty, Greene seems to imply, meant that Philby was not 'the pretending part of the proud world'. He goes further, in what Michael Brennan rightly describes as a 'sly rhetorical question', to suggest that we can all be excused for putting personal loyalties ahead of loyalty to our country, whatever the cost, 'but who among us has not committed treason to something or someone more important than a country?' he asks.[21]

details of the ceremony. This included the texts of both recipients' speeches in both German and English. See *Verleihung der Shakespeare-Preise* (Hamburg: Conti, 1969).

The text of *The Virtue of Disloyalty*, including the preface, was published in 1972 by The Bodley Head. It also appeared, along with the preface, in the *Observer Review*, 24 December 1972.

19 Michael Shelden, *Graham Greene: The Man Within* (London: William Heinemann, 1994), p. 5. Shelden quotes from John Wilmot, Earl of Rochester's 'A Satyr on Reason and Mankind'. Greene admiration for Wilmot is evident in his biography *Lord Rochester's Monkey: Being the Life and Work of John Wilmot, Second Earl of Rochester*, which he wrote in the early 1930s but was published only in 1974.

20 Preface to 'The Virtue of Disloyalty', *Observer Review*, review, 24 December 1972, p. 17.

21 See Michael Brennan, *Graham Greene: Political Writer* (Basingstoke: Palgrave Macmillan, 2016), p. 133; Kim Philby, *My Silent War* (London: MacGibbon & Kee, 1968), p. vii. See also Richard Greene, *Russian Roulette: The Life and Times of Graham Greene* (London: Little Brown, 2020), p. 383.

Greene's Hamburg speech had a much wider focus than simply a defence of his views on Kim Philby. Topical references within the speech to modern-day 'martyrs' such as Pasternak, Sinyavsky, Solzhenitsyn, Bastos and Seferis imply that the 'different offensive' was a political one. Indeed, it has been pointed out that during this later stage of his career, politics 'displaced religion at the forefront of his fiction'. One might add that this was true across the breadth of his writing, constituting a trend which became increasingly evident during the course of the 1960s. Interestingly, Greene's remark in his preface that his speech 'disquieted the professors, but, I think, pleased the students' was entirely prescient. This was 1968, the year of student protest in the United States, London, Paris, Berlin and elsewhere, and Greene had caught the mood of the moment.[22]

During the 1960s and beyond, Greene became increasingly active, and indeed strident, in political causes, as *The Virtue of Disloyalty* attests, in the form of articles, speeches and letters to newspapers – a trend which was to continue for the rest of his life. Prominent examples, closest in date to his Hamburg speech, include *Authors Take Sides on Vietnam* (1967), *Viva Che! Contributions in Tribute to Ernesto 'Che' Guevara* (1968), 'And a Happy New Year', remarks by Greene at the P.E.N. Writers' Meeting concerning the imprisoned writers Sinyavsky and Daniel (1968) and the introduction to *Papa Doc: Haiti and Its Dictator* (1970) by Bernard Diederich and Al Burt.[23]

Graham Greene received, in an act of remarkable beneficence by this German university, not the Johann Wolfgang von Goethe Prize but rather the William Shakespeare Prize for outstanding achievement in the field of literature. In his speech he had the audacity and moreover the renewed commitment to the power of the spoken and written word to turn what might have been expected to be an easy exercise in Bardolatry into a platform for vigorous and topical political protest.

Greene's foreword for *My Silent War*, entitled 'Reflections on the Character of Kim Philby', is a slightly shortened version of an article which appeared in *Esquire* magazine in September 1968. The conflict between personal loyalty and loyalty to one's country was a conundrum Greene would have been preoccupied with at the time. He had started writing *The Human Factor* (1978), which deals with this theme, the previous year.

22 See Greene, *Reflections*, p. 267; Neil Sinyard, *Graham Greene: A Literary Life* (Basingstoke: Palgrave Macmillan, 2003), p. 17.

23 Over forty letters of a political nature, principally highlighting [illegible]

‘A hot cookie, if a minuscule one’: *The Comedians*, the Haiti Government and the Foreign Office

Jon Wise

On 3 November 1967, Graham Greene issued a press statement in which he challenged President François Duvalier of Haiti to ‘take a vacation, in the outside world away from the security of his Tontons’. Greene went on to state that the ruler of Haiti was responsible for the murder and exile of thousands of his countrymen. This was a rebuttal for Duvalier’s official protest to the US State Department about the film based on his novel *The Comedians* (1966) which had been first screened in the United States that month. Although, at the time, the Republic of Haiti was described disdainfully by one British Foreign Office (FO) official as ‘a hot cookie, if a minuscule one’, the matter was significant enough for the whole affair to be recorded in the government’s official documents of the time.[1]

The Haitian government also released its own press statement strongly protesting against Metro-Goldwyn-Mayer who had produced and distributed the film. It claimed that ‘no effort had been spared to slander the people, the Government and the entire Haitian Nation. It is not less than, “a character assassination of an entire nation”’.[2] The British embassy in Washington was in immediate communication with the American Department at the Foreign Office, assuring them that the Americans could do nothing under the terms of their Constitution and that in their opinion the Haitians were behaving in a ‘ridiculous’ manner and would only draw further attention to the film. It was thought that the FO might receive a similar protest as the cast, director and writer of the film were all British.[3]

This essay was first published in an abridged form in *A Sort of Newsletter*, Issue 85, February 2020.

1 The National Archives (TNA) at Kew, London, holds the British government’s Foreign and Commonwealth Office records. The relevant file is FCO7/249, Relations with US and UK: Protest over Graham Greene’s book and film *The Comedians* (1967–8).

The ‘Foreign and Commonwealth Office’ (FCO) came into existence on 17 October 1968 following a merger between the Foreign Office (FO) and the Commonwealth Relations Office (CRO). Therefore, the events described in this article took place during the last days of the old FO, and the chosen nomenclature for these documents is not wholly accurate.

The novel sold over sixty thousand copies in its first edition. The film had a mixed reception despite its star cast. Quentin Falk expresses considerable reservations about its merit in *Travels in Greeneland: The Cinema of Graham Greene*, revised and updated 4th ed. (Dahlonga: University Press of North Georgia, 2014), pp. 105–11.

2 TNA FCO7/249: Press Statement, Embassy of Haiti, 3 November 1967.

3 TNA FCO7/249, Letter: British Embassy Washington DC to American Department [illegible] November 1967

There was reaction elsewhere. The British High Commission in Kingston, Jamaica, reported that the ambassador had not received any official protest when visiting Haiti in December 1967 despite the fact that there were articles in the Haitian press at the time critical of the film and decrying the fact that the Duke and Duchess of Kent would be attending the London premiere of *The Comedians* later that month.[4]

The whole matter erupted again in late February. The same high commission reported that a note had been received by the chargé d'affaires in Haiti regarding the offending film. It was couched in fairly strong terms. It was thought that the protest was surprising given the lack of criticism hitherto, despite the local protests. Opinion was that Duvalier had decided to take offence rather belatedly and this was a way of venting his feelings. A 'dead-pan' acknowledgement would be issued unless the FO wanted an official refutation made which included a statement that Graham Greene 'reserved the right to write *fiction* [original emphasis] as he chooses'.[5]

The same communication contained a memo reporting on reactions received from the American and Canadian missions. The Canadians felt that the matter needed to be taken seriously as it might threaten the security of their citizens, particularly those working in outlying areas of Haiti. The Americans, on the other hand, considered the wording of the Haitian protest over the film too strong 'for the relatively unimportant nature of the matter'. There was surprise because President Duvalier had hitherto appeared to regard the issue lightly. For example, he had been photographed earlier with a copy of the novel in one hand and his own book *Oeuvres Essentielles* in the other and had jokingly asked reporters to say which 'gave a truer insight in the Haitian way of life and philosophy'.[6]

Matters came to a head on 23 February when M. Delorme Méhu, the Haitian chargé d'affaires in London, requested an interview with Mr Diggines, the head of the American Department at the Foreign Office. Adopting a previously formulated 'official line', Mr Diggines stressed that *The Comedians* was an American-made commercial film for which Her Majesty's government held no responsibility. It had been shown in the UK where there was no political censorship. It was not exceptional that President Duvalier was featured as a great number of political figures, including heads of state, had appeared in entertainment films.[7]

Méhu, having lodged his complaint, reluctantly acquiesced but requested an official written note of the meeting. There was some concern in the FO that the appearance of Duvalier constituted defamation of character, but the legal department assured otherwise.[8] Essentially, that was where the matter rested as far as the FO was concerned.

4 TNA FCO7/249, Letter: British High Commission, Jamaica to American Department FO, London, 2 January 1968.

5 TNA FCO7/249. Letter: British High Commission, Jamaica to American Department FO, London, 21 February 1968.

6 TNA FCO7/249, Letter: British High Commission, Jamaica to American Department, Enclosure, FO, London, 21 February 1968.

7 TNA FCO7/249, Letter: DJ Swan FO to CD Sanderson, High Commission, Jamaica, 4 March 1968.

8 This was not the case in France where a three-year lawsuit culminated in a court ruling that the film constituted a libel against President Duvalier. Parts of the film were ordered to be cut. See Bernard

However, as Bernard Diederich points out, the book and the film *The Comedians*, and Graham Greene in particular, had a lasting impact on President Duvalier.[9] Later in March, the FO received its copy of *Graham Greene: Demasque Finally Exposed.* Diederich writes, 'Styled as an official Haitian Foreign Ministry bulletin, the 92 page document was devoted entirely to denouncing Graham Greene.' Greene was highly amused but disturbed by the cost to the fragile Haiti economy of this lavishly produced publication.[10]

The last document in the FO file contains the booklet itself accompanied by a handwritten note which reads, 'You may wish to see. This is an infantile publication, but its attack on ex-Ambassador Corley-Smith … is extremely inappropriate for an official publication.'[11] The file abounds with similar derogatory words and phrases about the Haitian government: 'ridiculous' behaviour, 'preposterous' remarks, 'outlandish' points and so on. Although many of these comments were made in internal memoranda they nevertheless demonstrate the contempt in which their Haitian equivalents in government were seemingly held. Despite its leader, Haiti was not an upstart nation; its origins as an independent and sovereign country stretch back to independence in 1804 when it became the first country to abolish slavery and the only state in history to be established through a successful slave revolt.

It comes as something of a surprise to find included in the file quotations from a broadcast made at the time by Ralph Story on the CBS Radio network, '*The Comedians* must be the first big budget movie of our times – obviously aimed at destroying an existing government … In this one there's no fiction … President Duvalier is frequently mentioned by name … and at one point is even represented on screen.' Story goes on to accuse the film-makers of showing aggression against a government representing the masses and the 'peasantry' in a fight for religious and economic freedom. He adds that the film's release was timed to scare off American tourists at the start of the season.[12]

Story's words chime today with the Black Lives Matter movement. It was a different case fifty-three years ago when a black nation dared to confront and admonish the still formidable, white, ex-imperial power Britain. This had not been Graham Greene's intention at all with *The Comedians*, arguably the most overtly political novel of his career, which was aimed instead at unsettling a malicious dictatorship in a country whose long and pitiful history had been a catalogue of cruelty, persecution and bloodshed.[13]

Diederich, *Seeds of Fiction: Graham Greene's Adventures in Haiti and Central America, 1954–1983* (London: Peter Owen, 2012), pp. 134–7. See also Richard Greene, *Russian Roulette: The Life and Times of Graham Greene* (London: Little Brown, 2020), pp. 379–80.

9 Diederich, 'Papa Doc Reacts to The Comedians', in *Seeds of Fiction*, chapter 9.

10 Diederich, *Seeds of Fiction*, pp. 120 and 125. Diederich calculated the extraordinary cost in dollars of Duvalier's campaign against the film; see p. 131.

11 FCO7/249. Titled 'Protocol & Conference', the note is attached to the copy of the Haitian booklet.

12 Ralph Story was a TV show host and radio personality. Duvalier was indeed anxious to attract tourism to the island at the time. See Diederich, *Seeds of Fiction*, pp. 115–16; and Greene, *Russian Roulette*, pp. 372 and 379.

13 Richard Greene states, 'Although Greene hoped that his book would [illegible]

Although Greene succeeded in some respects, regrettably Duvalier remained in power until he died in April 1971. Of course, it was the ordinary people of Haiti who ultimately bore the burden: 'ce petit coin de terre ou l'esprit de liberté donna le premier signal de révolte contre le joug colonialiste'.[14]

[14] FCO7/249. An unsigned note was attached to the FCO copy of *Graham Greene Demasque*, which included the above quotation in French.

'Unfilmable': 'The Basement Room' becomes *The Fallen Idol*

Mike Hill

The Fallen Idol, directed by Carol Reed and with a screenplay by Graham Greene, was released in UK cinemas on 25 October 1948 and was soon attracting good reviews. The *Monthly Film Bulletin* judged it 'outstanding', C. A. Lejeune called it 'the best thing [Reed] has ever done … full of heart as well as intelligence, wisdom as well as wit … a very lovely heartfelt picture',[1] while the *Daily Mail* critic saw 'British screen talent at its very best'. The pattern continued after the film's release in the United States on 15 November 1949: 'All that is so deeply satisfying in the best British pictures, the subtlety, intelligence, unforced humor and tragedy free of theatrical posture is on view in *The Fallen Idol*', wrote the *New York Post.*

Soon the film featured in awards ceremonies. In the UK, it won the BAFTA award as best British film in 1948. Greene was nominated for an Oscar for his screenplay (the only time in his career that this happened), and he won the award for Best Screenplay at the Venice International Film Festival and from the National Board of Review in the United States. Carol Reed was also nominated for an Oscar for his work as director and was voted Best Director by the New York Film Critic Circle. The film's reputation has not diminished over the years – David Hare has described it as 'a great overlooked masterpiece of the British cinema',[2] while David Lodge wrote that it is 'a film of exceptional distinction'.[3] Graham Greene himself said that '*The Fallen Idol* is my favourite screen work because it is more a writer's film than a director's'[4] and also because it was not originally written for cinema.[5]

The film has a simple story to tell. While his parents are away for the weekend, a young boy, Phillipe, is being cared for in a big embassy building by a butler and his wife, the embassy's housekeeper. Phillipe idolizes the butler, Baines, and becomes aware of his relationship with another woman, without realizing its full meaning. He witnesses what he takes to be the killing by Baines of his wife, but in the ensuing police

1 *Observer*, October 1948.

2 *Guardian*, 14 December 2001.

3 David Lodge, 'Did the Butler Do It?', *Guardian*, 4 November 2006.

4 *Graham Greene: On the Screen*, interview by Gene D. Phillips, *Catholic World*, August 1969. Reprinted in David Parkinson (ed.), *The Graham Greene Film Reader: Mornings in the Dark* (Manchester: Carcanet, 1993), p. 525.

5 [illegible]

investigation he almost secures the arrest of the innocent Baines by telling lies on his behalf.

This tale of childhood innocence and secrets and lies was in turn based on a Graham Greene short story – 'The Basement Room', written and first published in 1935. While retaining many of the original story's themes, however, the film is very far from being merely a faithful cinematic rendering of it. In 'The Basement Room', Baines is indeed guilty of killing his wife – Greene describes it as 'murder',[6] though manslaughter is equally plausible – but that guilt is only exposed through the inadvertent betrayal of his friend by Philip (as he is named in the story). So while the film ends with the butler being exonerated, the story concludes with Baines 'coming clean'.[7] There is a further important difference. In the short story, Greene as narrator inserts a number of comments relating to sixty years after the main action, with the boy now an old man; his whole life has clearly been scarred by the trauma of his childhood experience – he had, Greene writes, 'never built anything, never created anything, died, the old dilettante, sixty years later with nothing to show'.[8] (In this inclusion of 'what happened after', the short story thus prefigures L. P. Hartley's classic novel *The Go-Between*, published in 1953, and indeed Greene's own unfinished novel *Lucius*, from 1958.) The film has none of this looking forward to an older Phillipe, so the resolution of the plot is much less bleak than in the original story.

This translation of a written story into another medium deserves some investigation. Graham Greene was notoriously critical of many of the adaptations of his work for the cinema, particularly those done in Hollywood. Here he was himself involved in such an adaptation, writing a screenplay which very significantly diverges from his own story and being very happy with the outcome. How did this happen?

The simplest answer is that it occurred through a process of sympathetic collaboration between Greene and Reed. In his days as a film critic, Greene had spotted Reed's talents as a film director, writing of him in 1936 as 'a new English director … who has more sense of the cinema than most veteran British directors'.[9] Moreover, Reed was a writer's director, an attribute essential to Greene: in an interview in 1959 Reed said, 'I think it is the director's job … to convey faithfully what the author had in mind.'[10] In 1947, the two men were brought together by Alexander Korda, who suggested they might make a film of 'A Basement Room'. The three met in May 1947, and things went well. Korda did not interfere, leaving the two men to get on with it. Soon Greene and Reed took a suite of rooms in a Brighton hotel with connecting doors and a secretary between them. Greene wrote, Reed revised and suggested and Greene would discuss and write

6 Ibid., p. 101.
7 Ibid., p. 130.
8 Ibid., p. 114.
9 *Spectator*, 3 January 1936. The review was of Reed's *Midshipman Easy*.
10 Quoted in Nicholas Wapshott, *The Man Between: A Biography of Carol Reed* (London: Chatto & Windus, 1990), p. 196. Wapshott gives a full account of the Reed-Greene collaboration on *The Fallen Idol* (pp. 193–8).

more. This seems to have taken around ten days in July 1947, with Greene's work on the script continuing until early September.[11] In this way Greene's screenplay gradually took shape. It was, in Quentin Falk's words, 'a perfect collaboration',[12] which was to continue with *The Third Man* (1949) and *Our Man in Havana* (1959).

In 1950, to follow up on the phenomenal success of *The Fallen Idol* and *The Third Man*, Heinemann published an edition containing the two stories, with Greene writing prefaces to both. In the one on *The Fallen Idol*, Greene dealt with the change of name from 'The Basement Room'. It was, he said, 'a meaningless title for the original story'.[13] That in itself is a strange judgement: Philip in the story undoubtedly idolizes Baines, and Baines's arrest for killing his wife is a pretty spectacular fall. The best that can be said for Greene's view is that the title changes the emphasis from Philip and the long-term consequences for him of the events of the story, to Baines as seen by Philip; but this is hardly a matter of meaninglessness. In fact, Greene seems to have been unhappy with *The Fallen Idol* as the title of the film, too. The title 'was chosen by the distributors', he wrote bluntly in his preface. One of the surviving scripts for the film has *Lost Illusions* as a working title, with the final 's' crossed through, apparently by Greene, and he has added *A Very Simple Case* and *The Child on the Staircase* as other possible titles.[14] Whether any of these is a better title than *The Fallen Idol* is extremely doubtful. The film shows Philippe witnessing Baines's repeated lying, and being found out in lying, and Baines admitting that he lied to the boy in his many tales from Africa (there is no such admission in the short story). Phillipe has a dim awareness of Baines's clandestine affair with Julie, and the boy believes that Baines really did kill his wife. *The Fallen Idol* seems not such a bad title after all.

In one respect, however, Greene had a point. Collections of his short stories often include 'The Basement Room', rightly titled thus.[15] After the success of *The Fallen Idol*, however, it became common to reprint the story of 'The Basement Room' as *The Fallen Idol*, beginning with the Heinemann edition of 1950. What readers of that and subsequent editions with this title get is not a story reworked to reflect the story as told by the film – Greene never wrote such a story, except as a screenplay – but 'The Basement Room'. If *The Fallen Idol* is issued without Greene's preface to make clear what they are actually reading, the confusion is compounded. In this respect, Greene's assertion that *The Fallen Idol* is 'a meaningless title for the original story' is all too appropriate.

From Greene's preface we also get some indication of who did what in converting 'The Basement Room' into *The Fallen Idol*. It was Greene who suggested that the police

11 On the dates of Greene's work of the screenplay, see Norman Sherry, *The Life of Graham Greene Volume 2:1939–1955* (London: Random House, 1994), p. 241 and note, p. 526.

12 Quentin Falk, *Travels in Greeneland: The Cinema of Graham Greene*, 4th ed. (Dahlonega: University Press of North Georgia, 2014), p. 41.

13 *The Fallen Idol*, p. 101.

14 British Film Institute (BFI) Special Collections: Carol Reed Collection [illegible]

15 [illegible]

interview Baines's 'girl' Julie beside the bed they had shared, producing dialogue where she describes dressing quickly after Mrs Baines's fall and making the nature of their relationship explicit; in the short story, the girl is not seen at all by the police. Greene too suggested another element completely absent from the story – Phillipe's pet 'snake' McGregor. 'I have always liked snakes,'[16] Greene wrote by way of explanation, and he got his way against Reed's initial opposition, giving critics of the film a Freudian field day. Reed in his turn invented the moment when the police investigation of the death is interrupted by a clock winder who insists on doing his work; it provides an amusing interlude, while extending the tension as Baines is gradually found out in his lies. (In his 1954 film *Rear Window*, Alfred Hitchcock's cameo appearance is as an equally inconsequential clock winder: a nod to *The Fallen Idol*?) More importantly, Reed also suggested that the film should be based in an embassy – the short story is set in a large Belgravia house – on the grounds that in post-war Britain that was a more plausible grand setting. The whole business of a boy who speaks fluent French, has an ambassador father and lives in 'foreign territory' flows from that; it also allows Julie ('Emmy' in the story) to be a secretary at the embassy and to be, it seems, a foreign national – all different from the short story.

The film *The Fallen Idol* changes the short story in other ways. Some elements are given a tweak. When Phillipe is questioned in the police station, it is in the presence not of policewoman Rose but of a local prostitute, whose stock patter and tone of voice make for a wonderful bit of comedy (as does her aside, on hearing that the boy's father is the ambassador, that 'Oh, I know your daddy' – a sly suggestion that all may not be well in the marriage of Phillipe's parents?). Some changes involve new elements, like the splendid game of hide-and-seek between Baines, Julie and Phillipe. Parts of the film are an expansion of what is originally there. In the story there are brief mentions of a visit by Baines and Philip to London Zoo, which in the film become a whole sequence showing the boy enjoying himself among the animals as Baines and Julie talk. The police investigation of the death back at the house, which covers barely two pages in 'A Basement Room', becomes the whole of the last third of the film, as policemen swirl around the embassy. Phillipe puts doubts in minds about the nature of Mrs Baines's death, Baines is caught out in lying, his relationship with Julie is exposed and the circumstances of the fall are questioned. Greene's original swift resolution of the story, in which the boy inadvertently implicates his hero, now becomes a tense unravelling, a suspense thriller involving mounting terror and confusion for Phillipe. All these developed elements resulted from the creative partnership of Reed and Greene, bouncing ideas off each other over ten days in Brighton. And they reflect Greene's preference for a film which worked outwards from a short story – as he once wrote, 'Condensation is always dangerous, while expansion is a form of creation.'[17]

16 *The Fallen Idol*, p. 102.

17 Quoted in Gene D. Philllips, *Graham Greene: The Films of His Fiction* (New York: Teachers College Press, 1974), p. 51.

Above all, Reed and Greene had to confront the most problematic issue arising from 'A Basement Room': as Greene put it, 'It seemed to me that the subject was unfilmable – a murder committed by the most sympathetic character and an unhappy ending.'[18] The issue seems to have been one not of possible censorship (though the American censors did force some changes to the finished film[19]) but rather of such a downbeat theme not being popular with the viewing public. Greene really struggled to get beyond the idea that the story was unfilmable – as he later reported, 'There was always a moment when one thought, "this is hopeless". It was always I who thought it was hopeless.'[20] It was always Reed who reassured him that a solution could be found: in his preface Greene commends Reed's 'power of sympathizing with an author's worries and an ability to guide him'.[21]

The materials in the Carol Reed Collection at the British Film Institute – a 'First Treatment' by Greene dated 10 July 1949, two undated scripts and detailed script notes by Reed – give some insight into the processes involved in the Reed-Greene dialogue. Reed's notes, for instance, include an overall schematic layout for the film in six parts, from '1. Philip's relationship with Baines and Mrs Baines' to '6. Police take charge'. In the First Treatment, there is Phillipe hearing the voice of Mrs Baines's ghost 'speaking from the shadows in a tense whisper' after her death – a section which has been deleted, although at one point in the film, Phillipe does say of (the still alive) Mrs Baines, hiding in the embassy to spy on the lovers, 'I thought I saw a ghost.'

On the central issue of how Mrs Baines dies, there are clues about what Reed and Greene discussed before settling on their solution. Most intriguingly, one of the scripts has a note, in Greene's hand, '? Mrs B. really kills herself?' Though there is no further indication of how seriously this possibility was discussed, it finds echoes in the film. During the argument in which Baines asks his wife for his 'freedom', she certainly strongly hints that if he leaves her she will commit suicide. There is also a moment in the film when the desk sergeant at the police station whispers, 'Woman killed herself – fell down a flight of stairs', as if suicide is thought to have been a possibility. Among Reed's script notes, there is also a '3rd Version' by Greene, with the boy saying 'I did it' to exonerate Baines – but realizing that this will draw the blame onto Baines, Phillipe writes a note stating that no one killed Mrs Baines, then considers himself jumping from an upstairs window. Reed responded to these suggestions in his script notes, disagreeing with the notion of Phillipe's suicide note and attempted suicide.[22] So the ideas were dropped. But there are echoes of these ideas, too, in the finished film – at one point Phillipe, when asked who did it, does indeed desperately tell the police, 'I did', to try to clear Baines; and, of course, no one does kill Mrs Baines. So ideas were worked around

18 *The Fallen Idol*, p. 101.

19 Wapshott, *The Man Between*, pp. 203–4.

20 *Guardian Film Lecture* (Greene interviewed by Quentin Falk at the National Film Theatre, London), 3 September 1984. Reprinted in Parkinson, *The Graham Greene Film Reader*, p. 539.

21 *The Fallen Idol*, p. 102.

22 BFI Carol Reed C[illegible]

until a believable solution was found. Reed and Greene had their way forward: 'a small boy who believed that his friend was a murderer and nearly procured his arrest by telling lies in his defence'.[23]

Separate from this decision to make Baines an innocent man was the exclusion from the film of another element of Greene's short story. As already noted, 'The Basement Room' includes a number of authorial references to the boy Philip sixty years later, whose traumatic childhood experience has left a mark on him. These forward references to the adult Philip are entirely missing from the film. David Lodge has suggested this was due to a dating anomaly in the original story. 'In describing Philip on his deathbed, 60 years after the main action,' Lodge argues, 'the narrator is not prophesying but reporting. Since the story was first published in 1936 [*sic*], the character cannot have died at a later date; therefore the main action, when Philip was seven years old, must be taking place no later than 1876.' And since the story is clearly set in the mid-1930s, Greene has obviously committed a dating error in the story, Lodge writes. As he further says, this 'problem would have been obvious' to Reed and Greene in converting the story into a film. 'If the 67-year-old Philip were to be shown on his deathbed, it could be no later than "the present day" (i.e. 1947) and the main story would therefore have to be pushed back to 1887. Perhaps', Lodge concludes, 'his was the crucial factor that prompted Greene to undertake a radical reworking of his story in the screenplay, in which the essential meaning of the original (the psychological damage caused by suppressed memory of trauma) was displaced by a less bleak resolution of the plot.'[24]

Since Lodge's critique results in the suggestion that a dating anomaly in the short story forced Greene into a whole reworking of it for the film version, it is worth examining the argument. Professor Cedric Watts has rightly pointed out the fundamental error of his contention: 'David Lodge says of Philip that "the character cannot have died at a later date" than the date of the publication of the tale. To which I reply, "*There is no such rule!*" No rule forbids, in a fictional work, the description of an event which takes place after the time of publication of that work.' Watts then mentions a number of examples which contradict Lodge's supposed rule – Wells's *The Time Machine* and Dickens's *Christmas Carol* and *Hard Times*. Fiction writers, Watts concludes, have a 'chronological flexibility', and this includes Greene in 'The Basement Room'.[25] This is clearly common sense, and it applies equally to the adaptation of Greene's story for the cinema. If Greene and Reed had wanted to incorporate into *The Fallen Idol* 'flash forwards' to the end of Phillipe's life in the early twentieth-first century, there is no reason they could not have done so. They simply chose not to do it. To have had such insertions would have interrupted the flow of a very tightly constructed narrative and gone against the whole idea of producing a story which was less downbeat than

23 *The Fallen Idol*, p. 101.

24 Lodge, 'Did the Butler Do It?'

25 Cedric Watts, 'The Problematic Chronology of Greene's "The Basement Room"', *A Sort of Newsletter*, issue 84, November 2020, pp. 9–11.

the original. They chose not to have 'looks ahead' for quite other reasons than some notional rule of dating.

The idea of producing a more 'filmable' story that was less downbeat also involved consideration of the ending. This again prompted Reed and Greene to try out possibilities. The First Treatment of the script has a final line of dialogue in which the policeman says to Phillipe, 'We can all begin to forget poor Mrs Baines,' followed by the young boy trying (unsuccessfully) to turn cartwheels on the embassy floor[26] – as optimistic an ending as could be imagined. A later script has the policeman saying, 'Now shall I tell you a secret,' at which Phillipe shakes his head[27] – a potentially comic moment and one which did make it into the film, with Phillipe emphatically answering, 'No.' That is followed by the final image – Phillipe hearing that his parents have returned, as he slowly makes his way down the stairs and out of shot. This is generally taken to be a happy ending. Though Mrs Baines is dead, this was an accident. The boy's idol has been cleared, we may reflect that Baines is now able to marry Julie and normality returns for Phillipe with the return of his parents.

Things may not actually be so simple. The film of Greene's *Brighton Rock*, released the year before *The Fallen Idol*, famously had a superficially happy ending which contained the potential for something more awful, once Rose gets the record beyond the scratch and hears Pinkie's true message. *The Fallen Idol* too has this potential for a more downbeat reading. Towards the end of the film, Baines is seen looking at his gun in a drawer in the basement room, and he might be considering suicide; at the very least, we are being encouraged to consider what is going on in his troubled mind. At least one film reviewer in 1948 saw the complexities of the film's ending, including the impact on the adulterer Baines, whose wife has died and who comments on his marriage, 'There were faults on both sides.' The review in the Catholic paper the *Tablet* commented,

> The unthinking may, if they must, accept the proffered hint of a happy ending … Only the unthinking will miss the point that Baines is going to suffer an agony of conscience more painful than legal punishment; and that the child, watching his parents arrive at the embassy door below, has learnt his first bitter lesson of 'omnis homo mendax' [every man is a liar].[28]

This downbeat reading applies above all to the boy. As Phillipe descends the stairs at the end, calm but unsmiling, we might reflect on what he has gone through. He has had his pet 'snake' killed by a woman he has said he hates. He has witnessed his hero caught out in an affair, even if as a child he does not fully comprehend what that involves. He has seen a marital argument, as Baines asks for his freedom. He has been sworn to secrecy by Baines, then been unable to keep the secret under an attack by a demented

[26] BFI Carol Reed Collection.

[27] Ibid.

[28] *Tablet*, October 1948

Mrs Baines. He has been sworn to secrecy by Mrs Baines, giving him a conflict of loyalties. He has heard that Baines's tales of Africa are all lies. He has seen Baines lie to the police and tried to cover for him, even to the extent of trying to confess to being Mrs Baines's murderer himself. He is told by Baines not to tell the police what he knows, then by Julie that he must tell the truth. Above all, he has, he believes, witnessed the killing of Mrs Baines by his idol, and run in terror into the night, unable to speak of what he has seen. As Baines is exonerated by the footprints in the soil, Phillipe is so shocked and confused that he tries to set the record straight by trying to tell the police he made the footprints, not Mrs Baines – thereby implicating Baines afresh – only to find that the police will not listen. So the film ends with Phillipe still believing that his hero is a murderer. A boy of eight might not recover speedily, or ever, from such a series of events. Perhaps Reed and Greene realized that they did not need 'flash forwards' to a scarred adult for us to know that lasting damage has been done.

Graham Greene's work on the screenplay of *The Fallen Idol* was finished in early September 1949, and filming began on 17 September. Greene was not present at any of the shooting, so his script was left to others to bring to the screen. What was added were the brilliant sets of Vincent Korda; the striking photography of Georges Perinal; pitch perfect acting from the whole cast, from Ralph Richardson as Baines to Dandy Nichols as a cleaning lady; the subtle sound work of John Cox and the expressive music of William Alwyn; and the sharp editing of Oswald Hafenrichter. Shaping it all was Carol Reed as director and producer, pulling all these contributions together and coaxing an astonishing performance from Bobby Henrey, the non-actor who plays Phillipe. So Greene's screenplay came to life, and the unfilmable 'The Basement Room' became *The Fallen Idol*, one of the finest British films ever made.

‘Murder didn’t mean much to Raven’: *A Gun for Sale* in context

Mike Hill

I read my first Graham Greene novel, I think, sometime in the 1970s. I liked what I read and read some more, so by the 1990s I had read them all, including his two suppressed novels. This was true of all his other published writings, too. So when the centenary of Greene’s birth came round in 2004, there was nothing new to read. My solution was to reread all the novels, but this time in the order in which he had published them, starting with *The Man Within* and ending with *The Captain and the Enemy*. It is an approach I can thoroughly recommend – reading the novels in order gives a strong sense of the progress of his career as a writer, the gradual development of his distinctive voice and style, his concerns and outlook, and yields the occasional dead end. Since doing that in 2004, I now realize that when I come to reread any Greene novel I am always half-consciously doing this contextualizing, putting the work in question in the more general context of his development as a writer.

There is another context for me. My own academic training was not in literature but in history, and at least one of the attractions of Greene’s writing for me is the historical context of his novels – with only a couple of exceptions he was a chronicler of the twentieth century, and there is generally in his novels a very strong historical background of which I am aware or keen to know about.

So now I am explicit about it, I am always these days rereading a Graham Greene novel with these two frameworks in my head – how it fits into Greene’s progress as a writer, and how it fits the history of the time in which it is set. And I would like to look at these two contexts in relation to an unjustly neglected Greene novel – *A Gun for Sale*, from 1936.

Part 1: ‘I like thrillers’ (Anne Crowder, *A Gun for Sale*)[1]

The literary context concerns where the novel sits in Greene’s development as a writer. *A Gun for Sale* was published in July 1936, his seventh novel. He had started writing it

This is a slightly adapted version of an essay posted on the Graham Greene Birthplace Trust website, 2 October 2020.

[1] Graham [illegible]

after his return from his trek across Liberia in 1935 and finished it, we know, on 4 January 1936, during a very busy period, which also included seeing through to publication his previous novel *England Made Me*, the writing of his travel book *Journey Without Maps* and of various short stories, extensive book reviewing and, now, film reviewing for the *Spectator*. *A Gun for Sale* was written with all the confidence and speed of youth – he was now in his early thirties – and a growing experience as an established writer who was finding his voice. He had a wife and daughter to support, and soon, a son too, and he was making the most of his writing talent. In 1935 Greene and his family had moved from Oxford to 14 North Side, Clapham Common, now perhaps for the first time confident of being able to earn a full-time living with his pen. *A Gun for Sale* helped in that – sales of the hardback were not remarkable (5,000 copies in the UK, 2,100 in the United States), but startlingly the film rights to the novel were sold to Paramount even before publication for the tidy sum of £2,500. (It was eventually made into a film in 1942.)

There is one other thing to point out about the publication of *A Gun for Sale*. It was the first Greene book to be given the formal title 'Entertainment', signalling the intention of something popular and commercial; *Stamboul Train* was similarly now listed as an Entertainment, while *The Man Within*, *It's a Battlefield* and *England Made Me* were Novels. These categorizations suggest that by the mid-1930s Greene was for the first time publicly acknowledging that his career was that of a writer, someone whose works could be listed and put into different categories of literary aspiration. In calling *A Gun for Sale* an 'Entertainment', Greene's priorities with the book were clear: he was indulging his penchant for melodrama and aiming at a commercial market, without much pretension of literary merit. Greene referred to *A Gun for Sale* as a 'thriller'[2] or a 'shocker'; whether it is more than that remains to be seen.

What Greene had come up with, in plot terms, was a John Buchan-style double chase. James Raven, a hired killer, assassinates a central European politician and thereby sparks off a general European crisis leading, it seems, to war. However, he has been paid in stolen currency, so he pursues those who have tricked him, and he finally tracks down the Mr Big – Sir Marcus, head of a steel firm in the English Midlands who had ordered the killing precisely to provoke a war crisis and boost his company's profits. In turn, Raven is pursued by the police. He comes across a showgirl and a whole range of secondary characters and situations, leading eventually to a denouement in which Raven kills two more people, including Sir Marcus, but is shot himself. The war crisis subsides as quickly as it has arisen.

Such a bald plot summary scarcely does full justice to the book, but it does point to one element of Greene's progress as a writer – that by 1936 he still had not got a proper sense of a plausible plot. Critics are right to point, for instance, to some pretty big coincidences in the story. The showgirl Raven kidnaps, Anne Crowder, just happens

2 Graham Greene, *Ways of Escape* (Harmondsworth: Penguin, 1981), p. 54.

to be the fiancée of Mather, the policeman pursuing Raven. Davis, Raven's paymaster, is also the financial backer of the revue Anne is appearing in. Davis, pursued by Raven, happens to catch the same train out of London as Anne. Various characters involved in the plot intersect by chance at a church jumble sale. Much later, we learn that Sir Marcus attended the same orphanage as the politician he has had killed. Most comical of all is an extraordinary plot detail: Davis discovers that Anne Crowder is in cahoots with Raven, and, in a manner not described, he pushes her up a chimney; there she is discovered accidentally the following day by Raven himself; and within moments of being released, Anne is as briskly cheerful as if nothing has happened. By my reckoning it is easily the most bizarrely implausible plot detail in all Graham Greene's books. Perhaps it is some kind of private joke on Greene's part.

So like the later 'Entertainments' *The Confidential Agent* and *The Ministry of Fear*, Greene's thriller is rather too reliant on coincidence and implausibility, but it nevertheless forms a tightly structured, gripping tale: *A Gun for Sale* is under much firmer authorial control than, in particular, *The Confidential Agent*. The opening section, in which Raven kills the Minister and his secretary, is a brilliant tour de force – short sentences, action clearly and concisely rendered, a classic example of the cinematic qualities of Greene's writing; perhaps the best opening section in all of Greene's novels. Much of the novel is set at night and/or in fog, giving it a suitably noir feel. The book also shows Greene's command of the cliffhanger and keeping the reader waiting – at one point we are left wondering what has happened to the endangered heroine Anne for over thirty pages; and later, a student rag day plays out while we are unsure of Raven's whereabouts in his pursuit of Sir Marcus. Here is Greene in control of the thriller form.

By 1936 Graham Greene had also mastered one of his trademark skills as a writer – the depiction of place. Much of the novel is set in Nottwich, his name for the Nottingham he lived and worked in in the mid-1920s, and here is his wonderful description of early morning Nottwich one December, as a train pulls in:

> There was no dawn that day in Nottwich. Fog lay over the city like a night sky with no stars. The air in the streets was clear. You had only to imagine that it was night. The first tram crawled out of its shed and took the steel track down towards the market. An old piece of newspaper blew up against the door of the Royal Theatre and flattened out. In the streets on the outskirts of Nottwich nearest the pits an old man plodded by with a pole tapping at the windows. The stationer's window in the High Street was full of Prayer Books and Bibles: a printed card remained among them, a relic of Armistice Day, like the old drab wreath of Haig poppies by the War Memorial: 'Look up, and swear by the slain of the war that you'll never forget.' Along the line a signal lamp winked green in the dark day and the lit carriages drew slowly in past the cemetery, the glue factory, over the wide tidy cement-lined river. A bell began to ring from the Roman Catholic cathedral. A whistle blew.[3]

3 Greene, *A Gun for Sale*, p. 26

That seems to me to be a Graham Greene who has found one part of his authorial voice.

There is another feature of *A Gun for Sale* which is quite typical of Greene the novelist and little remarked on. Writing about the 1930s in *Ways of Escape*, Greene refers to 'my early passion for playwriting which has never quite died'. He continues,

> In those days I thought in terms of a key scene – I would even chart its position on a sheet of paper before I began to write. 'Chapter 3. So-and so comes alive.' Often these scenes consisted of isolating two characters ... It was as though I wanted to escape from the vast liquidity of the novel and to play out the most important situation on a narrow stage where I could direct every movement of my characters. A scene like that halts the progress of the novel with dramatic emphasis, just as in a film a close-up makes the moving picture momentarily pause.[4]

Greene suggests that this typical set-up began for him in *Stamboul Train*, with the scene of Coral Musker and Dr Czinner in a railway shed; and there are other examples in his later fiction, from Harry and Rollo atop the Prater Wheel in *The Third Man*, to Fowler and Pyle in the watchtower in *The Quiet American*, to Jones and Brown alone in the cemetery in *The Comedians* and the long scenes of kidnappers and victim in a hut in *The Honorary Consul*. In *A Gun for Sale* the equivalent scene takes place between Anne and Raven in a railway shed in the course of a cold night. Their conversation gives us background to Raven's poor upbringing and his sour outlook on life and gives the hired gun a new insight into the man he has killed; it even covers belief in God and the nature of dreams. Crucially, it leads Raven to trust Anne, and to enlist her help in evading the police and hunting down Sir Marcus. It is a remarkable scene, one which occupies about 10 per cent of the whole book, and it is part of a long tradition in Greene's writing.

Raven's conversation with Anne about God and prayer is part of a religious theme in the novel that is worth mentioning. Graham Greene was famously irritated when critics suddenly labelled him a 'Catholic writer' after discovering religious themes in *Brighton Rock*, rejecting the label and feeling as if no one had read any of his earlier work. *A Gun for Sale* bears out this irritation. It is perhaps no coincidence that the plot unfolds in the days leading up to Christmas, which allows Greene to put into Raven's mind and mouth his reactions to the Christian story. In particular, there is a long passage where Raven stops outside a religious shop in whose window is a plaster display of Madonna and Child in the stable and books of devotion. He reacts with bitter anger, remembering his own brutal treatment in a children's home, reflecting: 'They twisted everything; even the story in there, it was historical, it had happened, but they twisted it to their own purposes. They made him a God because they could feel fine about it all, they didn't have to consider themselves responsible for the raw deal they'd given him.' So Raven feels a 'horrified tenderness' towards 'the little bastard', born like Raven to be double-crossed.[5] The religious element in *A Gun for Sale* is not as thoroughgoing as in *Brighton Rock*, but it is there nevertheless, embedded in the thriller format.

[4] Greene, *Ways of Escape*, p. 25.

[5] Greene, *A Gun for Sale*, p. 85.

Finally on matters literary, some words about Greene's characterizations in *A Gun for Sale*. It is striking how many of the support characters are caricatures or grotesques or have tantalizing backstories, as if Greene has more imagination than he can quite cope with. There is a stammering policeman. There is Dr Vogel, the backstreet surgeon. There is Mollison, Sir Marcus's valet, who hates his master. There is Joseph Calkin, the fat, excitable Chief Constable of Nottwich who yearns once more for the power to run the local military tribunal. There is Davis, a man with a greed for cakes and showgirls. There is Buddy Ferguson, the second-rate medical student who organizes the student rag in Nottwich. And there is Acky, the deranged, defrocked clergyman and his evil wife, Tiny, who run a bawdy house – characters so startling that they jump off the page and threaten, like Minty in *England Made Me*, to highjack the story.

In contrast there is Jimmy Mather, the policeman who hunts down Raven. Greene writes in *Ways of Escape* that he can imagine Mather 'to have been trained as a police officer under the Assistant Commissioner of *It's A Battlefield*';[6] in just the same way we might think his girlfriend Anne Crowder to be a friend of the plucky, good-natured chorus girl Coral Musker in *Stamboul Train*. Mather is a PC Plod who has been promoted – efficient and dull, ordinary and predictable. The closest he comes to a personal motto is 'it's the routine which counts',[7] and we are told that his response to his fiancée Anne is not love, but 'a dumb tenderness'.[8] As for Anne: that good-natured, resourceful chorus girl knows how to get out of a tight corner, survives three attempts on her life and having spent a night wedged up a chimney is within minutes of her rescue able to turn a gun on Acky and effect her escape. I think Judith Adamson's wait for Aunt Augusta would not have been so long had she considered *A Gun for Sale*: Anne Crowder is easily the sparkiest Greene female before *Travels with My Aunt*.[9] And though the book ends with Anne returning home with Mather and sighing, 'Oh … we're home',[10] it is impossible to believe that their marriage will be contented. Anne would have to leave her plodding hubby or just die of boredom. Her future is little brighter than Rose's at the end of *Brighton Rock*.

Then there is the central character James Raven, a lonely, tormented young man, emotionally cold and alienated from society. He has a harelip and has never been with a woman; his criminal father was hanged, and his mother committed suicide. He has had a brutalized childhood; he is as efficient a killer as that other James, Mather, is a policeman; and he has no moral scruples – 'Murder didn't mean much to Raven.'[11] He responds to Anne, the first person who ever trusts him, but ultimately he remains a

6 Greene, *Ways of Escape*, p. 57.

7 Greene, *A Gun for Sale*, p. 33.

8 Ibid., p. 68.

9 See Judith Adamson, 'The Long Wait for Aunt Augusta', in *Dangerous Edges of Graham Greene: Journeys with Saints and Sinners*, edited by Dermot Gilvary and Darren J. N. Middleton (New York: Continuum, 2011), 210–21.

10 Greene, *A Gun for Sale*, p. 182.

11 Ibid., p. 1

cold-hearted killer who must meet justice. Most critics have seen Raven as an earlier version of Pinkie in *Brighton Rock* – as Graham Greene himself did. This is Greene on Raven, in *Ways of Escape*:

> Raven the killer, seems to me now a first sketch for Pinkie in *Brighton Rock*. He is a Pinkie who has aged but not grown up – doomed to be juvenile for a lifetime. They have something of a fallen angel about them, a morality which once belonged to another place. The outlaw of justice always keeps in his heart the sense of justice outraged – *his* [original emphasis] crimes have an excuse yet he is pursued by the Others. The Others have committed worse crimes and flourish. The world is full of Others who wear the mask of Success, of a Happy Family. Whatever crimes he may be driven to commit the child who doesn't grow up remains the great champion of justice. 'An eye for an eye.' 'Give them a dose of their own medicine.' As children we have all suffered punishments for faults we have not committed, but the wound has soon healed. With Raven and Pinkie the wound never heals.[12]

Raven as a Pinkie who has aged but not grown up is an interesting idea – Raven seems to be in his late twenties, while Pinkie, remarkably, is only seventeen. There is another link with Pinkie, too, in that Raven confesses to Anne that he cut the throat of a rival racecourse gang member, Kite – a murder which of course provides a mainspring for the plot of *Brighton Rock*, since Pinkie is a protégé of Kite. As for Raven believing that his crimes have an excuse, as Greene writes, there is of course his brutalized childhood and background, and Raven certainly comes to believe that 'others have committed worse crimes and flourish' – specifically Sir Marcus, the man behind Raven's assassination mission to central Europe. So Raven becomes not so much a fallen angel as a vengeful one, and while we do not exactly approve of his activities, we have perhaps sympathy for his vengeance, and certainly none for Sir Marcus. From the very first pages of *A Gun for Sale*, Raven is an interesting and memorably chilling character and one well depicted by Alan Ladd in the 1942 Hollywood film version of the book.

The man Raven tracks down and finally kills, Sir Marcus, is the most controversial of all in the novel. He is next in the line of Greene's big businessmen, after Carlton Myatt in *Stamboul Train* and Erik Krogh in *England Made Me*. A very old, frail man, Sir Marcus is one of the wealthiest in Europe. He has mysterious origins: Greene tells us, 'He spoke with the faintest foreign accent and it was difficult to determine whether he was Jewish or of an ancient English family. He gave the impression that very many cities had rubbed him smooth.' In him, too, 'there was a touch of Jerusalem'.[13] We are elsewhere told that 'Sir Marcus had many friends, in many countries',[14] including it seems those in positions of power – friends who like him would do very well from the slide to war and the increased demand for metals and armaments. All this, and the

12 Greene, *Ways of Escape*, pp. 56–7.
13 Greene, *A Gun for Sale*, p. 103.
14 Ibid., p. 111.

added detail that Sir Marcus was a Freemason, has led Cedric Watts to conclude that 'it seems depressingly obvious that Greene is offering the old anti-Semitic myth of a world-conspiracy of wealthy Jews to profit by war and death'.[15] It was a conspiracy theory current in the 1930s and had been applied also to the war of 1914. Greene seems to go out of his way to avoid saying that Sir Marcus was a Jew – his origins are shrouded in mystery, obfuscation, contradiction, but Greene does not help his case with the phrase 'his nose was no evidence either way'.[16] Certainly in later editions of the novel, Greene made no alterations to his depiction of Sir Marcus, and one is left at the very least with an uncomfortable feeling on the matter. I will return to Sir Marcus later.

Part 2: 'Men were fighting beasts, they needed war …' (A thought of Anne Crowder, *A Gun for Sale*)[17]

My second type of context is that of the historical background to *A Gun for Sale*. The book was written in 1935 and published in 1936, and the immediate historical context is the growing threat of war in Europe. In particular, there was a growing feeling that if Europe did get plunged into war, civilians would be under threat of air attack. In the First World War, British civilians had been bombed from the air by German Zeppelins and Gothas. In 1924 the Committee of Imperial Defence set up a subcommittee called Air Raid Precautions (ARP) to see how the civilian population could be protected from aerial attack, and over the next ten years the need was identified for gas masks, air raid shelters, evacuation of children and the blackout. Nor was this merely a bureaucratic concern: the threat of the bomber was part of ordinary people's consciousness by the mid-1930s. As early as 1932 Stanley Baldwin had famously remarked on the uselessness of air defences in protecting civilians: 'the bomber will always get through'. The Italian use of poison gas during the invasion of Abyssinia in 1935–6 reminded people of the dangers. In 1936, the year that Greene's novel was published, the popular and influential film *Things to Come*, based on the book by H. G. Wells, presciently showed a great world war breaking out in 1940 and characterized that war as the indiscriminate slaughter of civilians in an air raid. Greene's own review of *Things to Come* in 1936 comments on the 'horribly convincing detail' of the raid – 'the lorry with loudspeakers in Piccadilly Circus urging the crowd to go quietly home and close all windows and block all apertures against gas, the emergency distribution of a few inadequate masks, the cohort of black planes driving over the white southern cliffs, the crowd milling in subways, the dreadful death cries from the London bus, the faceless man in evening dress dead in

[15] Cedric Watts, *A Preface to Greene* (Harlow: Longman, 1997), p. 119.

[16] Greene, *A Gun for Sale*, p. 105.

[17] Ibid., p. 17[illegible]

the taxi'.[18] These appalling scenes in a widely seen film told British filmgoers what to expect if war happened, and the events of the Spanish Civil War soon confirmed their worst nightmares: the air attack on the Basque town of Guernica in 1937 saw to that.

In *A Gun for Sale*, Greene has a long scene in Nottwich in which there is an air-raid drill during which civilians are required to put on their gas masks – which in turn gives an opportunity for Raven to hide his harelip as he seeks out Sir Marcus. Writing this scene in 1935, Greene himself was being remarkably foresighted. Despite the fear of air attack on civilians, air-raid drills were scarcely heard of in 1935, and it was only in that year that a Home Office Committee was set up to coordinate the response to possible gas attack by air; and that same year saw the first government circular inviting local authorities to plan to protect people in times of war. But the Air Raid Wardens Service was not to be created until 1937, and local councils were not compelled to create ARP services until 1938. The readers of *A Gun for Sale* would thus have found Greene's extensive depiction of a gas air-raid drill novel, frightening and, as time went on, remarkably prescient. Yet there is an irony here. Civilians were indeed targeted by bombs in the Second World War, in Britain, Germany and elsewhere, but these were bombs that caused destruction and fire, not gassing. For reasons never wholly explained, gas attacks on civilians were not a feature of the new warfare of the Second World War. Greene's emphasis on preparing for gas attack on civilians may have accurately foretold things to come, but such attacks never actually happened. Forty million gas masks in Britain proved unnecessary.

In the historical context of 1935–6, *A Gun for Sale* may also be seen as prescient in foreseeing a war on the horizon. War is averted in the novel, but there is a feeling at its end that the political tensions in the air will not go away and that peace may be no longer-lasting than the upcoming marriage of Anne Crowder and James Mather. 'This darkening land', Greene writes, 'was safe for a few more years'[19] – not a very comforting assurance.

Certainly, in the world outside Greene's novel, there were plenty of suggestions in 1935–6 that peace was under threat. Japan had invaded Manchuria in 1931, and Italy invaded Abyssinia in 1935. Hitler remilitarized the Rhineland in March 1936, breaking the terms of the Versailles Treaty, and the Spanish Civil War began a few months later. Noises of war were all around. Yet here again there is something of a paradox, for the war crisis in Greene's *A Gun for Sale* does not look forward to the Second World War but back to the First. In the novel, a Czech Minister for War is assassinated, for which a Serb is blamed, followed by an ultimatum which is accompanied by mobilization and increasing war fever as the clock ticks down. This is 1914 being replayed – Princip's assassination of the Archduke, Austria's ultimatum, the countdown to war into which

18 *Spectator*, 28 February 1936. The full review can be read in *The Graham Greene Film Reader: Mornings in the Dark*, edited by David Parkinson (Manchester: Carcanet, 1993), p. 78.

19 Greene, *A Gun for Sale*, p. 181.

many countries will be drawn. In fact, Greene's novel repeatedly goes out of its way to emphasize the parallels with the crisis of 1914 and its aftermath. Speaking of war, Anne says, 'The last one started with a murder.'[20] 'It always seems to be the Balkans,' another character says.[21] There are repeated references to No Man's Land and one to 'the front trench'.[22] The Mayor of Nottwich wears his Mons Medal and his Military Medal, and we are told that he had been wounded three times in the last war. The Chief Constable seems to relish the prospect of a new war in which he can resume his First War role of presiding over the local military tribunal and giving the pacifists a hard time. Sir Marcus reminiscences about the armaments needed for Haig's assaults on the Hindenburg Line and reflects how in the war crisis Midland Steel is now more valuable than ever since November 1918, the end of the last war. And in the extract earlier describing early-morning Nottwich, there are references to Armistice Day, Haig poppies and the local War Memorial. If there is to be a second war, Greene seems to be saying, it will be one in the shadow of the first one, indeed one not unwelcome to all. Graham Greene of course belonged to that generation which was too young to have fought in the First World War, but old enough to have heard the long lists of former pupils of his school who had lost their lives in the war. So his war crisis has none of Hitler and Mussolini but much of Franz Ferdinand and Field Marshal Haig.

Then in *A Gun for Sale* there is the specific motive behind the war crisis. There are vaguely drawn political tensions in Europe, but these are brought to the point of war by a political assassination, deliberately engineered to boost the profits of the makers of steel and armaments. Sir Marcus's company is in a bad way: 'It's Midland Steel made this town,' a character says; 'But they're ruining the town now. They *did* employ fifty thousand. Now they don't have ten thousand.'[23] So Sir Marcus concocts his plan to have a politician shot and provoke a war. 'Probably within five days,' Sir Marcus muses, 'at least four countries would be at war and the consumption of munitions have risen to several million pounds a day.'[24]

If this plot device of Greene's seems far-fetched, some historical context may be of help. The treaty-makers at Versailles in 1919 saw the arms race among European powers as a background cause of the First World War, and the restrictions on German military might were intended to be part of a much more widespread process of disarmament, in which all countries would take part. More specifically, there was a left-wing critique which by the 1930s saw the last war, and possible future war, as the product of capitalism itself, in its drive for profits. Some authors identified and criticized the close links and vested interests shared by European governments and big arms companies such as Vickers in Britain, Krupp in Germany, Skoda in

20 Ibid., p. 5.

21 Ibid., p. 27.

22 Ibid., p. 9.

23 Ibid., pp. 54–5.

24 Ibid., p. 11[illegible]

Austria-Hungary/Czechoslovakia and Schneider-Creusot in France. In the years before Greene published his novel, a whole series of books was written exploring these links – these included *Death and Profits* (1932), *The Bloody Traffic* (1933), *Salesmen of Death* (1933), *Iron, Blood and Profits* (1934) and *Merchants of Death: A Study of the International Armaments Industry* (1934). In the United States, there were claims that profit-hungry arms manufacturers had unduly influenced America's decision to enter the First World War and that this might happen again in the future, so the Senate created the Nye Committee in 1934 to investigate the sale of munitions in that war.[25] At the same time in the UK, a so-called 'Peace Ballot', organized in Britain during 1934–5 and focusing on issues of the League of Nations and Collective Security, asked as one of its questions, 'Should the manufacture and sales of armaments for private profit be prohibited by international agreement?' Over eleven million people responded to the question, and over 90 per cent said 'yes'. With these books and that vote as a background, a Royal Commission enquiry was set up in Britain in 1935 to look at the issue of making and selling arms for private profit.

The Royal Commission on the Private Manufacture of and Trading in Arms met in Middlesex Guildhall, the building in Parliament Square which now houses the UK Supreme Court. In 1935–6 it had twenty-two sessions of evidence-gathering and cross-examination, with contributions from a range of organizations and individuals. Lord Robert Cecil, who had attended the Disarmament Conference at Geneva in 1927, testified that

> the influence of armaments firms tends to dampen the actual effort for peace. There had been cases in which active steps had been taken by great armaments interests to prevent the conclusion of disarmament negotiations. The most startling case was that of Mr Shearer who was employed by certain great firms in America to prevent the conclusion of the disarmament conference in Geneva in 1927.

In further testimony, Lord Cecil referred to the Chaco Wars between Bolivia and Paraguay, during which British armaments manufacturers had been supplying both sides and, effectively, fomenting the war. Former prime minister David Lloyd George asserted that rearming doubles the holding value of a company, whereas disarmament halves it. He argued that profiting from the sale of arms was immoral and called for a state monopoly of arms production and sales. When the Royal Commission published its report in October 1936, it recommended unanimously that there should be more state control over the armaments industry. The report was quietly shelved, and little done.[26]

This is the background to Graham Greene's tale of Sir Marcus and war fever. And Greene himself had a direct interest in these goings-on. One of the witnesses before

25 More details on the Nye Committee can be found at https://en.wikipedia.org/wiki/Nye_Committee.

26 More details on the Royal Commission can be found at https://armingallsides.org.uk/case_studies/the-arms-trade-on-trial/. The full minutes of its proceedings can be found at https://archive.org/details/np00610010/page/n21/mode/2up.

the commission was Fenner Brockway, whose book *The Bloody Traffic* had been critical of the armaments manufacturers Vickers in particular. Brockway was giving evidence on behalf of his left-wing political party, the Independent Labour Party (ILP). Greene himself was a member of the ILP for a few years in the mid-1930s, and he attended some of the sessions of the Royal Commission on armaments in the Middlesex Guildhall. In *Ways of Escape*, Greene writes that he cannot remember whether he attended because he was writing *A Gun for Sale*, or whether it was his attendance that gave him the idea. Either way, his attendance testifies to his interest in the issues surrounding the armaments industry. In *Ways of Escape*, he comments on the lacklustre nature of the commission's proceedings, writing:

> My chief memory of the hearings is of the politeness and feebleness of the cross-examination. Some great firms were concerned and over and over again counsel found that essential papers were missing or had not been brought to court. A search of course would be made … there was a relaxed air of *mañana*.[27]

Although he was critical of the proceedings, Greene realized from the hearings that here was a useful background to his planned thriller. His readers may not be as well versed in these issues as Greene himself, but the books on the armaments industry, the Peace Ballot and the Royal Commission would give his plot a plausible topicality.

Did Greene have any real-life equivalent in mind for his evil industrialist Sir Marcus? One of the likeliest candidates seems to be the notorious arms dealer Sir Basil Zaharoff. Born in Greece in 1849, Zaharoff died peacefully in his bed, protected by bodyguards, in 1936, the year *A Gun for Sale* was published. He was one of the richest men in the world during his lifetime and was described as a 'merchant of death' and 'mystery man of Europe'. His success was forged through his cunning, often aggressive and sharp business tactics. These included the sale of arms to opposing sides in conflicts, sometimes delivering fake or faulty machinery and reportedly sabotaging trade demonstrations. He sold munitions to many nations, including Britain, Germany, Russia, Turkey, Greece, Spain, Japan and the United States. Zaharoff worked for Vickers, the British munitions firm, from 1897 to 1927, including during one of its boom periods during the First World War. And he cultivated political friends – by 1915 he had close ties with David Lloyd George of the UK and Aristide Briand of France. Graham Greene is known to have read a biography of Zaharoff, and he was willing to declare in *Ways of Escape* that 'Sir Marcus in *A Gun for Sale* is not, of course, Sir Basil, but the family resemblance is plain'.[28]

What are we to make of this historical context of Greene's 1936 novel? My suggestion is that we should see *A Gun for Sale* as more than just a thriller but as having real political bite. In particular, I would draw attention to two features of Greene's plot. The

27 Greene, *Ways of Escape*, p. 54.

28 Ibid., p. 55.

first revolves around Sir Marcus. He is an emotionally empty, misanthropic bad man, but Greene is at pains to emphasize that he is part of a wider network of power. He is able to try to blackmail or bribe the chief constable into ensuring the police shoot to kill Raven, for instance. And his network is international: as war fever grows and Midland Steel's share price rockets, Greene tells us this:

> Sir Marcus had many friends, in many countries; he wintered with them regularly at Cannes or in Soppelsa's yacht off Rhodes; he was the intimate friend of Mrs Cranbeim. It was impossible now to export arms, but it was still possible to export nickel and most of the other metals which were necessary to the arming of nations. Even when war was declared, Mrs Cranbeim had been able to say quite definitely, that evening when the yacht pitched a little and Rosen was so distressingly sick over Mrs Ziffo's black satin, the British Government would not forbid the export of nickel to Switzerland or other neutral countries so long as the British requirements were first met. The future was very rosy indeed, for you could trust Mrs Cranbeim's word. She spoke directly from the horse's mouth, if you could so describe the elder statesman whose confidence she shared.[29]

Here we have Sir Marcus not as an isolated misanthrope but as part of an international nexus of powerful people with friends in high places. As already mentioned, Cedric Watts is distressed by what he sees as the tired anti-Semitism of this passage, and it is hard to disagree. But beyond that, what we have depicted here is international capitalism, red in tooth and claw and utterly amoral, unable or unwilling to see the dead bodies behind the glowing figures of the company balance sheet. *A Gun for Sale* at heart has a remarkably left-wing view of the world.

The second feature of Greene's plot that feeds into this world-view concerns Raven himself. He is a hired killer, no more, no less, and we are told at the very beginning of the book that 'Murder didn't mean much to Raven'. He was good at his job, he was being paid, so he did not need to ask who he was killing, or why. But in the long confessional scene with Anne in the railway shed, Raven begins to change his mind. Anne tells him about the politician he had killed:

> Old what's-his name. Didn't you read about him in the papers? How he cut down all the army expenses to help clear the slums? There were photographs of him opening new flats, talking to the children. He wasn't one of the rich. He wouldn't have gone to war. That's why they shot him. You bet there are fellows making money now out of him being dead. And he'd done it all himself too, the obituaries said. His father was a thief and his mother committed –
>
> 'Suicide?' Raven whispered.[30]

[29] Greene, *A Gun for Sale*, pp. 111–12.

[30] Ibid., p. 118.

So the scales fall from Raven's eyes. Here was a man from a similarly poor background as himself, a self-made man who has become a socialist politician and done good in the world. And Raven had killed him, at the behest of profiteering capitalists. Raven is apolitical no more; he becomes aware of social and political realities, becomes more than just a hired killer. As Raven later prepares to take his revenge and kill Sir Marcus, he tells him, 'I wouldn't have done it … if I'd known the old man was like he was.'[31] By the end of the novel, Raven has become a left-wing avenger, killing the international capitalist who had set him up.

We should not push this analysis too far. *A Gun for Sale* is, as Greene says, an Entertainment first and foremost, a thriller or shocker, melodramatic and designed to sell film rights to an American studio; hence, no doubt, a scene of British policemen firing guns on British streets. But just as Greene later dropped the division of his works into Entertainments and Novels, seeing it as having no fundamental validity, so also we should not be blinded by the thriller form into ignoring what else *A Gun for Sale* offers. In *Ways of Escape*, Graham Greene wrote of the period 1933–7 as 'the middle years for my generation, clouded by the Depression in England … and by the rise of Hitler. It was impossible in those days not to be committed.'[32] Impossible not to be committed: Greene's own words. Critics have seen *It's a Battlefield*, published in 1934, as Greene's first political novel, part of this commitment. But we should see *A Gun for Sale* in the same way, the product of a writer who had joined the ILP and attended meetings on the trade in armaments. *A Gun for Sale* is a thriller, but it is a left-wing political novel too, a critique of international capitalism and what it does to the disadvantaged. In the end, at least, murder did mean much to Raven.

31 Ibid., p. 161.

32 Greene, *Ways of E[illegible]*

'Treating the contemporary world with poetic realism': Graham Greene and *It's a Battlefield*

Jon Wise

Greene wrote *It's a Battlefield* (1934) in just under eleven months – an extraordinary feat when compared, for example, with the twelve years he took to write *The Human Factor* (1978). Naturally, circumstances were very different in the late 1960s and 1970s when the wealthy novelist could afford the time to labour over what he freely admitted was a very difficult book to complete.[1] By contrast, Greene describes 1932 and 1933 as a period of great personal anxiety. *The Name of Action* (1930) and *Rumour at Nightfall* (1931) had lost money and *Stamboul Train* (1932) was still in manuscript form. His biography of the Earl of Rochester had been rejected, he had just twenty pounds in the bank and his wife Vivien was expecting their first child.[2]

Although Greene recalls *It's a Battlefield* as making 'slow progress', examination of the original holograph shows comparatively few changes made.[3] This fact, together with the very short time spent writing, might well be explained away as a combination of the urgency he felt about his precarious financial situation and a youthful absence of inhibition. On the other hand, this novel shows the writer experimenting with an ambitious shift in style. More so than its immediate predecessor *Stamboul Train*, the novel moves dramatically away from the imagined world of *The Name of Action* and *Rumour at Nightfall* he came to deplore to one firmly grounded, in the case of *It's a Battlefield*, in the London of the 1930s. He had partially achieved the realism he was seeking in *Stamboul Train* through the experience of travelling as far as Cologne by train. Greene notes in *Ways of Escape* that the allotments outside Bruges really existed

This essay was first published in an abridged form in *A Sort of Newsletter*, Issue 65, February 2016.

1 Greene voiced his overall dissatisfaction with *The Human Factor* to several people. The Harry Ransom Center (HRC), University of Texas, Sybille Bedford Papers, 1973–8. In 1978, in thanking the writer and journalist Sybille Bedford for her generous review he told her how he had nearly abandoned the novel after twenty-five thousand words and after eventually finishing was still unhappy with it.

See also Georgetown University (GU), *Leopoldo Durán Papers*, Box 1, 1964–90. In 1977 he told Durán that he had just completed *The Human Factor* but was not satisfied with it and was undecided whether or not to offer it for publication.

2 Graham Greene, *Ways of Escape* (London: Bodley Head, 1989), pp. 30–1. Greene's biography of John Wilmot, Second Earl of Rochester, was eventually published in 1974. HRC Graham Greene Collection, Box 37, Folder 1, Diary, 1932–3.

3 HRC Graham Greene Collection, Box 20, Folder 1, *It's a Battlefield*, [illegible]

in April 1931. On the other hand, he adds, his readers should not have any confidence in his description of Subotica on the Yugoslavian border.[4]

He was able to draw on recent experience of living in the capital city when writing *It's a Battlefield*. He moved from Nottingham to London in 1926 having secured a job with *The Times* and found lodgings in South London. Although other locations in the capital feature frequently in the novel – Soho, Trafalgar Square, Camden Town – Greene's descriptions of the neighbourhood around his flat in Battersea stand out. This was 'blue-collar' London, its narrow streets full of densely packed, terraced houses. Thus Candahar Road, Kabul Street, Khyber Terrace, each name resonant of the era in which it was built, are not figments of Greene's imagination or even an amalgam of experiences.[5]

In one episode in the novel Conrad Drover, whose brother is facing a death sentence for killing a policeman, walks from Central London to Battersea. The precise details of his route from Oakley Street in Chelsea, along the Thames Embankment and over 'the curve of Battersea Bridge', are described with the compression yet minute attention to detail for which the writer subsequently became famous.[6] Greene would have passed that way on countless occasions. In a passage in an early typescript of *A Sort Life*, later deleted, he describes 'escaping' the newspaper offices around ten o'clock in the evening, spending some time in the West End before hopefully catching the late bus back to Battersea. Otherwise he faced the long walk home which would have taken him along a similar route to that described in the novel.[7]

Greene mentions in his 1932–3 diary that he paid research visits to two London prisons, Wormwood Scrubs and Wandsworth, in October and December 1933: 'Took a bus out to Wandsworth Prison to inspect the terrain for Opus V.'[8] The establishment described in the episode where the Commissioner visits Drover is unmistakably Wandsworth Prison with its 'square buildings' and 'tall hexagonal tower'. His eye for verisimilitude is impeccable as in the phrase 'a train went by unseen past the allotments, and the nursery gardens'. Although the allotments have disappeared, the Victorian-era plant nursery thrives to this day while the Victoria Line runs next to the prison in a cutting. ' "Odd to hear that in your cell," the secretary said with a touch of gloom.'[9]

The only feature in the Battersea area which seems not to have existed was the match factory off Battersea Rise. Research fails to reveal a factory in the locale which might fit Greene's description. However, the first Bryant and May factory in Bow in the east end of London did feature a tall, square tower. The knowledge of the interior workings of such a place, where the character of Kay Rimmer endures the long hours until her shift ends, was gained through Greene's visit to a match factory in Gloucester while he

4 Greene, *Ways of Escape*, p. 27.

5 Battersea has changed considerably since the 1920s, and 141 Albert Palace Mansions in Lurline Gardens, an extensive Victorian-era red-brick block where Greene rented a one-bedroom apartment, is now an expensive and highly desirable address.

6 Graham Greene, *It's a Battlefield* (London: Heinemann, 1934), pp. 14/15 and 78/79.

7 HRC, Graham Greene Collection, Box 31, Folder 9, *A Sort of Life*, undated, typescript.

8 HRC, Graham Greene Collection, Box 37, Folder 1, Diary, 1932–3.

9 Greene's description of the locale is particularly precise as he describes the last part of the car journey to Wandsworth Prison. The straight Spencer Park Road runs alongside the railway cutting, and the bulk

was living in nearby Chipping Campden. He was invited to tour the factory following a letter of complaint about a box of the firm's products which had 'exploded' in his hand.[10] Greene's description in *It's a Battlefield* based on his visit shows that little had changed in the intervening forty-four years since the London match-girls strike of 1888 at the Bow factory, which had been caused by poor working conditions, including fourteen-hour work days, poor pay and excessive fines. Norman Sherry quotes a letter Greene wrote to Vivien about his experience in Gloucester. He thought the working conditions for the girls far worse than incarceration in Wormwood Scrubs prison.[11]

The building exists to this day in Bristol Road, an unadorned district of Gloucester, yet still within sight of the gothic splendour of the city's medieval cathedral. In 1913 Bryant and May took over the business previously owned by S.J. Moreland and Sons whose distinctive red, white and blue 'England's Glory' matchboxes featuring the pre-dreadnought HMS *Devastation* had been a household brand for a number of years. Greene describes in the novel how the 'hundred blue-and-white match-boxes jumped from the machines on to a great moving stair'. The Gloucester factory closed in the 1980s.[12]

In *Ways of Escape* Greene admits that, following the two notable failures mentioned above, he needed to escape the influence that Joseph Conrad had imposed on his writing. He expresses embarrassment at his weak imitation of Conrad's style and particularly his clumsy overuse of metaphor and simile.[13] But what drew him to experiment instead with an entirely different approach to novel writing, to conveying realism in the way which is characteristic of *Stamboul Train* and *It's a Battlefield*? There are clues to be found which add to what he wrote in his autobiographies. In September 1965 Greene was asked to write a tribute to François Mauriac. A typescript copy of his short essay has survived. He notes that in 1932 he had read Mauriac's novel *Le Noeud de Vipères* (*The Knot of Vipers*) (1932) when it first appeared in translation, 'with an excitement which I can remember to this day'. It was not the religious theme which had stirred his imagination but rather 'the possibility of treating the contemporary world with poetic realism, the poetic realism which I had admired in the Elizabethan and Jacobean dramatists'. Greene writes that Mauriac's novel had enabled him to find a fresh purpose which aided him in the arduous task of writing.[14]

In 1934, a few months after *It's a Battlefield* was published, Greene wrote an essay entitled 'The Seed Cake and the Love Lady'. It was published in *Life and Letters* magazine as a riposte to the writer Charles Morgan whose own essay championing the

of the Gothic Revival Royal Victoria Patriotic School for Girls could have been mistaken for the prison. Greene, *It's a Battlefield*, pp. 14–15.

10 Ibid., pp. 29–33; Paul Hogarth, *Graham Greene Country* (London: Pavilion, 1986), p. 28.

11 Norman Sherry, *The Life of Graham Greene: Volume 1, 1904–1939* (London: Jonathan Cape, 1989), p. 461.

12 Greene, *It's a Battlefield*, p. 29.

13 Greene, *Ways of Escape*, pp. 13–20.

14 Boston College, Graham Greene Papers, Box 17, Folder 35, Correspondence with François Mauriac, 1951–70. Greene had responded to a request by Michel Droit, one time [illegible]

virtues of the aesthetic novel had appeared in the previous issue.[15] Quoting Henry James who had said that the object of novel writing was about 'catching the very note and trick … the strange irregular rhythm of life',[16] Greene argues the case for a middle course to be set between what he describes as 'extreme aestheticism' and the kind of 'extreme social preoccupations' to be found in overly politically focused novels. He makes an oblique reference to that exchange of views in *Ways of Escape*, describing himself as 'a reformed rake' when he had attacked Morgan – barely three years after *Rumour at Nightfall* had been published with its disastrous and false obsession with style.[17]

It's a Battlefield is certainly not written as straightforward narrative; in places Greene adopts what was at the time the fashionable modernist approach. Yet Roger Sharrock considers the novel's themes to be the closest he came to writing a political novel in the interwar years.[18] Taken together, these two elements suggest that the writer was indeed trying to adopt the 'middle course' he had advocated in 'The Seed Cake and the Love Lady'.

It is often claimed that in Greene's fourth published novel, *Stamboul Train*, the writer had 'found his voice' thus implying that thereafter his unique style became fixed. There is enough evidence to show that this was not the case. Rather the period between 1932 and 1936 might be regarded as a time of experimentation. *Stamboul Train*, *It's a Battlefield*, *England Made Me* (1935) and *Journey Without Maps* (1936) together with the short story 'A Day Saved' (1934) and the startlingly different yet strangely neglected *The Bear Fell Free* (1935) all attest to this fact in varying degrees. Before Greene became a published writer he was already experimenting with the novel form. *The Episode*, which most likely dates from 1925–6, was a historical novel whereas the fragment of *Fanatic Arabia* (*c.*1927–8) that survived is firmly set in current-day 'Boxstead', which, with its canal, common and castle, is unmistakably Berkhamsted.[19]

His lasting admiration for Mauriac is expressed in his essay 'Francois Mauriac', in Graham Greene, *The Lost Childhood and Other Essays* (London: Eyre and Spottiswoode, 1951), pp. 69–73.

Greene was particularly admiring of Jacobean drama. He singles out John Webster's *The Duchess of Malfi* and 'the keen, economical, pointed oddity of the dialogue'. Graham Greene, *British Dramatists* (London: William Collins, 1942), pp. 22–5.

15 Graham Greene, 'The Seed Cake and the Love Lady', in *Life and Letters: The florin Magazine*, vol. x, no. 56 (1934): 517–24.

'Graham Greene, a Personal View'. An 'Unlocking Archives' talk given by Nicholas Dennys at the Balliol College Historic Collections Centre, 8 June 2015. Dennys described 'The Seed Cake and the Love Lady' as his uncle's 'manifesto for all his later writing'. Greene told him that fiction was about 'catching the reality of all human life'.

Charles Morgan had given a talk entitled 'A Defence of Story-Telling' to the Royal Institute of Great Britain in February 1934; his essay in the July edition of *Life and Letters* was no doubt based on that talk.

16 Henry James, *The Art of Fiction* (Longman's Magazine, 1884).

17 Greene, *Ways of Escape*, p. 19.

18 Roger Sharrock, *Saints, Sinners and Comedians: The Novels of Graham Greene* (Tunbridge Wells: Burns & Oates, 1984), pp. 58–70.

19 GU, Graham Greene – Catherine Walston Collection, Manuscripts, Box 57, Folders 1–6, undated, holograph. Greene based his narrative on the nineteenth-century Spanish Carlist Wars. He subsequently used material he had gathered from the rejected novel in both *The Name of Action* and *Rumour at Nightfall*. HRC, Graham Greene Collection, Box 12, Folder 2, 'Fanatic Arabia', undated, holograph fragment.

A House of Reputation: Graham Greene's 'last significant play'

Jon Wise

On 15 December 1987, Greene wrote to Roger Sharrock, a retired English professor at King's College, London, 'I have in fact got another play already although it has not yet found a producer but it will be published anyway sometime in the New Year. It is called "A House of Reputation" and the setting is a brothel in Central America. Perhaps that should be called my last significant play.'[1]

The three-act play has only been seen once on stage in front of a live audience in the form of a rehearsed reading.[2] This essay examines the surviving manuscripts, its long and unusual genesis and Greene's lifelong fascination with the theatre. It ends with a discussion as to whether this writer, at a very late stage in his life, was justified in his determination that this work should be published and performed.

A House of Reputation takes place on the ground and first floors of what Greene describes as an old-fashioned 'house' or brothel in an anonymous Central American city. The first act introduces us to the various members of a large cast and advances the plot involving a rich but naïve young student (Martín) who falls hopelessly in love with Marta, a sex worker at the brothel.[3] Martín's growing obsession becomes the focus in Act 2 as he tries to persuade her to leave her place of work and marry him. We gradually learn that his father is the Minister of the Interior, part of a repressive dictatorship which rules the country. In Act 3, Martín, frustrated by Marta's continuing

1 The British Library (BL), Western Manuscripts. Letter: Graham Greene to Roger Sharrock, 15 December 1987. Greene thought highly of Professor Sharrock's book of literary criticism, *Saints, Sinners and Comedians: The Novels of Graham Greene* (Tunbridge Wells: Burns and Oates Press, 1984), calling it 'easily the best critical study of my work'.

2 The rehearsed reading took place in the Deans' Hall, Berkhamsted Collegiate School, 30 September 2000, in front of an audience of attendees of the Third Graham Greene International Festival, an event organized annually by the Graham Greene Birthplace Trust. The 2000 Graham Greene festival director was Roger Watkins who 'discovered' the play in the John J. Burns Library at Boston College. He commissioned Lee Marsh and David Pearce to prepare a 'script in hand' for a cast of local amateur actors who performed the rehearsed reading.

The event was introduced by Bryan Forbes, the film director and a friend of Graham Greene. He was familiar with *A House of Reputation* having been asked by Greene to read the script with a view to a possible TV or stage production. Subsequently, he purchased the rights to the drama. See BL, Bryan Forbes & Graham Greene Correspondence 1970–91: Letter Greene to Forbes, *c.*1987.

3 Originally, the cast numbered fifteen but various [illegible]

rejection, blackmails his father into closing down the brothel by threatening to pursue his relationship with the girl. However Marta, in a dramatic climax to the play, dismisses him finally in favour of an impoverished old man, confusingly also named Martín, who visits the brothel weekly mostly seeking solace and company rather than sexual gratification.

What sets *A House of Reputation* apart from most of Greene's other writings is that the dominant as well as the most rounded characters are both female: the brothel's Madame (Lili) and Marta.[4] Judith Adamson, in her seminal essay on Greene's female characters, 'The Long Wait for Aunt Augusta', analyses the succession of women who appear in his work and assesses the extent to which they are more than mere adjuncts of their male partners.[5] In effect, most of Greene's women characters are, to some degree, dependent on or linked emotionally to males – even, one could argue, Aunt Augusta herself. On the other hand, the 'disposable' prostitutes Lili and Marta, despite earning their livings through selling their bodies to men, are only dependent through financial exchanges.[6] For Marta, there is an element of choice.

Marta: It's work like any other work. I haven't the talent for nursing, and I'm bored with embroidery. What do you want me to do? Learn to type and earn two hundred a day?[7]

When Marta does not have sex with Martín, she says,

Marta: You can have your fifty back. I haven't earned it, have I?
Martín: 'If I take it back, I haven't bought you, have I?'

For a moment she does not understand. Then she smiles – it is a professional triumph – and holds out her hand.[8]

The 'reputation' of Lili's brothel rests, it seems, on the quiet reliability and safe service it provides for a small, regular clientele. The 'house' is unadorned and shabby in appearance as highlighted by Lulu, the madame of a rival establishment in nearby Jeronimos Street,

4 Professor Neil Sinyard describes the play as being 'a sympathetic piece, with unusually strong female characters'. See Neil Sinyard, *Graham Greene: A Literary Life* (Basingstoke: Palgrave Macmillan, 2003), p. 137 (endnote).

5 Judith Adamson, 'The Long Wait for Aunt Augusta: Reflections on Graham Greene's Fictional Women', in Gilvary, Dermot and Middleton, Darren J. N. (eds), *Dangerous Edges of Graham Greene: Journeys with Saints and Sinners* (New York: Continuum International, 2011), pp. 210–21.
In her essay, Adamson refers to Greene's 'writer-narrator' (p. 221). Uniquely in Greene, this play's narrative uses a woman's 'voice'. Interestingly, the Berkhamsted production took liberties with the script by 'creating' a female narrator.

6 Ibid. Adamson refers to '(Greene's) prostitutes, being, we might say, disposable' (p. 210).

7 Graham Greene, *A House of Reputation*, Manuscript dated 20 November 1986. Washington, DC, Georgetown University, Lauinger Library, The Graham Greene Papers, Series 5, Box 2,72. There are almost identical copies of *A House of Reputation*, in a mixture of holograph, typescript and photocopy formats, located in the Greene archives at Boston College, The University of Texas at Austin and Georgetown University, Washington, DC.

8 Ibid., p. 28.

Lulu: I came here to see if you might have thought up a few new ideas. And what do I find? A pianola, an old gramophone – not even any pictures on the wall to stimulate the appetite. This isn't the 19th century, Lili.[9]

Lili, we are told, 'has a determined face and a manner accustomed to authority. She might well be the headmistress of a fashionable school'. The Doctor, paying his weekly visit to examine the health of the girls, remarks that their well-being is because 'she looks after her family properly'. To which Lili sharply retorts, 'I teach them to look after themselves.'[10]

Indeed, far from being simply a caricatured 'tart with a heart', Lili's ruthless side emerges triumphant in the verbal duel with her old rival Lulu from their streetwalking days on National Square. A set-piece scene in Act 2 climaxes when Lili plays a recording of 'The Jeronimos Street Blues', parts of which are played or sung intermittently to highlight the reality of the lives of these women,

They fished me out for good near Jeronimos Street
From beneath one bridge or the other.
The men in the bar heard police cars bleat,
But who bothered to turn?
it was only another
More naked
than the law allows.[11]

The bluntness of the lyrics seems to reference the recent 'accident' involving one of her girls: 'A client struck too hard. Too many times. The girl went out and drowned herself.' This proves too much for Lulu. She flees amid a torrent of acrimony on both sides. Lili does not appear in Act 3 once her brothel has been shut down. Had she, too, taken her own life? Marta says simply, 'She didn't seem desperate when she left here. Just reasonable. Thinking of the future.'[12]

If the Madame's character is both pragmatic and enigmatic, Marta, beneath her professional façade, emerges as a brittle and rather disturbed individual. For her, the house is a refuge. We are told she is older (in her early thirties) and is certainly more mature and intelligent than the other girls. When asked by Lili why she works in a brothel, she remarks, 'For easy money, For a home. Because I hate all this fuss people make about love.'[13] The words 'home', 'hate' and 'love' betray the inner turmoil which seems to have driven this character beyond even the realms of despair. In the course of a diatribe against

9 Ibid., p. 58.
10 Ibid., pp. 2 and 4.
11 Ibid., p. 61.
12 Ibid., p. 75.

all forms of emotion, she says, 'I'd like to lie down before men as I would before a charge of cavalry. I want to have no features left. Something men have ridden over and gone.'[14] Marta provides some evidence of the root of this negativity, bordering on nihilism, 'My mother taught me how to hate. She hated me, she hated the man she couldn't remember whom she got me with, she hated the surgeon who refused to wash me out.'[15]

Even if Lili, who has to listen to this bilious outpouring, says at the end, 'You talk of hate all the time. Sometimes I think you've got your words mixed up and what you mean is love,' this does not come close to changing Marta's mind. The ending of the play, with Marta seeking womb-like comfort with the impotent 'old Martín', may seem both trite and sentimental, but it does not detract from a powerful portrayal of a troubled woman.

The other girls in the establishment are by comparison minor characters, one-dimensional in contrast to Marta's developed personality. Likewise, there are no male characters to match the complexities of Marta and Lili. Young Martín, who claims at one point to have learned a great deal in the past week 'watching how the world wags', shows little sign of character maturity beyond the archetypal lovelorn youth.[16] The Police Captain who appears briefly at the start of Acts 1 and 3 is simply used by Greene as a kindly and sympathetic ear for Lili in her battle to keep the house functioning.

Dr Candolo is perhaps the exception. He is yet another dentist in a succession of Greene's fictional creations and interestingly follows on from Dr Victor Rhodes in the 1959 play *The Complaisant Lover*.[17] However, unlike the tragi-comic personality of Greene's earlier play, Candolo cuts an unpleasant, unctuous figure. He is strongly disliked by the girls: when the Maid spots him she automatically 'spits on the floor'.[18] When Lili tells him he is no longer welcome, he protests that he is an old and regular customer. He then reveals, 'I am ashamed to pay money to a woman like this. I am ashamed to do – a thing like that.' Lili probes the source for this self-deprecation,

Madame: Is this wisdom you learn from looking into people's mouths?

Candolo: Perhaps it is. One scrapes and drills and repairs. Tartar, pyorrhoea, the effect of rich foods. I peer into the crannies for decay – it's not a pretty job. And I can't make love prettily, Madame. No – I am ashamed.[19]

[14] Ibid., p. 52.

[15] Ibid., p. 53.

[16] Ibid., p. 65.

[17] Michael Billington, 'The Plays of Graham Greene', in *Dangerous Edges of Graham Greene*. Billington writes about the character of Victor Rhodes in Graham Greene, *The Complaisant Lover* (London: Heinemann, 1959), pp. 244–5.

In 1964, Greene wrote a collection of short passages about himself, later abandoned, which may have been preliminary work for his autobiography. Amongst them are comments on his apparent predilection for including dentists in his writings. 'I always seem to come across dentists. In life and in my work. They always crop up. The first person I met in Mexico City was one. He took me to a brothel and showed me his own girl's teeth. Like most things, one doesn't invent one's own dentists – they happen.' The Mexican dentist may well have been an inspiration for Dr Candolo. See the University of Texas, The Graham Greene Collection, 'Places, Etc.' (undated).

[18] Greene, *A House of Reputation*, p. 2.

[19] Ibid., pp. 30–1.

Candolo returns briefly to the house in Act 3 and is similarly rejected, this time by Marta. Again he tries to explain,

Candolo: You don't understand, Miss. Those ugly dreams. Here, too I used to have dreams, but happy dreams. But when I woke I was always afraid someone, one of my patients, would see me here – one of those mouths. And those mouths would laugh.[20]

These two grimly comedic scenes involving Candolo provide rare lighter moments in the play. Nevertheless, Lili's 'house of reputation' is at the top of the city's pecking order: superior to the modern but risky 141 Jeronimos Street or the downright dangerous National Square. But in Act 3, with the brothel closed down, Marta is faced with the prospect of returning to the National Square. She asks for protection from the Police Captain. Benevolently, if cautiously, he agrees, 'Yes, I'll try to protect you. If the high-ups allow me.'[21] The reality of that proposition is neatly summarized earlier in Lili's recollection of her streetwalking days on National Square:

> My beat was fifty yards – west east. North and south belonged to others. I mustn't trespass unless I wanted a bunch of keys across my face. When a man spoke to me, he spoke to me out of the corner of his mouth. … Will you do this and that? Ashamed to be seen with me, and we carried the shame with us in our cab, and up the stairs to my room – a bed, a ewer and basin, one hard chair, used for business only.[22]

Inevitably, given its Central American location, the Catholic Church is seen as integral to people's lives. Ironically, Lili's party at the brothel is to be held to mark the Feast of the Immaculate Conception. The maid sits telling her rosary beads between customers while prostitution generally is an accepted part of the warp and weft of society, alongside other parts of the economy. Martín recalls a conversation at home,

> One day at dinner a charitable Monsignor said to my father it would be unjust if the penalties against the street walkers were increased and people like you (Lili) should go relatively free. The street walkers were good girls who went often to Confession and didn't work on a Sunday but came to Mass. Money again, you see, in the collection bag.[23]

Greene introduces an atmosphere of anonymity by using homophonic names and pseudonyms for his characters. The effect might well confuse an audience watching the events of the play unfold for the first time. Young Martín is 'christened' by Marta after his older namesake, but we never learn his true identity. In turn he calls Marta 'Elena' in

20 Ibid., p. 77.
21 Ibid., p. 78.
22 Ibid., p. 31.

honour of the Ancient Greek beauty Helen of Troy. Marta herself uses a pseudonym and refuses to reveal her birth name. The names Lili and Lulu are not only almost identical like their occupations but both are referred to throughout as 'Madame' while the Police Captain, though a weekly visitor, is known only by his occupation.[24]

A House of Reputation was first mentioned in a letter from Greene to his theatrical agent Jan van Loewen on 12 August 1957,

> If Binkie wants a play for the Watergate let him wait a few weeks and take my brothel play! The first draft of the first two acts will be in type in the course of the next ten days and the third act will only take a fortnight to do – this apart from revising of course, but he could get some idea whether he wanted it.[25]

Greene then made a mistake by sending a copy of the unfinished script to the American theatre director Carmen Capalbo in New York. During November 1957 two letters were sent by Greene's secretary to Capalbo asking for its return. One read, 'Mr. Greene was most anxious that it should be floating around New York.' A final one followed couched in a much firmer tone, 'He also says that unless it is returned at once he will not feel under any obligation to show you further drafts.'[26]

Greene received no reply. Norman Sherry interviewed Capalbo concerning the script. He had been granted first refusal rights on Greene's next play following the success of *The Potting Shed* but weighing up the likely financial prospects against the artistic merits of *A House of Reputation* decided to turn it down. He attributed Greene's later denial of the existence of such a play to the 'hurt and upset' he felt at this rejection.[27]

Greene appeared to abandon the play in a matter of weeks. Writing from Canada on 6 January 1958, he told his French agent Marie Biche that it had 'not progressed at all' and

24 The various manuscript copies of the play show evidence that Greene changed the names of several of his characters at different times. Martín was originally Maurice, Marta was Marie, Dr, plain Señor Candolo.

One can only speculate on the choice of Jeronimos Street for the site of the notorious brothel. There are the obvious associations with St Jerome, said to be patron for virtually every cause, country, profession or special interest, which might be considered appropriate given the cosmopolitan nature of brothel life. On the other hand, when choosing the name, Greene could have recalled from his wartime SIS service on the Portuguese desk. The magnificent Jerónimos Monastery, now a World Heritage site, is situated west of central Lisbon.

25 Boston College, Boston, Massachusetts (BC): Graham Greene Papers. Letter: Graham Greene to Dr Jan van Loewen, 12 August 1957.

Greene makes reference to Binkie Beaumont, who was one of the most successful and influential manager-producers in the West End at the time, and to the New Watergate Club. In 1957, in a theatre world overshadowed by the Lord Chamberlain's powers to ban or edit a play deemed to be unsuitable, a number of 'Theatre Clubs', private membership clubs, were formed, among them the New Watergate Club which was based at the Comedy Theatre (now the Harold Pinter Theatre). Given the subject matter of *A House of Reputation*, it is hardly surprising that Greene would make this suggestion as a suitable venue for his play.

26 Ibid. (BC), Letters Doris Young to Margaret McCall 27 November 1957 and 2 December 1957 to Carmen Capalbo 2 December 1957. There is no evidence to show that the script was ever returned.

Greene had been impressed by Capalbo's work on *The Potting Shed*. (BC) Letter to Donald Albery, 30 January 1957. Capalbo was noted for his revival of *The Threepenny Opera* for which he won a Tony Award in 1956 and another Tony in 1957 for *The Potting Shed*.

27 Norman Sherry, *The Life of Graham Greene Volume 3, 1955–1991* (London: Jonathan Cape, 2004), p. 302.

he was not completely sure he would 'ever go with it'. The play required a great deal of rewriting although he admitted that perhaps it was his current black mood that made him dubious.[28] In a brief public statement published as a letter to *The Stage* newspaper on 5 June of that year he sought to quash speculation which had circulated that it had existed in the first place.[29]

After that there is no mention of *A House of Reputation* in Greene's correspondence or other papers until a note he made in his diary in December 1984 where he commented that he had been busy all day working on a cassette of the last act of the play, 'something to leave behind although insufficiently revised'.[30] A further three years then elapsed before, in December 1987, following the remark made by Roger Sharrock (quoted above and presumably referring to the disastrous *Carving a Statue* [1964]), Greene informed him that he had finally completed his brothel play, some thirty years after he wrote the first two acts. If his notoriously faulty memory is to be believed, he finished it sometime between June and December of that year. He had mentioned an 'unfinished play' in a letter to Sharrock on 16 June 1987 adding that he doubted whether an agent 'would be able to place it' as the play required a sizeable cast of twelve.[31]

Why had it taken so long to write? It would seem that the task of completing the last act proved far more difficult than expected despite the hubristic comment in his letter to van Loewen in 1957. He admitted as much to Christopher Hawtree the next year,

> I think in 1958 I had abandoned A House of Reputation because I couldn't find an ending to it. About a year ago I took it up again, liked it, and the ending seemed obvious. However, I haven't been able to find a producer perhaps partly it necessitates a difficult set and a lare (*sic*) cast.[32]

Close examination of the manuscripts held at the University of Georgetown particularly provides the best evidence that the play was worked on in two distinct phases. An undated photocopy of acts 1 and 2, thirty-eight and thirty-one pages in length, respectively, appears to date from the 1950s. There is evidence of revision with occasional handwritten pages substituted for typescript and holograph character name changes. Other folders in the same file more obviously date from the 1980s as a different typescript to the photocopy has been used and holograph corrections are inserted in blue rather than the earlier black ink. These include a heavily corrected, seven-page holograph version of act 3 and folders containing revised pages from all three acts. One folder is conveniently dated 20.11.86.[33]

28 Balliol College Archive, Marie Biche Papers, Letter: Greene to Biche, 6 January 1958.

29 Sherry, *The Life of Graham Greene Volume 3*, p. 301. Greene wrote, 'Not only have no arrangements been concluded, but no play has been written and I am not planning to write any play with this title. I have no plans whatever for a play in the foreseeable future.' Almost exactly a year later *The Complaisant Lover* was first performed at the Globe Theatre in London suggesting that Greene was being either deliberately secretive or deliberately disingenuous in this statement about his future plans.

30 BL, *Graham Greene Diaries Volume 2 1986-87*, Diary Entry, 4 December 1984.

31 BL, Letters, Graham Greene to Roger Sharrock 16 June 1987 and 15 December 1987.

32 The University of Texas: Harry Ransom Center (HRC), Graham Greene Collection. Letter to Christopher Hawtree, 19 December 1988.

33 Jon Wise and Mike Hill, *The Works of Graham Greene Volume* [illegible]

Greene had a lifelong passion for the theatre. He wrote in 1961, 'My life as a writer is littered with discarded plays, as it is littered with discarded novels.' In the same introduction to a collected edition of his plays he enthuses over the 'excitement and frustrations of casting, the grim interest of auditions when every line became more leaden, the first reading with the complete cast, the conferences and changes over coffee, the delight of working with players interested not only in their own parts but the play as a whole'.[34]

Although no trace remains of a comedy involving a kidnapping during the Japanese occupation of Manchuria in 1931 which is mentioned in the same preface, there is evidence of at least three other abandoned dramas of various lengths in the Greene archives. *The Clever Twist* consists of eight pages of dialogue together with two pages of notes for what was planned to be a three-act 'melodrama' set in an unspecified democratic republic, 'somewhere in the Far East'. It is undated but the fact that two pages are on Greene's headed Albany notepaper indicate that it was written after 1953. *Horror Comic* comprises three holograph pages of another planned three-act play, this one dated 1 November 1956. The setting is a 'middle-class living room' with a 'bedroom/ workroom above'. Only one foolscap page of script exists of *Oh Damn Your Morality!* Greene's notes indicate that this was to be yet another three-act play; an amusing three-way conversation between removal men and a woman, who is simultaneously holding a conversation on the telephone with an unseen person, points to a comedy.[35]

The dates on two of these 'fragments' suggest these abandoned projects may well have been written in the flush of success following Greene's first West End play, *The Living Room* (1953). By contrast, the failure of *Carving a Statue* a decade later seemed to bring an end to his involvement with this medium. Greene's notes in his accompanying 'Epitaph for a Play' appear conclusive: 'This play was never fun and I earn my living in another field.'[36] However, this was not to be the end of his career as a playwright. *The Return of A.J. Raffles* followed in 1975 and the double-bill *Yes and No* and *For Whom the Bell Chimes* in 1980.

Neil Sinyard states that *A House of Reputation* has 'something of the flavour and atmosphere of Jean Genet's "The Balcony"'. It seems more than coincidental that the first translated version of *Le Balcon* was performed at the Arts Theatre Club in London in 1957, the same year as Greene first mentioned his 'brothel play'.[37] Did he watch the production with its similarly powerful leading female character? Genet's sinister and unsettling depiction of brothel life is more akin to Jeronimos Street than Madame Lili's genteel establishment although both plays share the premise that the customers are encouraged to leave their troubled lives behind them when they step over the threshold.

34 Graham Greene, *Three Plays* (London: Mercury, 1961), pp. vii and x.

35 HRC, Graham Greene Collection.

36 Graham Greene, *Carving a Statue: A Play* (London: Bodley Head, 1964), p. 7.

37 Sinyard, *Graham Greene: A Literary Life*, p. 137 (endnote).

Interestingly, Genet's own very early childhood, born to a prostitute in a brothel and subsequently rejected by his mother, has echoes of Marta's upbringing and the source of her sour outlook on life.

For someone who seemed to frequent brothels on his trips round the world as others might take holiday snaps or 'selfies', Greene used such places sparingly in his prose fiction. In *The Comedians*, Mere Cathèrine's is a shack located on some scrubland outside the capital. Brown describes Cathèrine as 'the kindest woman I knew in Port-au-Prince'. There are other similarities with Lili's brothel in *A House of Reputation*, including the way the clientele are expected to behave and the care taken with the well-being of the girls. However, in the novel, the level of menace is much greater during Brown's visit with the presence of the dreaded Tontons Macoute inside the building itself - 'making a night of it'.[38] In contrast, Señora Sanchez's establishment in *The Honorary Consul* has the airy, relaxed feel of a country club. Any threat is far less evident, although we learn that despite the brothel being 'protected by the authorities' it was best not to leave one's car outside in case the number was noted by a policeman – 'Such an addition to one's police file might one day prove undesirable.'[39]

Graham Greene appeared to be very optimistic when he claimed in late 1988 that *A House of Reputation* just lacked a sympathetic producer prepared to take on a production requiring a large cast and complicated set. On the evidence of the surviving manuscripts, his play needed an amount of work before being ready for performance. More pertinently, despite the economic recovery that followed the early 1980s recession in the UK, one might question whether there would have been the necessary financial backing at the time for an ambitious drama by an ageing author much better known as a novelist.

Michael Billington, in the course of a perceptive assessment of Greene's plays, states that date-wise *The Living Room* and *The Potting Shed* (1957/58) respectively stand astride the point when 'the English theatre underwent a series of profound changes', adding that 'in London the balance of theatrical power gradually began to shift away from the West End … towards the Royal Court in Sloane Square and the Theatre Royal in Stratford'. Plays such as Samuel Beckett's *Waiting for Godot* (first staged in Paris in 1953) showed that it was possible to dispense with such traditional theatrical 'staples' as plot, action and elaborate scenery.[40] In truth, *A House of Reputation* is heavily reliant on those supports. Indeed, all his dramas, with the possible exceptions of *Yes and No* and *For Whom the Bell Chimes*, lean towards that centuries old 'proscenium arch'

38 Graham Greene, *The Comedians* (London: Bodley Head, 1966), p. 155. Greene naturally enough uses his experience of brothels to add verisimilitude. In his description of such an establishment, in a suppressed chapter of *A Sort of Life* in which he recalls one in Conduit Street, Central London, 'the door was always opened by a tidy maid' and 'unlike a French brothel no one was pressed to order champagne'. There is a maid in *A House of Reputation* while the sale of 'champagne' to the customer is considered mandatory. HRC, Graham Greene Collection, *A Sort of Life*, no date, typescript.

39 Graham Greene, *The Honorary Consul* (London: Bodley Head, 1973), p. 65.

40 [illegible]

convention which Greene had grown used to in his youth rather than towards the avant-garde movement that grew from the theatrical revolution of the mid-1950s.

Norman Sherry devotes a chapter to this play which for those who missed the performance at Berkhamsted referred to above must have come as a revelation when they first read his book being an unknown complete play. Sherry mainly devotes the chapter to recounting the plot, but he does offer an opinion as to whether the brothel depicted is merely a figment of the writer's imagination. In a rather tentatively worded critique, he writes, 'the play is quintessential Greene: curious, witty, fascinating and reflecting his view of brothels (at least the type represented here) as being both unique and necessary. One might think that such a place deserves to exist, but surely, in life, could not'.[41]

A close reading of the surviving text of *A House of Reputation* reveals the familiar occasional shortcomings of Greene the playwright: the dialogue is sometimes laboured and 'stagey', lacking the acuity of observation and economy of language which typify his prose. Nevertheless, the play, with its pertinent social commentary, unusual setting and particularly its strong female characterization, is a fascinating and an almost completely unknown part of the Greene canon which regrettably is likely to remain that way.

41 Sherry, *The Life of Graham Greene Volume 3*, p. 301.

An old man's memory: The strange case of *The Tenth Man*

Mike Hill

In March 1985 Graham Greene's short novel *The Tenth Man* was published in the UK with great fanfare. Here was a new work from the Grand Old Man of English Literature, now eighty years old – and, remarkably, a work actually written in the 1940s and, it was reported, newly discovered. Greene wrote a short introduction to the published novel, relating how he had heard of the sale of the story in 1983 and remembered only 'an outline' he had written for the film company MGM towards the end of the Second World War: an outline of 'two pages of typescript'. When sent the complete typescript, Greene found to his amazement 'not two pages of outline but a complete short novel of about thirty thousand words'. Moreover, Greene wrote, he found 'this forgotten story very readable – indeed I prefer it in many ways to *The Third Man*'.[1] No wonder *The Tenth Man* became something of a publishing sensation in 1985.

The idea that Greene had simply forgotten about the novel – that it was the victim of 'An Old Man's Memory', to use the title of one of Greene's own short stories – has been questioned. In particular, Michael Shelden, in his 1994 biography *Graham Greene: The Man Within*, as ever led the case for the prosecution against Greene. 'There was nothing wrong with Greene's memory, and the novel had not been lost,' Shelden wrote, quoting some evidence to this effect; 'The "discovery" of *The Tenth Man* allowed Greene to have some fun at the expense of journalists who think only in terms of headlines. And, of course, there was always the added benefit of increased sales from the publicity.'[2] In turn, Shelden's account has been challenged by W. J. West in his 1997 book *The Quest for Graham Greene*. 'Greene's papers at Boston College', West wrote, 'demonstrate beyond doubt' that Shelden's version of the case was untrue. *The Tenth Man*, West asserted, was simply an 'astonishing example of Greene's very weak memory of his own work'.[3]

Where is the truth in all this? The natural instinct in researching such matters relating to Greene's life and work is to refer to the late Norman Sherry's monumental

This is a slightly amended version of an article which appeared in *A Sort of Newsletter*, Issue 81, February 2020, pp. 2–8.

1 Graham Greene, 'Introduction', in *The Tenth Man* (Harmondsworth: Penguin, 1986), pp. 9–11.

2 Michael Shelden, *Graham Greene: The Man Within* (London: Heinemann, 1994) [illegible]

3 [illegible]

three-volume biography, at least as a starting point. In this case, no help is forthcoming. Astonishingly, Sherry mentions *The Tenth Man* just once, in a parenthetical reference of less than two lines,[4] and there is no reference to the novel in the index or even in the listing of Greene's work. If Greene was guilty of forgetting about the novel for very many years, his first biographer went one better.

For guidance we must instead look at the various archives containing Greene material, in particular the one at Boston, referred to by West. It is worth pointing out at the outset that Michael Shelden did not visit the archives at Boston College, for the simple reason that Boston had not yet then (1994, when Shelden's work was published) acquired its Greene material.

The Boston archive gives some detail of Greene's original writing of *The Tenth Man.* There is a typescript of the novel, sent by Greene's literary agent Laurence Pollinger to MGM's agent in London, Ben Goetz, on 19 December 1944.[5] This was in part fulfilment of what Greene later described as 'an almost slave contract',[6] wherein he had agreed with MGM to provide story ideas for two years. Greene had returned to England from duty with the Secret Intelligence Service (SIS) in West Africa in 1943 and resigned from the service altogether in June 1944. He was aware of the need to generate some income. He started work at the publisher Eyre & Spottiswoode in summer 1944, and in February 1944 he had signed a contract with MGM. Greene would produce ideas for stories which might become films, and the stories would then become MGM's copyright – hence perhaps his reference to a 'slave contract'. Under the contract, MGM would pay him £250 per week for not less than ten consecutive weeks in two years. (And rather bizarrely, the contract specified that Greene would not be called upon to 'work on the script of WAR AND PEACE by Leo Tolstoy'.)[7]

Nothing seems to have come of this contract by the time Greene left the SIS in June 1944, but in that month, V-1 flying bombs began to fall on London, where Greene was living most of the time. His wife and children were safe in Oxford, but Greene seems to have been genuinely concerned that he might die at any moment with his family unprovided for. 'All our expectations of life these days are a little uncertain,' Greene wrote to Laurence Pollinger in July 1944, and he suggested ways his family might be provided for 'in the event of death', by various reissuings of his existing writings.[8] But the MGM contract represented another way of making money, by Greene writing something new.

What might he write? In a fragmentary diary he kept in the 1930s, Greene had recorded this:

4 Norman Sherry, *The Life of Graham Greene: Volume I, 1904–1939* (London: Jonathan Cape, 1989), pp. 589–90.

5 Burns Library, Boston College, Graham Greene Papers: MS1995-03; Series V: Literary Works; *The Tenth Man*, Box 60, Folders 20–3.

6 Greene, *The Tenth Man*, p. 9.

7 Burns Library, Gerald Pollinger to Graham Greene, 22 July 1983.

8 Harry Ransom Center, University of Texas at Austin, David Higham and Associates papers, Box 11, Graham Greene to Laurence Pollinger, 1 July 1944.

> December 26.[9] Discussed film with Menzies [an American film director]. Two notions for future films. One: a political situation like that in Spain. A decimation order. Ten men in prison draw lots with matches. A rich man draws the longest match. Offers all his money to anyone who will take his place. One, for the sake of his family, agrees. Later, when he is released, the former rich man visits anonymously the family who possess his money, he himself now with nothing but his life.[10]

Here, of course, is essentially the plot of *The Tenth Man*, originally conceived in the context of the Spanish Civil War, but nothing had come of it in the 1930s. Now, in the summer of 1944, in need of ideas for possible films, the story emerged from what Greene called 'the dark cave of the unconscious'.[11] Following D-Day, France was being swiftly liberated – the German garrison in Paris surrendered on 25 August – and Greene now conceived his story based in France and in the context of the Second World War. By August 1944 Greene was writing to Ian Dalrymple at MGM's London office, suggesting that he might be able to write 'a long short story' of about twenty thousand to twenty-five thousand words, to be finished in around three months.[12] By 6 November a new contract was signed to cover the story, with Greene being paid £1,500 and copyright in the story assigned to MGM.[13] By that date Greene was within seven thousand words of finishing the story (having gone through 'a very sticky phase' with it, as he wrote[14]). He seems to have been put under pressure by MGM to get the story finished and sent off, and there is evidence that some of the writing was rushed – the character Thérèse is sometimes called Pauline; Greene had no time for revision, it seems.[15] By December the story was at last finished, copies were made and it was on its way to MGM in Hollywood.[16]

MGM never made *The Tenth Man* into a film, and Greene's contract with the company finally came to an end. He moved on to pastures new, and the typescript of *The Tenth Man* gathered dust in the MGM archives in Hollywood. Then in 1981, a man called Sam Marx discovered the manuscript at MGM, and in the two years following, Greene began to hear stories about it. In June 1982, he was interviewed by the academic Judith Adamson for her book on Greene and the cinema: the interview resulted in the sentence 'And MGM is reconsidering making a film of *The Tenth Man*' in her book.[17]

9 Greene puts the year as 1937, but it is actually 1936.

10 Lauinger Library, Georgetown University, Graham Greene Papers 2, Series 5, Manuscripts for Major Works, Boxes 2–3. Box 3 has the original journal, which was reprinted as 'While Waiting for a War' in *Granta* 17 (Autumn 1985).

11 Greene, *The Tenth Man*, p. 11.

12 Harry Ransom Center, David Higham and Associates papers, Graham Greene to Ian Dalrymple, 22 August 1944.

13 Burns Library, Gerald Pollinger to Graham Greene, 22 July 1983.

14 Harry Ransom Center, David Higham and Associates papers, Graham Greene to Laurence Pollinger, 6 November 1944.

15 Lauinger Library, Box 2.

16 Burns Library, Gerald Pollinger to Graham Greene, 22 July 1983.

17 Information from Professor Judith Adamson in emails, 4, 6 and 7 November 2020. The interview was conducted on 21 June 1982, and the quotation is from Judith Adamson, [illegible]

Whether Greene already knew this, or learnt it from Adamson, is not clear. In January 1983, Greene received a letter from Professor David Leon Higdon, a fellow Conradian with whom he corresponded. Higdon reported that the work had been discovered, that it was to be published in England later that year and that a film studio had secured the rights. Interestingly, Greene's secretary replied in April that rumours about the work had been heard – but tantalizingly, with no details. Greene heard in May that the British publisher Anthony Blond had bought the publication rights for £12,000, and Greene's agent Gerald Pollinger gave him details of his 1944 contract with MGM. Greene did not want the book to be published, but in November 1983 he read the story, provided for him by Blond. Greene's publisher Max Reinhardt became involved, and by January 1984 it was agreed that it would be jointly published by The Bodley Head and Anthony Blond. This is what happened in 1985. In the meantime, Greene had heard from Sam Marx, telling his tale of the discovery and inviting Greene to write the screenplay for a film version. Greene turned him down.[18]

And so the 'discovered' book was published in 1985, alongside two 'film sketches' of other Greene stories, *Jim Braddon and the War Criminal* and *Nobody to Blame*. Greene wrote a brief introduction, recording his surprise at learning that what he had remembered as 'an outline' covering 'two pages of typescript' was in fact a substantial novella.[19] The publication, and the tale of the discovery, caused quite a stir in literary circles. Keith Waterhouse wrote, 'I was struggling over a half-cooked novel when I read that someone had turned up a 60,000-word [*sic*] manuscript that Graham Greene had written years ago and *forgotten about* [original emphasis]. I thought briefly about doing away with myself. To me, forgetting having written a book is like forgetting having had heart surgery.'[20] For Michael Shelden, as we have seen, Waterhouse's incredulity was well founded. To forget a very substantial story, even after a gap of almost forty years, was inconceivable, he believed.

In the Greene archives in Boston and Texas is evidence that might seem to support Shelden's scepticism. A manuscript copy of *The Tenth Man* at the Harry Ransom Center in Austin, Texas, was sold to the university in June 1967,[21] so the idea that the story simply gathered dust at MGM until 1981 is certainly untrue. As Shelden points out, a bibliography of Greene's work by R. A. Wobbe published in 1979[22] included a reference to the unpublished work *The Tenth Man*, and it seems certain that Wobbe had seen the manuscript in the Austin archive. There is no evidence to show that Graham Greene himself knew of the bibliography's reference to *The Tenth Man* and, more frustratingly, no evidence that he knew of the sale of the manuscript to the Harry Ransom Center in 1967. That sale was a single-item purchase, and there is no record of where the

18 Details in this paragraph are drawn from Burns Library, Gerald Pollinger to Graham Greene, 22 July 1983.

19 Greene, *The Tenth Man*, pp. 9–11.

20 *The Times*, 6 September 1984.

21 Harry Ransom Center, University of Texas at Austin, Graham Greene Collection, Box 34, Folder 3. The typescript is undated, but it is accompanied by a letter dated 1967.

22 R. A. Wobbe, *Graham Greene: A Bibliography and Guide to Research* (New York: Garland, 1979).

copy came from. The sale was brokered through Lew Feldman's House of El Dieff in New York, which in itself is suggestive: from 1964 onwards, Greene sold a series of manuscripts of his novels via Sotheby's Auction House in London and El Dieff. But did Greene use this route again for the sale of a single manuscript of *The Tenth Man* in 1967? The answer is that we simply do not know.

However, we do have clear evidence that Greene became aware of *The Tenth Man* as a substantial story in the mid-1960s. In April 1966, a man called Charles Morris wrote to Greene from Stepney in London. Morris reported that 'some time ago' he had found a manuscript of *The Tenth Man*, inscribed with the words 'by Graham Greene'. 'Until recently I am afraid you were not known to me,' Morris wrote, in a blow to Greene's self-esteem, but now he had become aware of the novelist, and Morris offered to send him the manuscript.[23] 'The whole thing is rather a mystery,' Greene replied in May 1966, asking him to send it on to him in Antibes.[24] After some delay, Morris sent Greene the manuscript in October, referring in his letter to an 'East End stall'[25] – apparently where he had first purchased the manuscript; it is not the least of the mysteries surrounding *The Tenth Man* as to how the story came to be on the stall where Charles Morris found it. Greene sent Morris a copy of his most recent novel, *The Comedians*, by way of thanks, and in his cover letter referred to 'the strange missing manuscript', adding, 'I don't ever remember having copies of this made [interestingly, he did not say he could not remember having written such a long story] and I am certainly glad to be able to destroy one!' There is no record in the archives of whether Greene actually destroyed this copy. However, there is a handwritten note on Greene's reply to Morris saying, 'Found by E.D. [presumably Elisabeth Dennys, Greene's sister and, by then, secretary] in 1985 in an old and irrelevant file!', as if the whole Charles Morris episode had by then been long forgotten.[26]

Hard on the heels of the Morris discovery, another copy of *The Tenth Man* came to Greene's attention. Jill Phillips of Camberwell, London, wrote to Greene in February 1967 saying that she had a copy of *The Tenth Man*; perhaps she too bought it on an East End stall, but since her original letter has not survived, we do not know. What we do have is a reply to Mrs Phillips in March 1967 from Greene's agent Laurence Pollinger informing her that the copyright in the story rested with MGM and that 'you should take no action with your typescript copy without first having obtained permission from MGM'. Pollinger's letter added that 'this is the second time the subject of a typescript outside the possession of MGM has come up in the last twelve months'[27] – clearly a reference to Charles Morris's earlier purchase. Sadly, there is no further evidence of what Jill Phillips did with her copy. There is no indication that Graham Greene came

23 Burns Library, Charles Morris to Graham Greene, 27 April 1966.
24 Burns Library, Graham Greene to Charles Morris, 2 May 1966.
25 Burns Library, Charles Morris to Graham Greene, 14 October 1966.
26 Burns Library, Graham Greene to Charles Morris, 20 October 1966.
27 [illegible]

in possession of it, but the exchange again clearly made Greene aware of the existence of the story.

What did Greene do with the copy he received from Charles Morris? Destroyed it, as he said he would? Sell it the following year to the archive in Texas? We do not know, but we have further evidence of what he knew when. In October 1970, Greene was visited in his flat in Antibes by Judith Adamson, who told him that a manuscript copy of *The Tenth Man* was in the archive in Texas. (She reminded him of this in her later interview in June 1982.) So in 1970, he knew of its existence there, even if we do not know whether he had been responsible for its sale in 1967.

In Judith Adamson's notes from that day in October 1970, she also recorded Greene as saying that he was going to look for the manuscript of the story 'above his cupboard where he kept old papers and a tennis racket!'[28] This it seems was done, though not by Greene himself. In Yvonne Cloetta's memoir, *In Search of a Beginning: My Life with Graham Greene*, published in 2004, she writes about the winter of 1970. She looked in the bedroom of his flat in Antibes, on the top of some cupboards, in search of some radiators. On finding 'a whole lot of papers' behind the radiators, she brought them down. 'I started to pull out the papers and handed them to him,' Cloetta writes. 'What were they? Well, he had a vague memory of some pages that he had completely forgotten from *The Tenth Man*. He thought it was only the synopsis. In fact, he discovered the entire manuscript.'[29] No more is made of this discovery in Cloetta's book – she continues the story by talking about a dozen or so pages of an early draft of what eventually became *The Human Factor*, which were also found on top of the cupboard: it was these pages that caught Greene's attention, not the typescript of *The Tenth Man*. There is no sense in Cloetta's book of her story undermining the idea of Greene being surprised at the 'discovery' of *The Tenth Man* in 1983, merely a mention in passing that Greene had a copy of the manuscript, which he had clearly forgotten about. Was this the Charles Morris copy, which Greene had neglected to destroy? If so, it could not be the copy sold to the archive in Austin, Texas, in 1967. And what did Greene do with this copy, newly discovered on the top of the cupboard? Given his apparently greater interest in the discovery of some pages of the future novel *The Human Factor*, perhaps *The Tenth Man* was simply put back up on top of the cupboard and again forgotten about? Again as so often in this story, we do not know.

There is, therefore, a considerable body of documentary evidence dating from the mid-1960s that suggests that Graham Greene knew perfectly well that a complete story of *The Tenth Man* existed, indeed that there was one copy in his own possession. He received a copy from Charles Morris; he heard of another copy in Jill Phillips's possession; he had a copy in his Antibes flat in 1970; he knew in 1970 that a copy

28 Information from Professor Judith Adamson in an email, 12 February 2020, included in *A Sort of Newsletter*, Issue 82, May 2020, pp. 14–15.

29 Yvonne Cloetta, *In Search of a Beginning: My Life with Graham Greene* (London: Bloomsbury, 2004), p. 135.

existed in Texas and may even have been responsible for selling the copy to that archive in 1967. There are many references in the foregoing to Greene's hazy memory of the story ('the whole thing is rather a mystery', 'a vague memory of some pages that he had completely forgotten') but more than one occasion when Greene's memory had been jogged. Surely Shelden is right? Graham Greene was feigning ignorance in 1983 when *The Tenth Man* was discovered, was he not?

And yet, and yet. There is first the question of why Greene sat on his copy of *The Tenth Man* and did not try to get it published long before 1983. If he did not think much of it and considered it unpublishable, why did he later profess to thinking rather highly of it? As he wrote, 'I prefer it in many ways to *The Third Man.*'[30] Or perhaps we should merely join Shelden in his cynicism, assuming that Greene realized that since MGM held the copyright, he had himself no financial interest in seeing the novella published? Perhaps.

But there is another consideration. As mentioned earlier, W. J. West's defence of Greene over *The Tenth Man* is based on his research in the archives in Boston – archives Shelden never had access to. There is at Boston College a considerable collection of correspondence from 1983 to 1985 concerning *The Tenth Man* – its 'discovery', the developments leading to its publication and material relating to rights, serialization and a possible film version.[31] There is in all this correspondence not a single item where Greene admits to anyone that he already knew about the completed story *The Tenth Man.* More positively, when reading through this correspondence, there is an overwhelming feeling of Greene being genuinely puzzled by the gradual revelation of the existence of a finished novella. Professor Higdon's letter of January 1983, reporting the discovery of the story, has a scribbled note that reads, 'write and ask any more info?'[32] and this tone of Greene needing to be reminded of matters continues throughout the file. Greene's agent Gerald Pollinger was asked to investigate, and in May Greene was told that 'it seems MGM bought this in 1944 in manuscript'.[33] Later that month, Pollinger was able to give Greene fuller information about his 1944 contracts with MGM. In reply, in June, Greene wrote to Pollinger, 'I am completely puzzled by all this. I seem to remember writing a short possible outline for a film but which would not have had the length which I should have thought would be publishable.'[34] As he learnt of Anthony Blond's financial interest and intention to publish the story, Greene wrote to Blond in October, stating his opposition to having the novella published and asking him to send a photocopy of the

[30] Greene, *The Tenth Man*, p. 9.

[31] Burns Library, Boston College, Graham Greene Papers: MS1995-03; Series V: Literary Works; *The Tenth Man*, Box 60, Folders 20–3.

[32] Burns Library, David Leon Higdon letter to Graham Greene, 31 January 1983. This resulted in a letter from Greene's secretary to Higdon on 8 April, asking for more information.

[33] Burns Library, Letter from B. Franklin Kansler in Hollywood to Gerald Pollinger, 13 May 1983 – a letter then sent on to Greene.

story 'to refresh my memory'.[35] There is no indication that Greene believed he had had, or still had, a copy of the story on top of a cupboard in his Antibes flat.

This general tone of bafflement and vagueness could of course all have been bluff on Greene's part, though that then invites the question as to why Greene might act in this way and requires acceptance that Greene was willing to mislead not only the likes of Anthony Blond but even his own agent, Gerald Pollinger. Perhaps most tellingly, Greene's amazement carried into other letters with personal friends. To Michael Meyer in November 1983, Greene wrote that Blond had sent him a copy of the story 'which to my embarrassment seems to be rather good'. Greene continued, 'In my memory it was just a sketch of an idea for a film of a few pages, but it proves to be 100 pages of typescript and I think rather better than its successor *The Third Man* but not so filmable.'[36] And in a letter to his Swiss lawyer and friend Jean-Félix Paschoud in February 1984, Greene referred to 'a story of mine of which I had forgotten the existence called THE TENTH MAN!' Greene added, 'I apparently wrote it somewhere around 1945 under contract to MGM'[37] – a misdating of the writing of the story even after Pollinger had made clear the details to Greene. This misdating continued in the first draft of Greene's introduction to the novella, written probably in 1984 and held at Georgetown University, in which Greene wrote that the story had been written 'just after the war',[38] changed in the published introduction to 'towards the end of the war'.[39] Greene was genuinely unsure about the genesis of the story, and his letters continually reveal his surprise that a complete story actually existed.

We have therefore a conundrum in relation to *The Tenth Man*. To accept Greene's version of events we have to accept that his attention was more than once drawn to the existence of a finished story in the 1960s, and that indeed for a time he had a copy of the story in his Antibes flat – and yet that he managed not to realize all this in the early 1980s when the manuscript was discovered in the MGM archives. Yet the consistent tone of his letters of 1983–4 to a range of people is that this is precisely what happened. To believe otherwise is to assume an extraordinary level of deceit by Greene towards all those he corresponded with, for reasons that are not at all clear. Greene had a notoriously fallible memory for his own writings, and he seems in this case to have suffered from a persistent false memory of what work he had done on *The Tenth Man* story, which he stubbornly clung on to in the face of contradictory evidence. It may be hard to credit, but 'An Old Man's Memory' is perhaps the likeliest explanation after all.

35 Burns Library, Graham Greene to Anthony Blond, 6 October 1983.
36 Burns Library, Graham Greene to Michael Meyer, 9 November 1983.
37 Burns Library, Graham Greene to Jean-Félix Paschoud, 6 February 1984.
38 Lauinger Library, Box 2.
39 Greene, *The Third Man*, p. 9.

'No longer a by-product' but a 'main occupation': Greene and the short story, 1961–71

Jon Wise

Two episodes from the Thames Television series *Shades of Greene* (1975–6) were screened at Berkhamsted's Civic Centre on the Friday night of the 2016 Graham Greene International Festival. Discussion afterwards concluded that 'Two Gentle People' was more popular and accessible than 'Dream of a Strange Land'. 'Two Gentle People' was one of twelve short stories included in the collection *May We Borrow Your Husband? And Other Comedies of the Sexual Life* (1967) while 'Dream of a Strange Land' appeared in a lesser-known volume entitled *A Sense of Reality* (1963) along with just three others: 'A Visit to Morin', 'Under the Garden' and 'A Discovery in the Woods'.

When deciding on the composition of *A Sense of Reality*, it might have been expected that Greene would wish to publish most if not all of the twelve short stories which had appeared in various magazines and journals since *Twenty-One Stories* (1954) nine years previously. After all, that had been his custom hitherto. But this was not the case, and the gestation of this collection was subject to unexpected indecision and prevarication on Greene's part. It was seemingly out of character for an author who earlier in his career appeared to have shown scant regard for the short story format and in putting together a collection merely gathered together any suitable material that was at hand. In 1947, in a brief 'Author's Note' in *Nineteen Stories* (1947), he wrote, 'I present these tales merely as the by-products of a novelist's career.'[1] So why change his approach this time?

Seven volumes of short stories were published during Graham Greene's lifetime, eight if one includes *Shades of Greene* which was intended to 'tie-in' with the above-mentioned TV series and had appeared in other collections. The first three volumes, *The Basement Room and Other Stories* (1935), *Nineteen Stories* and *Twenty-One Stories*,

An abridged version of this essay was originally published in *A Sort of Newsletter*, Issue 69, February 2017, as 'A Sense of Reality – A Bibliographical Note'.

1 Graham Greene, *19 Stories* (London: Heinemann, 1947), author's note.
The curiously named *Nineteen Stories* was arrived at because Greene 'found' another (unnamed) story he had written in a magazine previously which required Heinemann at quite a late stage to make a name change from '18 Stories'. Rushden, Northamptonshire: Random House Archive and Library, The William Heinemann Archive. Letter: Graham Greene to Louise Callender, 4 November 1946.
The letter to Heinemann suggest a rather casual attitude to the formation of the collection, 'I am afraid another short story has turned up – which I very much hope [illegible]

should be considered as a group; these successive collections mostly reprinted stories from the previous book with some additions; a few were discarded altogether.[2]

By contrast, *A Sense of Reality* and *May We Borrow Your Husband? And Other Comedies of the Sexual Life* were discrete groupings. The very last collection chosen by the author, *The Last Word and Other Stories* (1990), was different as it included work which spanned Greene's entire adult life. Six rather than four of this selection, which the author erroneously claimed in his preface, had appeared previously in book form. *Collected Short Stories* (1972), as the name implies, was a compendium of the five collections which had been published thus far to which three new stories were added.

What became *A Sense of Reality* was to have constituted Greene's first major publication for The Bodley Head following his difficult departure from Heinemann. This slim volume must have seemed a scant return for Max Reinhardt, his new publisher who had recently encouraged the renowned author to leave Heinemann, with whom Greene had been associated for thirty years. Indeed, up until November 1962, Reinhardt would have been expecting to publish a very different set of short stories the following year.

The book was to have been titled 'Under the Garden and Other Stories' and, instead of four, to have consisted of at least twelve new stories plus an autobiographical 'fragment'. The content was to have been divided into three parts, as follows, with a short foreword of about one hundred words by Greene:

Part 1
Under the Garden
A Discovery in the Forest (later Woods)
Dream of a Strange Land
A Visit to Morin

Part 2
May We Borrow Your Husband?
Mortmain
Beauty
Mr Conway's Congress
A Shocking Accident
Awful When You Think of It
The Man who Stole the Eiffel Tower

Part 3
Church Militant
The Revenge

[2] See Jon Wise and Mike Hill, *The Works of Graham Greene: A Reader's Bibliography and Guide* (London: Continuum, 2012), p. 53, for a detailed listing of Greene's collected and uncollected short stories. Since that publication further published but uncollected short stories have been discovered, and these are listed elsewhere in this book.

Successive letters from Greene to Max Reinhardt in October 1962 setting out his plans advised that the then current word count for the collection amounted to 73,500, with the author adding that he would send more stories 'as they come ready'. Thus the finished volume would have been substantial.[3]

However, a closer look at the proposed contents suggests that the above selection was distinctly arbitrary; perhaps the list was assembled simply to satisfy Reinhardt at the time. For instance, the inclusion in Part 3 of 'The Revenge', the autobiographical 'fragment' noted above, seems out of place alongside 'Church Militant' which, with its gently ironic undertones, is more akin to the mostly comedic stories in Part 2, many of which later featured in the *May We Borrow Your Husband?* collection. The seven stories in Part 2 include the very slight 'The Man who Stole the Eiffel Tower' and, by contrast, the much longer 'Mr Conway's Congress'. In his letter of 17 October, Greene has written '? 10,000' alongside the latter story. The story has never been published. It is unclear from the approximately 11,000-word manuscript that survives whether or not 'Mr Conway's Congress' was ever actually finished.[4]

Greene wrote again to Max Reinhardt in early November. He told him that A. S. Frere had advised that he was 'dubious' about the combination of the more serious content in Part 1 and the 'comedies' in Part 2. Frere had suggested that the Part 1 group should be published on its own. Confirmation that Greene would be offering just the four stories with the title *A Sense of Reality* was revealed by Laurence Pollinger later the same month.[5] To engage Frere and his literary agent in what may be construed as 'deflection tactics' may suggest some degree of embarrassment on Greene's part at having to concede that a prospective major work had now shrunk to just four stories. Was it truly the concern expressed by his old mentor about the balance of the collection that swayed Greene, or were there other reasons for taking this quite radical decision?[6]

One mitigating factor is that, at the time, Greene was in the midst of his separation from Heinemann. His letter to Alexander Frere, dated 16 October 1962, is printed in full in Richard Greene's *Graham Greene: A Life in Letters*. It sets out in detail the circumstances which led to his decision to leave and his lasting admiration and affection for Frere. On the surface at least, Greene seemed caught in his familiar dilemma between loyalty and betrayal – loyalty to his mentor Frere who had been recently 'elevated' to the non-influential post of president of Heinemann and betrayal of the company which had played a central role in making him such a successful writer. But above all, the then

3 London, the British Library (BL): Department of Western Manuscripts, Max Reinhardt Collection. Letters: Greene to Reinhardt, 15–17 October 1962.

4 See Jon Wise and Mike Hill, *The Works of Graham Greene Volume 2: A Guide to the Graham Greene Archives* (London: Bloomsbury, 2015), p. 87. The holograph and typescript of 'Mr Conway's Congress' is in the Graham Greene Collection at the University of Texas, Harry Ransom Center.

5 BL: Letters: Greene to Reinhardt, 10 November 1962, and Laurence Pollinger to Reinhardt, 30 November 1962.

6 Richard Greene, *Graham Greene: A Life in Letters* (London: Little, Br[illegible]

recent sale of Heinemann to Thomas Tilling Ltd meant that Greene felt he now lacked 'a personal contact, a personal sense of confidence reciprocated' at a company 'of whom the directors are nearly all unknown to me'.[7]

Two letters from Greene, written much earlier in 1962, lend a further dimension to the affair. He wrote to his French agent Marie Biche on 26 January that he was planning a volume for Heinemann to be titled 'Three'. It would comprise 'Under the Garden', 'A Visit to Morin' and 'Can [later May] We Borrow Your Husband?' He informed her that 'Under the Garden' was finished and totalled twenty-three thousand words; he was part way through 'Can We Borrow Your Husband?' and expected the story to be twelve thousand to fifteen thousand words in length; 'A Visit to Morin' had six thousand words. He presumed that the three stories would make an acceptable collection for the French market. On 26 March, Greene also wrote to his South American publisher and friend Victoria Ocampo along similar lines although, by then, he was referring to three *or* four stories.[8]

The change of mind, at least twice, about the composition of the collection may be explained away by Greene's desire to please his new publisher, his respect for Frere's opinion, the turmoil caused by leaving Heinemann or just plain indecision. There is another factor to consider. By 1961, the emotional strain of 'living' with the character of Querry for two years had persuaded Greene that *A Burnt-Out Case* would be his last novel. He admitted as much on more than one occasion, most publicly in his introduction to *In Search of a Character: Two African Journals* (1961), where he wrote that, having completed *A Burnt-Out Case*, 'another full-length novel was probably beyond my powers'.[9]

Greene was clearly mentally exhausted at the time. In a typescript of the 'blurb' Greene wrote, but never used, for the moribund 'Under the Garden' volume, dated 30 October 1962, he describes the *Twenty-One Stories* collection of the previous decade as the 'by-product' of his work as a novelist. By contrast, he remarks that the current 'Under the Garden' collection was no longer the by-product but his 'main occupation, the fruits of a mood which he (had) described in his introduction to *In Search of a Character*'.[10]

[7] Ibid., pp. 262–3.

[8] Balliol College Library: Archives & Manuscripts, Papers of Marie Biche relating to Graham Greene. Letter: Greene to Biche, 26 January 1962; Harvard University, Houghton Library: Modern Books & Manuscripts; Victoria Ocampo Collection, Letter: Greene to Ocampo, 26 March 1962.

The comment in the letter to Ocampo is added as a postscript from which one may deduce that it was little more than a passing on of information. However, the far more detailed explanation given to his French agent Marie Biche suggests that Greene was properly focused on the composition of the short story collection and when it might be ready for publication in France – ahead of its release in the UK.

[9] Graham Greene, *In Search of a Character: Two African Journals* (London: Heinemann, 1961), p. 8. Greene had the opportunity to re-enter publishing on a full-time basis in early 1958 when he was offered the post of managing director at Eyre & Spottiswoode. Richard Greene states that Greene at this stage 'believed he was nearly finished as a novelist'. Richard Greene, *Russian Roulette: The Life and Times of Graham Greene* (London: Little, Brown, 2020), p. 220.

[10] University of Texas, Harry Ransom Center (HRC). Graham Greene Collection: Under the Garden (1962): Typescript of blurb.

Evidence shows that Greene had a number of short stories ready for publication at the end of 1962, his agent offering new fewer than four to the *New Statesman* in December of that year.[11]

Of course, this 'mood' did not last. By the following year Greene was pursuing two ideas for future novels. For example, there exist two abandoned projects from 1963: 'The Word Pterodactyl' and 'A Man of Extremes', which, with its part-Haitian setting and a character called Dr Magiot, is clearly the forerunner of *The Comedians*.[12] But the feeling that he was entering the last phase of his life did not entirely leave him. He spent his sixtieth birthday on his own in a rented studio flat in Antibes. He was struggling to complete *The Comedians* (1966) and was convinced that the novel that would follow it, provisionally to be called 'The Last Decade', would be his very last work. He began to make a series of morbid notes in a rather loose form of journal recording his thoughts, memories, regrets, convincing himself that 'the end of life faces us like a wall, and every day we must take a step towards it'.[13]

In a prologue to 'The Last Decade', written twenty years after the event and five published novels and one novella later, Greene speculated whether the act of writing the journal had 'served its purpose in loosening a writer's block'.[14] As for his concept of his own role as a short story writer, by 1971 Greene's position had shifted subtly yet again, 'I remain in this field a novelist who has happened to write short stories'.[15]

11 University of Sussex, *New Statesman* Archive, Letter, Greene's literary agent to editor, *New Statesman*, 31 December 1962. The stories in question were 'Dream of a Strange Land', 'A Discovery in the Woods', 'Beauty' and 'Reading at Night'. The first two were subsequently published in *A Sense of Reality* and 'Beauty' in *May We Borrow Your Husband?* 'Reading at Night' has never been published. In the end the *New Statesman*'s editor, John Freeman, decided instead to publish 'Mortmain' which was offered in a separate letter in January 1963.

12 University of Texas, HRC. A thirteen-thousand-word holograph of the unfinished novel 'The Word Pterodactyl' and notes for 'A Man of Extremes' are in this collection. The notes include the reference to Dr Magiot. Wise and Hill, *The Works of Graham Greene Volume 2*, p. 90.

Richard Greene states that 'A Man of Extremes' was later used as a working title for the novel *The Comedians*. He also remarks that Graham Greene's visit to Haiti in 1963 gave him fresh creative impetus, 'having lost confidence while writing *A Burnt-Out Case*'. Initially he envisaged an entertainment but this changed to a novel once he witnessed 'the moral and political urgency of Haiti'. Greene, *Russian Roulette*, pp. 359–60 and 362.

13 Graham Greene, 'The Last Decade', *Time and Tide*, Autumn 1984, p. 46.

14 Ibid.

15 Graham Greene, *Collected Short Stories* (1972), including

Index

Index of Greene's Work

Published Works

Unpublished Works

General Index